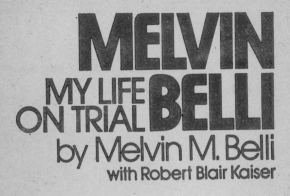

MELVIN
MY LIFE BELLI
ON TRIAL
by Melvin M. Belli
with Robert Blair Kaiser

POPULAR LIBRARY • NEW YORK

Published by Popular Library, CBS Publications, CBS Consumer Publishing, a Division of CBS Inc., by arrangement with William Morrow and Company, Inc.

November, 1977

Library of Congress Catalog Card Number: 76-12475

ISBN: 0-445-04025-4

WHAT KIND OF LAWYER CAN BATTLE AMERICA'S GIANTS IN COURT— AND PLAY IN THE SAME LEAGUE AS ERROL FLYNN IN PRIVATE?

Just one kind of lawyer. The most celebrated, vivid, and dramatic lawyer of our time. Melvin Belli.

Now Belli tells it all, revealing everything, hiding nothing:

- his most fascinating cases—with clients ranging from crippled children and convicts to famous names like Lenny Bruce, Mickey Cohen, the Soledad Brothers, Jack Ruby, Muhammad Ali, Martha Mitchell, and many others;

- his marriages, affairs, and international escapades— some would make a lesser man blanch and a shyer one blush;

- his friendships and feuds with the great and powerful. Mel Belli loves the law. Mel Belli loves life. And you will love him and his book.

"Melvin Belli is wise, compassionate, insightful—and so is his book . . . it deserves to be read!"
—*Chicago Tribune, Book World*

TO
Lia, Melia and Caesar

ACKNOWLEDGMENTS

To the University of California School of Law at Berkeley, Boalt Hall, a plus.

And a minus

To the Holy Grail Insurance Company and to all those insurance companies and banks and establishment organizations and the American Bar Association and various local bar associations without whose constant harassment I wouldn't have been motivated to write this book.

—MELVIN M. BELLI
San Francisco, May, 1976

Contents

PROLOGUE

I first met Mel Belli in Rome in the spring of 1962. I was acting bureau chief of *Time* Magazine in Rome, and he was on some kind of sabbatical, teaching forensic medicine at Rome University. By this time, Mel Belli had worked his way through the chairs of public opinion, from "well known" to "prominent" to "famous" to "celebrated"—not on the strength of a single case but because he had made blossom previously barren branches of the law. He too had blossomed from the once skinny, struggling graduate who defended the already condemned at San Quentin for free because those were the only cases he could get. He had become the ample, affluent trial lawyer with a building of his own which was and is now one of San Francisco's outrageously original tourist attractions. It seemed natural for Belli to invite a *Time* correspondent to dinner—and just as natural for a *Time* correspondent to accept.

I couldn't help but be impressed by Mel, his pretty blond wife, Joy, their five-year-old son, Caesar, and their warm, richly appointed villa on the Appia Antica. Mel was a raconteur, regaling his guests, an international though largely English-speaking cast of bankers, brokers, builders, barristers and journalists—and the rector of the

Irish College in Rome. That night he told them stories about his recent adventures in and out of court. He lingered on the details of a criminal case he had undertaken most recently for the sheer fun of it all, the defense of a judge in Southern California who had been accused of soliciting favors from attractive young ladies in trouble, in return for judicial clemency. The press had had a good time with the courtroom drama, which they dubbed The Case of the Kissing Judge. And so had Mel Belli. He got an acquittal for the judge and some pretty good headlines for himself.

When we sat down to dinner, however, and the talk turned to the import and implications of the upcoming Second Vatican Ecumenical Council, Mel simply rose from the table and, without a word of excuse, retired for the evening. (I wondered whether he had even caught my name. A year later, I learned he had. He sent me a note of congratulations on the publication of my first book, on Pope John and the Council.) I have since learned that Mel Belli seldom excuses himself. In the course of putting this book together, I confronted Mel with a vignette of himself from the distant past, one in which he came off looking like Dorian Gray. Mel simply said, "I did it because that's the way I felt at the time. There was no excuse for it." That's the way Mel is. He has little time for excuses—and even less time to audit the excuses of others. He bores easily. He won't stay at a cocktail party unless he finds someone fascinating to talk to. And when he is not in trial or about to go into trial, he is generally off on a trip. Where? Anywhere. He's been to every country in the world except Tibet, and by the time you read this, he'll have been there, too.

I saw Mel only a few more times during the 1960's. I watched him on TV in 1964, raging over a Dallas jury's verdict condemning his client, Jack Ruby, to death in the electric chair. I saw him as a generous host when I went to a huge party at his home on Twin Peaks in San Francisco on the eve of the Republican National Convention of 1964, a party attended mostly by members of the national press corps who had converged on the City to see the nomination of Barry Goldwater. A few years later, at Fifty-first Street and Lexington Avenue in New York City, I watched a truck driver lean out of his cab and call fondly to Belli: "Hey, Mel Belli! Give 'em hell, Mel!"

Clearly, Mel Belli was becoming something of an American folk hero. And a guy who wouldn't mind being an international folk hero, besides. The writer Alex Haley, who was traveling with Mel in 1967, told me that he had once caught Belli paging himself at Orly International Airport near Paris.

Mel Belli never needed lessons on how to attract attention to himself. He was a streaker in college at Berkeley almost fifty years before streaking became a national fad. Early in his law career, he was a darling of the San Francisco press, and it is now no accident that his best friends all over the world happen to be newspaper or magazine editors.

So it was not difficult for me to keep tabs on Belli as the years passed. I simply read the papers. Moscow—Belli visiting the Kremlin. Kenya—Belli on safari. Capetown—Belli watching Dr. Christiaan Barnard performing heart surgery. Los Angeles—Belli winning $675,000 for a child who caught polio from a vaccine designed to prevent it.

The press helped me keep track of Belli's colorful clients: Errol Flynn, Mae West, Lenny Bruce, Mickey Cohen, The Rolling Stones. And of some of his adversaries, too. In the 1960's he sued the U.S. Government on behalf of the Lime-Nondalton Hills Indians of Alaska for several hundred million dollars and he filed a $200-million antitrust suit against thirteen insurance companies who, he claimed, were conspiring to fix prices on medical malpractice insurance and to cut off insurance coverage from any doctor who testified against another physician. He even sued the president of the American Bar Association.

Belli was good copy. He was colorful. The Associated Press's favorite word to describe him (he could almost take out a copyright on the epithet) was *flamboyant*. I later learned that, except for his red carpetbag briefcase, Belli wasn't flamboyant in a trial situation; his approaches to judge and jury were weighty with respect, and he always wore gray in court.

Out of court, well, that was different. I was with him for a week at La Costa Spa and Country Club near San Diego in 1974, and but for the time we spent in the pool playing volleyball with a group of men that included Metrecal's Meade Johnson and the actor William Holden, he never wore anything but a bright-blue sweatsuit and sneakers. Once, he lost an election for president of the International Academy of Trial Lawyers (of which he was a cofounder) because he showed up at the Academy's convention wearing red slacks. The barristers couldn't see voting themselves a president who wore red pants. But what the hell? Mel was the King of Torts. If you're a king, you don't need to be a president.

In the late 1960's, the U.S. Ambassador to India, Kenneth Keating, set up Belli's visit to the Kingdom of Swat, now part of Pakistan. As Mel told the story, he was given the damnedest reception he ever had, with a big black limousine picking him up at the depot and a sumptuous banquet back at the palace with the Wali of Swat. Belli and the Wali gave each other courtly bows all afternoon and evening and addressed each other as

"Your Highness." "It wasn't until I got back to Delhi and saw Keating that I understood," Belli said. " 'Hell,' said Keating, 'when I sent word ahead that you were coming to Swat, I told 'em you were the King of Torts.' "

Life Magazine had given Belli that title in 1954, but, of course, "torts" was not a kingdom. The word *torts* comes from the French and means "civil wrongs." These civil wrongs (as opposed to crimes) were (and are) the raw material of much of Belli's practice. Crimes are offenses against society; torts are offenses against an individual. City and state officials prosecute crimes on behalf of society. Tort lawyers prosecute on behalf of an individual. There was an age when torts weren't worth much of a lawyer's time and trouble. But in the later forties and fifties, Mel Belli and a handful of other lawyers radically changed that. In representing lone (and frequently indigent) individuals against mighty corporations, they became knights on white chargers. They persuaded juries to give their clients big awards against previously almost untouchable giants like General Motors and the Southern Pacific Railroad—*when* these corporations were negligent. Mel's job, of course, was to *prove* that negligence in a court of law. He did it so egregiously that, to the press at first, then finally in his own mind, Mel Belli really did become the King of Torts.

Once he had assumed that role, everything else seemed to follow: Mel's continued successes in court, an increasingly regal lifestyle and, most flattering of all, a large following of younger lawyers who emulated his methods. Tom Girardi, an attorney and friend from Los Angeles, says, "Without Belli to show the way, I'd never be where I am today." Girardi has already won several million-dollar verdicts and settlements—and he's only thirty-six.

I see Belli, therefore, as someone who shows the way

to others—as a king, then, or, at least, kingly. I remember Shakespeare's King Henry V and his earnest remarks to Princess Katherine of France soon after the battle of Agincourt. Princess Katherine has informed Hal that he may not kiss her on the lips. Why? Because, she says (in French and halting English), such is not the fashion in France until *after* marriage. Then does the amorous Harry, like himself, assume the lawyer's cloak and argue, convincingly enough to win his kiss: "O Kate, nice customs court'sy to great kings. Dear Kate, you and I cannot be confined within the weak list of a country's fashion: we are the makers of manners, Kate; and the liberty that follows our places stops the mouth of all find-faults."

Belli's critics will no doubt cry a pox on me for the comparison. I am sure they would just as soon compare Belli to Falstaff, the youthful Harry's partner in sin, as to the newly sceptered king. And I imagine they could justify the comparison up to a point by instancing Belli's now ample girth, his proclivities for lots of wine, bawdy women, tall tales and a wit, like Falstaff's, which "will make use of anything" and "turn diseases to commodities." But the critics, judging only Belli's public image, would be wrong.

Those who know Belli outside the courtroom have generally seen him pursuing one of his life's overriding goals: having fun. But the wild flings, I think, were only a cover for an unjustifiable dissatisfaction with himself. Belli is a man of impossibly high professional and personal standards (learned too well from his mother, whom you will soon meet). He tries to live up to these standards as long and as well as he can—until the inhuman, self-inflicted pressures become too great. Then he explodes. He must raise hell in his office, or take a trip to Paris or Mexico City, or gobble up two dozen French pastries and/or twelve dozen oysters in a single sitting or buy a new Rolls-Royce or a half-dozen tailor-made suits. When he does so, he is Falstaff. But only for a moment.

The rest of the time, one sees another Belli. There is the serious legal scholar who haunts the British Museum when he's visiting London and stays up all that night writing down his new insights on the common law and their application to a current legal issue. There is the specialist in forensic medicine and pathology who puts on a surgical gown and gloves and actually helps with an important autopsy in Savannah to save a widow's will. There is the ascetic who abstains from strong drink through Lent and kneels for three hours through a Good Friday service at the Paulists' church in San Francisco's Chinatown. There is the curious seeker after truth who spends at least an hour questioning a group of youthful demonstrators in front of the Nixon White House.

There is, above all, Belli the barrister, the trial lawyer with uncommon common sense, who, like King Harry, has used his royal mind-set to overturn outmoded customs of the bar and bench. For most of his life, dating back to his case, *Escola v. Coca-Cola*—a California Supreme Court decision in the early forties that led to the consumer and environmentalist revolts of the 1970's— Mel Belli has helped *make new law*. And it was new law that helped make the powerful few accountable to the many who were previously weak and helpless. Lawyers the world over, even some who are envious of Belli, may concede this much. Readers of these memoirs will discover for themselves that the King of Torts, like King Harry and Princess Kate, was "a maker of manners" in the law, and that "the liberty that follows" his bold steps should stop the mouths of all the find-faults in the land. Because Belli dared to be different, there is greater liberty —and justice—for all.

It is not that Belli has committed no sins. Like King Harry (and like every man who aspires to greatness), Belli has sinned greatly. In his many conversations with me over a period of three years, he has tried to reveal himself in countless tales, drunk and sober. For these memoirs, Belli told all, and in the telling, he even gained some new perspective on himself. In the last three years, I have actually seen him mellow. His high ideals, often unattained, do not create as much pressure on him now as they did. He has learned to love his imperfect self.

And laugh at himself, too. One recent Chinese New Year's in San Francisco, Mel and Lia, his pretty young wife, Caesar, his son, a gang from Mel's office and I all met at Johnny Kan's Restaurant for a celestial feast of pressed duck and shrimp á l'orange and mushi pork and sweet-and-sour ribs and a dozen other dishes. Afterward, we looked for Mel's Rolls-Royce in front of his office. It was gone. He reported the theft to the police, and then I drove him and his family home. As soon as we arrived, he had to phone the police again. "Officer," he said, "this is Mel Belli. I reported my car stolen a while ago. I just found it. Some jackass parked it in my garage. The jackass," he added, "was Belli."

—ROBERT BLAIR KAISER
Mammoth Lakes, California

CHAPTER ONE

Ruffled Linen Collars

Hearsay is anathema to a lawyer, but they tell me I was born on July 29, 1907, in Sonora, California, in the western foothills of the High Sierras, toward the southern end of the Mother Lode. Sonora was a town where you could once pick up gold in the streets. Our principal, Maggie Fahy, used to let us out of school on rainy days so we could look for nuggets in the runoff. Sonora was a town that was settled by quick-thinking, self-reliant young men who didn't play it safe and who didn't go by the book. They rode in, took the town away from the Mexican miners who had already settled there, stole their gold and got out, leaving violence behind in the very names of their digs: Blood Springs, Black Leg Diggings, Dead Man's Bar, First Garrotte, Murphy's Defeat. Sonora, in the beginning, was a town where most of the single women were whores.

Both my parents grew up in and with Sonora and helped civilize it. My mother's father was a doctor. He died of pneumonia at the age of thirty-two when he was caught in a raging mountain stream after a midnight obstetrical call. Her mother, Anna Mouron, became the first woman druggist in California. My mother, Leonie, a pretty, frail woman, went to the most proper school on the West Coast, Mills College in Oakland. When her own brother, Otto, came to visit, they had to have a chaperone accompany them on the college grounds. I never heard her swear, nor would she tolerate my doing so. I was sitting in my favorite place one day in the kitchen, behind a Superior wood range with my Irish setter, Jack, lying next to me. I was looking at a picture of a fort in *The Book of Knowledge.* I started funning with the word *fort.* "Fort, fort, fort, fart, fart, fart . . ."

"What did you say?" demanded my mother. She didn't wait for an explanation, she thrashed me and washed out my mouth with Castile soap. I couldn't understand that and still can't. It was just a good Anglo-Saxon word describing a natural phenomenon, and it was awfully close to the word *fort.* How could one letter make it a "dirty word" that needed washing? And with Castile soap?

My mother was incapable of expressing any feelings for my father other than exasperation or disdain. Instead she doted on me, scrubbing me constantly and dressing me up all the time in velvet Little Lord Fauntleroy suits, or Norfolk jackets with ruffled linen collars. "Don't play in the leaves. Don't step in the mud. Don't slide down the hill. You can go swimming, darling, but don't get your feet wet." She never wanted me to play with the grubby little sons of the men who worked in the mines or the lumber mill. She never wanted me to have any fun. I have been trying to get even ever since.

My mother's idea of a good time was to get me dressed up like a diminutive six-year-old Uncle Sam, with striped pants, a swallowtail coat and a top hat so that I could ride on a float in the Fourth of July parade with Jackie Bromley, whose family owned one of our still-producing gold mines. Jackie wore a white pinafore, and she was supposed to be Miss Liberty. I had my fun anyway: I have a dim recollection that at some time during the day I thought about getting inside Miss Liberty's pantaloons. I think I even went so far as to kiss her on the cheek.

My father didn't put on airs like my mother. His father was just a laborer when he was born Caesar Arthur Belli in Eureka, Nevada. Grandfather Belli worked in the charcoal fields near Ely, Nevada, for several years until some explosive union wars drove him, his wife and their four children to California. They settled a ranch, raised cattle and chickens and grew everything for their own table. They worked hard and successfully enough so they could afford to send my dad, who was the quickest and the brightest of the kids, off to Bern College in Switzerland. He was sixteen when he left in 1897, and by the time he returned to Sonora at the age of twenty-two, he knew six languages and had become the quintessential gentleman.

He did everything with a flourish. He wrote with a cursive, ornate, flamboyant hand. He was well-groomed, had a barber shave him every morning and trim his brown, wavy hair. He always wore a suit and a vest and a pocket watch with a heavy gold chain and a high celluloid "Hoover" collar and his Shrine pin. When he went trout fishing, he would look as though he had just stepped out of the Abercrombie and Fitch catalog, straw hat, waders and a split bamboo rod.

The Bellis were Swiss. They pronounced their name Bally, like the famous Swiss shoe. And for some reason, they called me Pete. My mother, who probably dug up the name Melvin from some romantic novel about Englishmen drinking tea, cringed at the "Pete." I don't know how they ever made Bally into Belli or how the name got pronounced Bell-eye, but there it is. I rather like it when people give it the Italian pronunciation, Belly. I don't think of myself as of Swiss extraction anyway. Only money changers, cuckoo clock makers and hotelkeepers call themselves Swiss.

My father took his first job in Sonora at the Standard Lumber Mill, where he was a timekeeper, but he didn't stay there long. In 1904, at twenty-three, he helped organize a new bank in town and became the cashier. Two years later, when my father got the news that a great earthquake had almost destroyed San Francisco, he loaded up a large leather saddlebag with as much bullion as he could carry and rode west. When he arrived on the Oakland shore, he scanned the devastation of the City and smelled the smoke of a thousand fires on the other side of the Bay. He waited impatiently for a ferryboat, finally gave up and rented a rowboat, so he could deliver his gold to Mr. A. P. Giannini. The Bank of Italy was carrying on with business as usual, and my father wanted to help.

I have a picture in my mind's eye—of Caesar Arthur Belli, dressed in bankers' pinstripes and a vest and a bowler, rowing all by himself across the Bay with $12,750 worth of bullion at his feet, turning his lean torso from time to time to stay on a course heading for the City's financial district. I am sure that no anxiety creased his wide brow or clouded over his direct brown-eyed gaze and that a slight smile of anticipation parted his lips and squared his slightly dimpled chin. He docked the dory at the foot of Jackson Street, commandeered a wheelbarrow and wandered through the rubble and the smoke. From time to time, he could hear the shattering explosions caused by the militia. They were dynamiting the buildings on Montgomery Street in an effort to stop the sweep of the Great Fire that was consuming most of the City.

My father pushed his way past the place on Montgomery Street where there now hangs a small wooden sign that reads "MELVIN M. BELLI LAWYER." He continued walking to what is now the site of the towering Transamerica Pyramid where he watched O. P. Stidger, a giant of a man with blazing red hair and a full red beard, stand off the militia. Stidger was holding a long, loaded Colt .45. "You can't dynamite *this* building," he roared, presumably because the Montgomery Block was not only the biggest edifice west of Chicago, but because it was *his* building. The militiamen stood around grumbling and kicking the cobblestones with their boots looking down the barrel of that Colt .45.

My father, meanwhile, moved on with his wheelbarrow of gold and finally found Giannini himself. He was standing in front of a peddler's cart full of money on the corner of Kearny and California streets. "You'll probably be needing this, sir," said young Belli, after introducing himself to Giannini. The banker first expressed surprise then delight as he clapped Belli on the back and embraced him. Belli knew he had accomplished his mission: to establish his strength in the California banking community—and with a man who, as it turned out, would someday head the largest bank in the world. The two spoke their *ciao*'s and their *auguri*'s, and then Belli was off, his curiosity drawing him back to the Montgomery Block to see what had happened to O. P. Stidger and his building.

Stidger was still standing there, but the militia had moved on. Belli told Stidger that he'd come from Sonora and he wanted to shake the hand of the man who stood up to the dynamiters. Stidger smiled, stuck the gun into his belt and invited Belli into Duncan Nicols's Bank Exchange Saloon for a drink. They ambled up to the solid mahogany bar and had a Pisco Punch. And then they had another. (Today, Pisco Punch is the "house drink" in the Belli Building, my law offices, a couple hundred feet away from a new Bank Exchange.)

Caesar Belli could do marvelous feats like multiply 8,648 times 1,342,765 without pencil or paper. He would perform such calculations on the stage when a traveling vaudeville show came to town, facing off against the Chinese merchants who liked to do business with him. They would use an abacus while he did the calculations in his head. My father even learned to speak Chinese. At Christmastime, these merchants, dressed in their finest brocade kimonos and black slippers, would come knocking on our door—we lived in a huge brown-shingled house on a hill, a big yard front and back—with gifts for my dad, turkeys, some pyracantha berries, Chinese lilies for my mother and Chinese candy and litchi nuts for me.

Christmas was a big time, a time of special smells in the kitchen, of furtive visits by relatives bearing mysterious boxes, a time for wrapping gifts and decorating the huge tree in the living room with strings of cranberries and popcorn and lights, and a sense of expectation so strong I could hardly stand it and then—it was Christmas morning and it was snowing and I got up and ran to the living room and saw the presents under the tree and the filled stockings above the fireplace, and my father was standing at the front door waving to Santa Claus. For three or four Christmases, we'd go through that bullshit—that Santa Claus had just left and I had just missed him—again.

But if there was an air of phoniness about Santa, the food at Christmastime was real. No one worried about dieting then—and no one seemed to get fat. We always had a wonderful turkey. Nothing like the butter-injected, big, broad-breasted bird we buy today, but a leaner, wilder-tasting fowl. When it came out of the old wood range, it would be nice and brown. And the dressing would contain celery and sage and gizzards and onions and chestnuts. After dinner, I would lie on the floor in front of the crackling fire and listen to the men talk about Woodrow Wilson and the bank and militarism and new automobiles and places to hunt and fish. I listened until I fell asleep next to my dad's shiny, high-buttoned shoes.

It seemed that every Fourth of July we would have a fire in Sonora. I can still see the Volunteer Fire Department running down the street with their hose carts as if they were in a race. In fact, the fire companies did have a contest every Fourth of July. They would race down Sonora's main drag with their hose carts and vie with one another to see who could make the connection and throw water first.

Holidays were the happy times, they usually featured some big and fancy eating. Turkey for Thanksgiving and Christmas, suckling pig at New Year's, glazed ham at Easter. My parents weren't too religious. They would send me to church, except on Easter, a big day when they went, too. The pastor at St. James Episcopal Church handed out chocolate eggs from Mrs. Lick's and put on a big Easter egg hunt afterward. Then the Knights Templar would march down Washington Street. My father would be all decked out in a uniform, a big white sash across his chest and a sword on his hip and an ostrich-plumed hat. By paradetime, Dad would have had quite a few snorts, and he would trip on his sword and catch himself long enough to grab another little nip from his bottle and then he would trip again. He was wonderful.

I couldn't have been more than six or seven when the Shriners came to Sonora for some big pageant. Grandpa Belli and three uncles had all been Shriners and Dad was a candidate for the Shrine and this was the time for his "crossing the hot sands." They put him in a loincloth and clapped a bone on his head and black shoe polish all over his face. Then they locked him up and hauled him from the Sonora depot downtown right past our big brown-gabled house. "There's your father in the cage there," my mother said with a tinge of contempt in her voice. I recall bursting into tears. But I don't know whether it was because they had imprisoned my father in a cage or because of my mother's apparent sarcasm.

Except for the holiday times, I didn't live in a very happy house. There was an awful lot of arguing and fighting. My mother was always nagging my father about something. Sometimes, he'd reply, but most of the time he would just shrug and bury himself in the newspaper.

One day as the family was preparing to take a trip to Alaska, I went down to the barber shop and had all my hair cut off. Shaved shiny bald.

"What—have—you—done?" cried my mother. I didn't answer her. Wasn't it all rather obvious? Getting that haircut was probably my first subtle protest against the establishment—and against my mother, who was trying to take over more and more. Dad had bought this case of gin for the Alaska trip (it might get pretty cold up there) and when he was winding up things at the bank, mother poured half of the gin out of every bottle and replaced it with water. Watered the whole case. I saw her do it, and that's when I went down and had my head shaved. Dad didn't discover it until we'd set sail for Seattle, the first leg of our trip, and then you should have heard the howls from him.

Of course, it didn't do him any good. My mother just pursed her lips, put her coat on and went out on deck. My father stood there frowning at me, then reached over and removed my fur cap (mother having insisted I wear the cap at all times to cover my baldness). He smiled at

me and shook his head sadly. And I think he knew that
I had somehow "got my mother" by getting that haircut.
At that moment I think that if there'd been a barber on
board he would have gotten a shearing too.

My mother never spoke to me about sex. My father
didn't talk to me about it either, but I had the feeling
that there was only one reason why he didn't: my mother
wouldn't approve. But my father was brimming over with
life, and everywhere we'd go people would hail us. They'd
make a big fuss over me—"Caesar Belli's boy!" We'd
walk into Bill Burnham's ice-cream parlor, and Bill would
shout a big hello and give me a soda with an extra scoop
of chocolate ice cream in it, or a double sarsaparilla.

We'd get the big hello from Harold Ellsbee, too. Ellsbee's was right across the alley from my father's bank.
Ellsbee's great mahogany bar had been sloshed and aged
for years with good proof whiskey, and it had a great
big shiny brass rail you could rest your foot on while you
were having a drink. It had come from the East Coast
all the way round the Horn. That's the very bar that
keeps company with my memories in my office now in
the Belli Building.

My father and I would take jaunts in his car, always
a new Chalmers or an Oldsmobile. The cars were open
then, and the roads were a foot thick with dust, so we
wore khaki dusters over our clothes and great big leather
gloves and goggles and caps. If there was another auto
ahead of ours, the dust would settle down on us with
particles that would leave our teeth gritty. At nightfall,
Dad would get out and match-light the acetylene lamps
on the front of the car. What a great picture it was! The
two of us all dressed special for the drive, bouncing along
the dusty road at the great speed of ten or fifteen miles
an hour with the acetylene lamps sputtering in front and
casting a bouncing light on the tall pines that lined the

narrow road and seemed to stretch their branches out around us.

Mother didn't drive. Or smoke. Or swear. Or anything that was any fun. In the summers, however, she got a reprieve from what I imagine was the dullest kind of life. Each year, Dad would drive me and my mother and my aunt Edith Mouron and her son, Del, who was a year older than I, up to Strawberry Lake, where we would make camp and enjoy the mountain air.

We had a cabin on the South Fork of the Tuolumne River. The stream was full of hungry, fighting rainbows, but the meadows buzzed with rattlesnakes. Del and I caught a lot of trout up there, and my mother and my Aunt Edith had a special way of cooking them in a huge, iron Dutch oven sunk into a hole in the earth lined with hot coals. They put in the trout layer by layer, throwing on bay leaves, black olives, red wine, tomatoes, sage, rosemary and a few other spices. I think my mother even did some fishing herself, but I can't imagine how she could have scrambled up and down the stream and over the rocks (that sometimes harbored sunning rattlesnakes) in those ankle-length denim skirts and those long-sleeved blouses that buttoned up to her neck.

My mother was a closed person. She never let me know how she felt and made it very clear that any attempts of mine to let her know how I felt were *verboten.* I was a lone child in a usually silent household. The radio hadn't been invented yet, and I spent most of my time reading. One day my father brought home a set of *The Book of Knowledge,* and I'd hunker down reading the books in back of the wood·stove with Jack, my Irish setter, who found the warmth and the smells there as pleasant as I did.

The anonymous authors of *The Book of Knowledge* didn't just tell me how many miles to the moon, they told me in terms I could visualize for myself. If you could put X million railroad boxcars end to end, then the moon would be that many boxcars away from the earth. Miles I couldn't understand, boxcars I could. That modus operandi stayed with me ever after. It was the beginning of my "demonstrative evidence."

I was a curious child. I always wanted to know *why* a thing was so. I learned at an early age that very few people had good reasons why a thing was so. My mother had a whole barrelful of nonsense to feed me. She used to tell me never to get a drink of water in the dark because a snake might come out of the faucet into my glass. I had this insatiable urge to see new things and just stand back and enjoy them as they were without philosophizing about why they were or moralizing about whether they were good or bad. Everything that was, to me, was good: otherwise (and this is the closest, I think, I've ever come to elaborating any kind of coherent theosophy), God wouldn't have made it—or given us the capacity to make it ourselves.

What free spirit I have I got from my grandmother, Anna Mouron, who had been born in Shleswig-Holstein. My mother used to take me over to Grandma Mouron's Rexall Union drugstore on Friday afternoons to spend the weekends. Grandma Mouron was a salty, earthy woman who didn't see anything wrong with giving me an occasional glass of frothing German beer or in engaging everyone who came into the store in talk and laughter. When we went to bed at night in her big double brass bed with the fluffy Continental comforter on top, we said our prayers out loud together. Grandma and I would talk and maybe we'd laugh if we heard the cats scrambling and screeching on the back stairs and then, under the hypnotic ticking of the big grandfather clock that I have in my office now, I'd drift off to sleep.

One Saturday night, just before we were about to close the store, some cowboys who'd gotten snorted up rode their horses right into the drugstore. Grandma didn't shriek or call the sheriff. She just picked up a broom and went ofter those cowboys shouting good-natured imprecations at them in German and hitting their horses on the flanks, shouting them out of the store.

I used to study the patent-medicine bottles on her shelves. Each label had a lot of writing and a list of ingredients—all new names to learn and wonder about—and an intricate engraving of some bearded wizard or a bucolic country scene or a couple of animals or even an abstract fret that could have come from ancient Mesopotamia. Ayer's Cherry Pectoral, Lydia Pinkham's Compound, HHH Liniment, Perry Doan's Pain Killer.

In the dark brick-and-shale-lined basement below the store was a room where the condoms were kept. Some had snakes and warts and wasps raised in rubber on their surface and were sold by the gross to the ladies in the square block in back of the drugstore—Sonora's red-light district. Later, I was to first deny, then cry in indignation when I was told my grandmother owned these well-paying houses. But there was something even more interesting in that basement, a human skull. I dreamed that it was the skull of a dead Indian, and from then on neither money, ice cream nor candy could entice me down into that cobwebbed basement alone.

Grandma had her own remedy for malaria, and it was advertised on a sign that ran all the way across the front of the store: CHAMPION FEVER CURE. I guess most remedies of the time were 90 percent water, 9 percent alcohol and 1 percent a combination of herbs—but that's all people had. Their faith and imagination and the marvelous powers of the human body did the rest. But it was a time when appendicitis was fatal more often than not.

I had chicken pox and measles and sore throats and, when I was about ten, I was circumcised. Once, when I was sick in bed, my mother prevailed upon the Episcopalian bishop to come to our house to confirm me. His Grace was a big, jolly man who looked like Charles Laughton. He came huffing and puffing up this long flight of stairs and he never spoke directly to me. He kept looking at me and talking about "the boy." Gee, I was the only boy in the room, why didn't he talk to me? Finally, he got out his chrisms and he said to my mother (not getting any answers from the boy), "What's the matter with the boy?" Chicken pox, said my mother.

"Arggh" and "Harrumph," said His Grace with a mighty clearing of his throat and a scuffling of feet. He was waddling out of there and down the stairs in less than a minute, and I thought to myself, "Doc Hood has been here and he wasn't scared, but this guy comes with (supposedly) much heavier medicine and he is terrified!" Some of these "holy men," I thought, must be phonies. Later, I found out many of them were.

I will always remember my first visit to San Francisco in 1915. I was only eight, but it was love at first sight, the beginning of a romance that continues to this day.

They were celebrating the City's recovery from the earthquake and the fire with something called the Panama Pacific Exposition. The Exposition had twelve palaces, each one built to brag on some glory of the Far West. There was an amusement park called "The Joy Zone" with rollercoasters and Ferris wheels and a thousand sideshows. There was a track for racecars and some flyers who did stunts over the Bay that positively thrilled this little eight-year-old. Two men did loop-the-loops in their no-cockpit biplane and at night, too. William Jennings

Bryan spoke there that day. And John Philip Sousa and his band played "Three Cheers for the Red, White and Blue" in front of the resplendent "Tower of Jewels."

The Panama Canal had just opened a new gateway between east and west, and from a large platform at the Exposition I stood and looked at a great, dynamic water-filled model of the canal, with real locks, that worked. I said to my father, "Someday, I'll go through these locks."

"Indeed, you will," my father replied. At this time, he was well on his way to becoming a millionaire.

My dad was a good banker, because he liked people—and people liked him. He was one of the handsomest men I have ever known and he smelled of lavender or carnations and, at times, of Sen-Sen—and bourbon. He was outgoing and efficient. He brought an awful lot of business to the bank and from all manner of people, not only the old established shopkeepers of the town but other kinds of entrepreneurs who needed short- or long-term cash. He was one of the first men to drive a car over the Tioga Pass into Yosemite. And when the State of California was giving Tioga to the federal government, the state selected my dad to make the appraisal. Dad was always bringing home some grouse or sage hen, geese or ducks, trout and venison.

Caesar Belli had long since ingratiated himself with the Chinese merchants because he didn't treat them (or anybody else) as inferiors. No one at the bank could help a Chinese merchant except my father. Old Bob Teefee, who was president of the bank, would say, "Well, get Caesar," and my father would come. The patient Oriental would be all smiles and he would reach into his smock and pull out some ginger or an Easter lily.

One day, I remember my father returning early from the bank, changing his clothes, packing a big picnic basket and hopping into his Chalmers. He wouldn't say where he was going, but later that evening my classmates Pat Guerin and Sooey Ng told me about it. A hired killer had arrived on the stage from San Francisco to get Sooey's dad. We never did find out exactly who wanted Sooey's dad dead or why, but my father had heard about it moments after the killer, all dressed in black and carrying a violin case, with a big, black pigtail running down to his black slippers, had gotten off the stage and ambled on down to the Victoria Hotel. While this guy was signing the register at the hotel, Dad was already taking Bill Burnham and Sooey's father to a hideaway in Kennedy Meadows.

This killer seemed to be in no apparent hurry. He just sat on the porch of the Victoria Hotel rocking back and forth, with his violin case at his side, smoking cigarettes. Pat Guerin, Vernon McDonald, Sooey Ng and I watched him from a distance for a couple of hours and then finally we got enough courage to sneak up through the back of the hotel and spy on him while he rocked away on the porch. Closer up, we could see he was wearing black pantaloons under his black smock and we tried to figure out whether he had a gun in that violin case or a hatchet. "He's a hatchet man all right if I ever seed one," whispered Vernon McDonald. Of course, Vernon hadn't ever seen a hatchet man, but we knew what he meant. As we watched this villain rock back and forth, he smoked his cigarette right down to his yellow fingernails and the smoke curled up under his eyes. He wouldn't bat an eye or speak to anyone. Then he sensed our presence and very slowly started to turn toward us. He never saw us. Before he had finished moving around, we were already out the back of that hotel. We were scared. We knew his mission was death.

The hatchet man stayed seven days rocking away on

the front porch of the hotel. He never saw Sooey Ng's dad, and after a week (apparently, that was all the time he had to allot to this contract) the hatchet man got back on the stage to Stockton. Then my father and Bill Burnham went up and got Sooey's dad out of Kennedy Meadows and brought him back to Sonora. The hatchet man never came back.

Early school bored me. I never cared what $1,000 would bring me at 6 percent compound interest or how soon it would take two locomotives going fifty miles per hour to crash into each other. (I was more interested in wondering what stupid dispatcher would want to send two trains hurtling toward each other at fifty mph.) I liked to chew over things my own way and examine things upside-down. I liked to read. I discovered Edgar Rice Burrough's Martian stories and Robert Louis Stevenson. Mrs. Fahy took three of my best friends, Pat Guerin, Irving Symonds and Vernon McDonald, and skipped them to the sixth grade, but she didn't skip me. I really didn't care that much, but as soon as my mother heard about it, she rushed down to the schoolhouse to find out what was wrong with little Melvin and how come he got passed over. I could have told her if she'd asked me. I had a mind of my own and I didn't cotton to parroting stuff back to the teacher. That was all. But to hear my mother at that time you'd have thought she'd just gotten the news that I had just been pronounced the village idiot.

I remember when a traveling medicine man came to town once with a circus troupe. This fraud was selling some miraculous elixir in front of the gas lamps. He had something that was absolutely guaranteed to grow hair on the baldest pates. It seemed only natural to ask, "How do we know it will grow hair?"

This fellow frowned, and everyone else turned and

frowned at me, too. "How dare you ask such an impertinent question, little boy?" Well, the medicine man wasn't going to get angry at the little boy, was he? Hell, no, he was going to be big about it and answer the little snot's question. "Because, young man," he boomed, "it says so right here on the bottle." And he read the legend on the bottle. "This marvelous elixir"—there was an unmistakable note of triumph in his voice—"will . . . grow . . . hair!"

"Hooray!" shouted the crowd, congratulating the guy for putting me in my place. "It says so right on the bottle, kid!" Oh.

My cousin Del was kind of cruel, too. "It says so right on the bottle," he said accusingly over his cotton candy. I could only shrug. It seemed that I was the only one in the crowd who saw the flaw in the fraud's "proof," but I couldn't call it by its right name then.

However, Del would soon get his. We were walking behind this tent with a hole in the back of it and this carny was standing there with a silly grin on his face. He didn't say anything to us, just kind of smiled when Del stuck his head in the hole to see what was on the other side. He soon found out. It was the shortstop on the Sonora town team armed with a baseball. He caught Del right on the bridge of the nose. Broke it good. Del had a bump there for the rest of his life. We both learned something.

One summer evening in 1916, my grandmother rang us on the telephone—we were among the first families in town to have a telephone—to tell us in high alarm that the Kaiser was bombing Sonora. At the time, of course, the Germans were dropping some kind of primitive missiles on London from Zeppelins, and Grandma Mouron was quite certain that the Kaiser, knowing in some magical way about Grandma Mouron's anti-German sympathies, had sent the Zeppelins over Sonora in retaliation. We rushed outside to scan the evening skies. Indeed, we saw some strange lights, then realized what they really were: Several boys in town were flying huge box kites with candles in them. It took my dad lots of talk to convince Grandma Mouron that the Kaiser wasn't after her.

It was 1917. I was ten. A lot of the younger men were going off to war. But instead of going to war, my father went off to Stockton. For a big block of stock, he agreed to take over the San Joaquin Valley Bank. He was moving to bigger and better things and he wasn't in Stockton a year before he made a trip to San Francisco to sell his considerable holdings in the Valley Bank, 2,200 shares, for $200 a share to A. P. Giannini. The transaction would have given Giannini control of the San Joaquin Valley Bank—and, incidentally, would have given my father $440,000 worth of stock in Giannini's Bank of Italy, later to become the Bank of America. (Held and passed on to me, that block of stock would now be worth some $440 million.) The law didn't allow branch banking then and so Giannini, anxious to start a bank in Stockton, readily agreed.

But something went awry in Stockton. My father had second thoughts and didn't think it quite right to sell the other minority shareholders down the river. He wrote Giannini a note. "We . . . could not under any circumstances feel justified in accepting a bonus for our stock no matter how great that may be and then allow the minority interests to take care of themselves the best way they can at the solicitation you may afterward deem proper to make them." He signed off, ". . . regretting our inability to favorably consider your offer . . . with kindest personal regards, I am, Yours very truly, C. A. Belli."

Giannini was furious. In a note posted only one day after my father's letter, Giannini pointed out that it was Belli who made the original offer, that it was Belli who set a price of $200 a share on his holding and that it was Belli who hadn't thought of taking care of the minority interest when he made the offer, until he had the later misgivings. "Your letter to us," wrote Giannini, "doesn't quite jibe with the interview you had with the writer the other day in the presence of our friend, Mr. Wolf. We assure you that we are more than glad not to be connected up with anyone who distorts facts as you do. Yours respectfully, A. P. Giannini, President, Bank of Italy."

I have no idea how this unfortunate contretemps may have hurt my father in his banking career. I rather doubt that it could have helped, but the fact remains that the Belli family continued to live in the most comfortable style, now that my father branched out into ranching as well as banking. I was to spend my teenage years in the booming, big town of Stockton instead of sleepy little mountainous Sonora.

CHAPTER TWO

Bare-Assed Naked

My father bought a large ranch near Stockton in a place called Woodbridge. He grew grapes and raisins and pears, and he had about seventy-five workmen to run the vineyards and the dehydrating plant. During the fall, I'd pick grapes at twenty-five cents a box, cabernets, chardonnays, chenin blanc, pinot noirs. The place was called the Martha Washington Vineyard, and it was one of the great vineyards of California. Dad would sell these grapes to the wineries. Then, in 1919, the drys overtook the country's senses and forced Congress to make illegal the selling of beer, wine, whiskey and other of God's own fermented beverages. This law, the Volstead Act, didn't impress the folks up in the Mother Lode. Garrotte had thirteen saloons that never closed a day during Prohibition. The feds would come in one day and shut down the bars and put the proprietors in the local bucket, but the sheriff would turn them loose immediately. No local jury would touch the men who were making or selling booze. And so, down in Stockton, my father didn't even think twice before he put out raisin bricks about the size of a loaf of bread, along with a death's head label that read, "CAUTION: Do not put this in water at 105° temperature and do not add yeast and sugar because this will turn into excellent wine."

The feds came to the door to ask my father about these wine bricks. They put the squeeze on him and made him give all kinds of incriminating evidence against himself. Had the lawyer now been the boy then, he would have stopped this nonsense. What a scene it could have been. But that's daydreaming. Dad had to stop producing wine bricks. Even though the bricks were good in themselves, Congress made them bad by simply decreeing they were bad and forced people with common sense to become, technically at least, outlaws.

I think my father got overextended. Being a banker, he knew how to float everything. He bought too much land and got in way over his head. When a crop failure came, it hurt Dad more than it should have. He didn't have any cash to back him up. I remember how one rainstorm hit and took out a whole crop of Black Princes. My father was gambling on continued fair weather. But the grapes mildewed, and that was the end. With setbacks like that, the family fortunes began to decline. And maybe my father began to work a little overtime on his drinking.

He went to San Francisco to pick up a new Packard roadster, a consolation prize to himself. To celebrate getting the new car, he probably bent the elbow at his favorite St. Francis Hotel bar more than a little bit. It was quite late when he headed back for Stockton. And it just happened to be snowing there for the first time in years, so Dad's perceptions were off a bit. At any rate, when Dad got home, he zipped right up the driveway, drove smartly into the garage—and right out through the back of it, taking half of the splintered garage with him. It made one hell of a racket. I came tearing down in pajamas to see what happened, and my mother was right behind me. The two of us stood in the snow and watched my father ease himself out of his new Packard. He was smashed to the gills but he was, as always, full of dignity and not a thread on his immaculate person was out of place. He sized up my mother's blubbering and hysterics in a flash. With a stern gaze, he said, "Madam, what is the boy doing out here at this time of night in his pajamas?" I think this is where I first learned that the best defense is a good attack.

I, too, would soon have my first adventure in an automobile. My parents were off to a New Year's party. Ed Peckler, Don Carr and Percy Smith came over and helped me get my dad's car out of the garage. We pushed it out into the street 'cause we didn't know how to back it out of the driveway. Then I drove it across town and back, and we eased it back in the driveway and into the garage. My parents never found out. It was really quite a thrill. I may have been fourteen or fifteen years old. All that power and not knowing exactly whether I could control it.

I'd begun to feel the same way about sex. There was an undeniable power there, and I wasn't exactly sure what to do with it. Mother and Father conveyed the unspoken impression that sex was better left to the grown-ups, maybe by the time I was sixty-eight or so. Fortunately, I found a girl named Helen (a big girl with a pretty face, who later joined the Salvation Army), who led me out to the back steps of the high school science building one balmy night during a school dance and showed me a thing or two. (To say this opened up a new world for me would be as much understatement as to say "Columbus once took a trip.")

I hadn't been much of an orator or public speaker. After Helen, however, I had an extra measure of confidence in myself. I remember going on the stage and facing this sea of faces and going completely blank for a moment. Then I gulped and said brightly, "It's not that I can't remember what to say, it's just that I have so much to tell you I can't decide what comes next." That brought the house down. Then I was on my way—forevermore—and I finished with a flush and flourish. Minnie Howell, my English, drama and public speaking teacher, was crying tears of delight when I came off the stage. She was cross-eyed and bowlegged and as homely as a sluicebox but she was a great teacher and she loved me. She said, "Melvin, you'll have a thousand and one audiences, and they'll have a love affair with you." Soon she had me playing the lead in the high school plays. She also put me on the debating team and made me the sports editor of the school paper, *The Guard and Tackle.*

My senior year in high school came much too fast to suit me. I wasn't ready to grow up. My Irish setter, Jack, got run over by a car. My dad and I carried him back up to the house. All that poor Jack could do was look at me with those big, sad, brown eyes. He tried to drink some water I got for him, but that didn't help. He just lay down and started to die. I lay down with him and the two of us died together. "Come on, Pete," my father said. It was one of the few times he ever called me Pete. He was taking Jack out to the ranch to bury him and he wanted me to come. I didn't go. I wasn't going to cry anymore and I wouldn't share my sorrow with anyone, not even my father.

It was too bad I didn't go with my dad. That was an opportunity for me and my father to grow closer. Instead, we continued to drift further apart.

The following year, 1925, I became the class valedictorian and I was headed for Berkeley. My cousin Del Mouron was just finishing school in Sonora and he was going to go to Cal. So was his friend, Harry Cobden, whose father was postmaster in Garrotte (now Groveland). (He was called "Post Office Ed.")

In the spring play, *The Whole Town's Talking,* by John Emerson and Anita Loos, I was given the part of Donald Swift, flamboyant movie director. I liked that. And then I started working on my valedictory address, which I called "Respect for Law and Order." I pilfered half of it from one of the books on my shelf and improved on it considerably (I thought) by adding a lot of bigger words. I can still remember the opening lines of that speech: "Through the mist of the vast phantasmagoria of early life, justice reared its head." It was a beautiful beginning. I never gave it.

Shortly before graduation, my folks went off to San Francisco. About fourteen of my buddies and I went to see C. B. DeMille's *Ten Commandments.* It was pretty impressive seeing all ten of the commandments coming out of clouds and lightning and all, but after that smashing opening it really was more fun watching Gloria Swanson taking a milk bath right on the screen. After the movie, we felt like going out and breaking a few of the ten, but, failing to find any action, we went over to my house instead and borrowed several bottles of my dad's vintage and went up to *The Guard and Tackle.* Well, it got pretty drunk out that night. Somebody started laughing uncontrollably. Somebody started dumping files all over the office floor. Somebody started hurling wastebaskets out the window. Somebody called the principal, Mr. Garrison—who suddenly materialized before our eyes—a son-of-a-bitch. Somebody started running. Somebody fell down the stairs. It was Belli.

Next morning, about eight o'clock, Mr. Garrison phoned my mother and told her I better not come to school. "Oh," she said, "little Melvin won't be there today. He's a little under the weather. The doctor's here now." The principal said he had no doubts about little Melvin's being ill. He told my mother what had happened. It took him quite a long time to tell the story. Result: suspension, no valedictory and no diploma.

We had two weeks to go before graduation. I didn't know what to do with myself. Grandma Mouron was coming to visit. I couldn't let her know that I was suspended, my mother said. So when Grandma arrived, I got dressed every morning as if I were going to school and took off at 8:15 for the Stockton Public Library. During these last two weeks of no school I got in a lot of reading—more than I would have at school.

But what would happen to me without my diploma? I had to have that scroll to get into Berkeley. At this point, I had my first personal experience with The Law, in the person of an old codger my dad took me to see named Judge Rutherford. He had the florid complexion of a drinking màn. Red-veined, whiskey nose and a beer belly, he sat nodding portentously as my father explained what had happened at *The Guard and Tackle*. I wondered, why is everybody taking all of this so seriously? All I had done was get drunk and I had already been punished for that. I just wanted my diploma.

But no. We had to go through all this formal folderol. The judge mumbled a lot of juristic incantations which, to me, were a pull on my father's pocketbook. My first experience with the law, and I could see "fee" written all over this guy. But my father had already had a fruitless session with the principal, so we went along with the judge, who started rummaging around the whiskey bottles in his rolltop desk looking for a bunch of legal forms. He hauled out a couple of writs, a replevin, a bench warrant, a subpoena duces tecum, a habeas corpus, a habeas diplomam, and a handful of old bail bonds. He stuck them all together with notary public seals and a red ribbon, put on his W. C. Fields top hat, marched over to the high school (with me and my father tailing behind) and served the whole thing on the principal. I got my diploma on the spot. It was the most majestic legal encounter in my entire life at the bar then or since.

Some chroniclers of my life and hard times have attempted to say that this is when I decided that I must be a lawyer. I'm not so sure about that. In truth, I really don't know when I decided. I think I always wanted to be a lawyer—just as I always wanted to travel. Lawyers were leaders. Lawyers would settle disputes. Lawyers would do the talking. Lawyers would square things for those who didn't have the heat to do it themselves. Old Judge Rutherford undoubtedly helped me see that you could do things with the law—that the law, though "a ass," was an ass that you could yoke up to carry burdens for you, if you only knew how to do it. Judges (lawyers with notions of grandeur) are a lot like the Wizard of Oz. Some have a phony facade, and you can see through it if you're intelligent enough; once you do and know how to handle it, you can have a lot of fun in and with the law. When I realized that, I knew I'd be a lawyer. It was only later, after I started practicing, that I also learned that it would be more fun not to be just a run-of-the-court lawyer, but the best damned lawyer in the land.

But still the question I'm most usually asked I can't answer. "When did you *decide* to be a lawyer?"

I can remember, even as a child, that I already knew I'd be a lawyer someday. There was no particular trial lawyer or trial that inspired me, just the profession of lawyering itself. For me it's just a majestic business! And along the way I really faltered only once. That was because of my greatest passion for—TIBET:

Rowan Gaither, whose dad was president of the Pacific

Security National Bank in San Francisco, and I studied at law school together. Gaith graduated number one in our class and went along to become chairman of the Ford Foundation, but he died when he was quite young. I used to be a guest in his home quite frequently and became friendly with his dad, who was a real great guy. As a banker, Gaith's dad had friends and business associates all over the world, but none as interesting to me as the legendary "Mr. Benjamin," who came from Tibet. Benjamin was an importer-exporter and dealt in silver. One day he went to Mr. Gaither and asked if Mr. Gaither's son would be interested in coming with him to spend six months in Tibet while he, Mr. Benjamin, spent six months "outside"; then the positions would be reversed. Mr. Benjamin didn't have a son, and he made it clear that he wanted to treat whoever took his job as a "son." The opportunity to travel would be limitless, but living in Tibet for six months at a time—that was my fondest dream. I've always had some mystical liking for and romantic alliance with Tibet. I've read everything on Tibet I could lay my hands on, even manuscripts for doctors' theses. I envied the Lowell Thomas expedition to Tibet; my license plate is "TIBET." Once, in later years, when I was in Katmandu, I had the opportunity to take a Royal Nepalese Air Force plane over Everest and Tibet. How I would have liked to have parachuted down onto the Tibetan plateau!

Mr. Gaither's dad ruled against the job for Rowan and when Rowan turned it down Mr. Gaither halfheartedly offered it to me. I literally didn't know what to do, but I was definitely interested. However, I didn't have to make up my mind for, shortly after the job was offered, there was an international crisis in silver and the legendary Mr. Benjamin lost everything he had. It was such a disheartening blow to him that he didn't want to start over again, with or without a surrogate son. I still haven't set foot on Tibetan soil. I still very much hope to.

But I am leaping ahead too far, too fast. In the summer of my eighteenth year, in 1925, when I started at Cal, I wasn't all that serious or ambitious. I just wanted to have fun. And I did.

In early September, Del Mouron and Harry Cobden, both earthy, salty sons of the Mother Lode, stopped for me on their way to Berkeley in an old Model T Ford. They had one of Harry's Irish setters in the back seat. I think his name was Rocky. Rocky became a campus mascot, overfed and overloved and lazy. Harry and Del stayed at my house that night, and in the morning when I was starting to load my trunk into the Model T, I told Harry to go to the basement and draw some wine from my father's thirty-gallon cask. Harry already had some liquor in the Model T, but his eyes lit up at the prospect of adding some wine to the supply. So casual-like, he ambled downstairs. He'd gotten two gallon jugs filled and was working on a third when my mother caught him in the act. "Uhhh," said Cobden, "I thought my dog was down here."

"Is the dog going to drink all that?" my mother asked, tapping her foot. Soon, Harry emerged with a shit-eating grin on his face—and no jugs. I shook my father's hand, kissed my mother good-bye, pretended to listen to her last-minute admonishments and jumped into the back seat with Rocky. We careened down the street and then Harry stopped, reached for a bottle of good mountain whiskey, turned it upside-down and took a long pull. "One for the road?" he said. I took a good gulp of the stuff and handed it to Del. "I'm going to like Cobden," I said.

"Oh, Senator Cobden?" Del replied. "He's okay."

I don't know where Cobden got the name "Senator."

He was always Senator Cobden to me from that day forward. And somehow I was Doctor Belli. Anybody asked Cobden what state he was senator from, he said he was from the State of Goodwill. Cobden could have been a senator. He was a consummate politician and a great raconteur and, except for occasional attacks of backcountry sass, had a real way with people. We hadn't been in Berkeley for more than a couple of days when Cobden's way got us in—and out of—some real trouble.

We were walking through Sather Gate when we happened on a group of sophomores hazing one of the incoming freshmen. It was our old Chinese friend Sooey Ng, and these laughing boys had him dressed like an Indian. They were daubing their idea of warpaint all over his body. Cobden went over to the group and tried to persuade them to give up their captive. They wouldn't— which was what Cobden had been hoping for, because he hadn't gotten into a good battle yet at Berkeley and he needed a fight to keep him healthy.

We got into the goddamnedest slugfest, a fight that started small with four of us squaring off against four of them and ended up with half the freshman class coming to our aid against a gathering crowd of upperclassmen. They finally had to call out the campus gendarmes and the local fire department, who used high-pressure hoses to break it up. The gendarmes were resourceful enough to find the troublemakers, me and Cobden, and bring us to the dean's office for fitting punishment.

"This is too serious for me to handle," said Dean Hildenbrand. "You men aren't even an official part of the student body yet and you've already started a riot. You'd better go see General Barrow." Sending us to see the president of the university was the best favor the dean could have done.

"Where you from?" thundered President Barrow.

"We're from the mountains," Cobden said.

"Oh, mountain men, huh?" Barrow replied. "Come in and sit down." Then he ushered us into his inner office, which had a nice smell of strong cigars and good whiskey, and he said, "You men know horses?"

"Hell," Cobden said, "I was born on a horse." I allowed I knew which end of the horse you put the bridle on.

We stayed for lunch, as bedraggled as we were. The general introduced us to his wife, a chestnut filly named Mary, and to his horse, a snow-white mare named Thunderhead. "Take care of Thunderhead and you men won't get into any more trouble here," he said. What he meant, of course, was that if we got into any trouble, he'd be around to get us out of it, an arrangement which worked well until they canned General Barrow and installed President Campbell, an astronomer who didn't have any horses. Cobden and I spent most of our remaining undergraduate days on probation.

In December, 1925, I went home for Christmas and then up to Sonora for one of the family traditionals at Grandma Mouron's. I had the funny feeling when I kissed Grandma goodbye that I wouldn't see her again ever—alive. I was right. In March, I got a letter from Grandma at the Berkeley Inn. "I hope you can stay with it another year," she wrote. "The second year will not be as hard as the first." She enclosed five dollars so I could buy a shirt or a tie. "But do not loan one cent of it to nobody," she added. "Keep it for yourself." She admonished me to "associate with good company so as to keep out of trouble" and signed off "with lots of love." The day after she wrote this note she was dead of a heart attack. I still have the obituary that ran in the Sonora *Union Democrat*:

Death entered our city unannounced Wednesday and took from our midst Mrs. Annie Mouron, mother of Otto J. Mouron, Mrs. W. L. Hood and Mrs. C. A. Belli.

Mrs. Mouron was 74 years old, quite active, and was at the store of her son most every day, and always with a kindly greeting. Wednesday she complained a little of a slight pain in the chest, which soon afterwards proved to be the icy touch that extinguishes the mortal spirit.

I found Grandma Mouron in a coffin at Aunt Julie's in Sonora. I put a red rose in her hand as she lay there, choking back the tears—only to find my mother at my side asking why I looked so sad. I wasn't even allowed to feel sad because my dear grandmother, my closest friend on this earth, was dead.

Growing up with money was a definite advantage. I had high expectations. I'd never settle for less, a belief which has stood me in good stead ever since—in and out of court. There is, of course, another theory: "Growing up poor makes you suffer, and suffering of this sort only contributes to your greatment." Maybe my father subscribed to that theory. When he lost all his money, he disposed of that major impediment to my "greatment." In a couple of years, my father must have gone through a couple of million dollars. I don't know exactly how he did it. But he did it with aplomb. I didn't understand money then and still don't and I have now gone through much more money than he. Sometimes, I have thought, with my good friend, the late Lucius Beebe, that "money is to throw off the rear end of an observation car going over the Truckee summit."

By the time I was finishing my freshman year at Cal,

Dad didn't have much left. He got a job selling mutual funds and earned enough to keep me in college, but not enough to support me in the manner to which I'd become accustomed, so I started on a round of jobs. I became a recreation director at a local playground. I got fifteen dollars a month as a member of the Air R.O.T.C. Harry Cobden and I sold Real Silk hosiery door to door. We opened up a store in the fraternity house and sold clothes, but the brothers ended up stealing our stuff or sleeping on the shirts. I waited table at the frat house and the faculty club, which gave me an opportunity to experiment with about twenty-five different kinds of milkshakes. I was as skinny as Douglas Fairbanks in those days and I ate everything, even moths. The Delts had rushing night every Wednesday. It was difficult to entertain new people week after week, so I started eating moths for the edification of our guests. I would pop one into my mouth and swallow the dusty little creature. Then I'd take up a collection and pull in a couple of dollars to see Belli eat another moth. I would down a shot of whiskey afterward in the fervent hope that the whiskey would kill any plague virus, but I lost my job as entertainment chairman the night that Joe Chase (later a Pan Am Clipper captain) topped my act by eating a slug. I couldn't follow that. To make extra money in the summers, Harry and Del and I organized pack trips in the Sierras. Harry and Del were the wranglers and guides; I was the cook.

I didn't take my undergraduate days too seriously. I led a carefree, floating-in-the-stream existence. I got B's and C's, cut a lot of classes, read a lot of astronomy, helped the local girls, mostly nurses and waitresses, in the exercise of their new womanly freedoms. I'd been making a halfhearted shot at rowing in the California crew, but my athletic career ended when, coming home from a party, I fell off the bridge at Sather Gate into Strawberry Creek and broke my ankle. It wasn't until daylight that Cobden found me hung over and bleeding and hardly able to hobble over to the infirmary, where they put my leg in a cast. I became a manager on the track team and a some-time rooter for the Golden Bears' glory on the gridiron—although if it came to a choice between seeing a game or working in the parking lot for some extra spending money on Saturday night, I'd usually bypass the game.

We bought most of our booze in Emeryville, a grungy little town hanging onto the bayside of Oakland, which, despite Prohibition, was full of speakeasies. Sometimes we'd make our own gin with good whole grain alcohol, borrowed from the University's anatomy lab, then add distilled water and glycerin and the juice of the juniper berry to make some pretty awful gin. Most of my frater-nity brothers are dead now; it's probably because they drank too much of it. My own strong constitution made me immune to the stuff's more deadly qualities.

Other than suffering from an occasional bite from John Barleycorn, I have been sick very few times in my life. Once I was in the Cal infirmary for a sore throat. I stayed in the place for three days and no one did anything for me except make me gargle with saltwater. In presulfa, pre-antibiotic days, it was probably the only thing they could do for me, but I was angry, so I phoned Cobden to meet me on the street. I got my clothes and climbed out on the roof and shinnied down a drainpipe. Cobden was waiting and took me back to the Delt House, where I went to bed. They sent the campus police after me, and Cobden came rushing up and moved me down the hall to a closet until they left. But I had to go to the Dean of Men and apologize before I could get back into school for com-mitting such an anti-social act as to leave the hospital. Asinine. I had to apologize to the authorities because they couldn't do anything for me!

After I finished my basic R.O.T.C. they recommended I go on for basic flight training to get a commission in the Air Reserve. So the summer after my junior year I took the next step: I spent six weeks at Crissy Field in the San Francisco Presidio qualifying as an Army Air Corps observer. Then the plan was that after graduation I'd go down to March Field and become an army pilot. The plan went awry when the army and I both discovered that I didn't take too well to regimentation.

My six weeks at Crissy were a riot. I found a like-minded fun-loving companion named Jack Eggleston (he would go on to become editor of *Life*), and together we pulled every caper we could think of. We drained the alcohol from a huge nautical compass and made enough punch with it to throw a pretty good party. We put bowling balls in the sergeant's bed. We drove out to muster at six o'clock one morning, drunk, in my Dodge convertible. The commanding officer just didn't think we were officer material.

It was at Crissy Field that I met Colonel Edward V. Pettis, a dashing figure in a crew cut and jodphurs, doing his reserve-officer bit on leave from the California Highway Patrol. He was a man who took an immediate liking to me and treated me to special privileges. He used to take me up in his DeHavilland with a double cockpit and do stunts over San Francisco Bay. What a scene: both of us wearing these leather jackets and old leather helmets with the goggles and a white scarf tied around our necks, taking off from one of the most dangerous fields in the U.S. We took off right over the Golden Gate, and as soon as we'd raise up a little bit, the winds would lift us right around and we'd be headed back for Oakland.

Once Ed tried to see how much I could take: He did a series of stunts—immelmans, barrel rolls, loops. I loved it. Then he did a dizzying spin down, down, down, right straight toward Alcatraz, and pulled out at what I thought was just about the nick of time. It seemed I could have spit in the yard. But I wasn't scared. Hell, Pettis had as much reason to want to live as I did.

In Berkeley my fraternity brothers and I enjoyed our share of practical jokes. To liven up a dull party once, I suggested that somebody ought to take off all their clothes and run around the block. "Why not you, Belli?" someone challenged. I smiled. Indeed, why not? All I needed was ten dollars so that I would have something more to show for it than the mere notoriety. My brothers, chortling, quickly gathered the money and passed the word around the party that Belli was going to run around the block bare-assed naked. The idea was that I take my clothes off in the vestibule, make a dash for it and end up back at the Delt house.

Only trouble was that my brothers had also alerted all the other fraternity and sorority houses along the route. The brethren and sistern poured out to the street, many of them to their Peerlesses, Wintons, Darts, Moons and Roamers, so they could turn the headlights on me and honk their horns as I dashed by. Naturally, the local cops were in hot pursuit before I'd finished my circuit. Somehow, I got back to the Delt House still untouched by the law. I grabbed my clothes and kept on going right out the back door. The cops didn't get me.

But the dean of men did. He proceeded completely on hearsay evidence, didn't even give me a trial and condemned me to full probation for the rest of the year and for the succeeding summer of residence "for conduct unbecoming a student of the University." I have saved the order as an example of how institutions supposedly dedicated to the higher arts of civilization have always been prone to deny such elementary human rights as due process of law.

But I suppose my most supercolossal production as an underclassman was the free advertising samples I sent for in the name of my classmate Syd Thaxter. I didn't study very much as an undergraduate, that is, the prescribed courses. I did spend a lot of time in the Emerson Shakespearean Library at Cal, I haunted the astronomy buildings and used the telescopes when I should have been back at the fraternity house studying and I randomly searched the library stacks for offbeat books on old customs, weird laws, ancient civilizations, picture and illustration books of other ages.

After the four years of college and as soon as I set foot into the sacred precincts of Boalt Hall, my school of law on the Berkeley campus, I started really to study. I don't know whether I was struck with the learning lightning then or whether I started to study because it was the custom for students to put as many hours into the law books as they could—until they dropped. For the three years at Boalt Hall I studied from eight in the morning until twelve at night, including Saturday and Sunday, Thanksgiving, New Year's, Christmas and through the summer vacations. During summer vacations I took special courses in Roman law, international law, common law pleadings, and subjects which, though no one directly uses them now, provide tremendous background for the most modern law. Law, like history, is a continuous thing, one reform, one new law built upon an old one, or a new law discarded to be replaced by an earlier law.

I was a voracious reader. Ever since grammar school I had been particularly impressed by the many and varied advertisements in magazines. The advertisements of the old days—corsets, cosmetics, elixirs, deodorizers, menstrual regulators, pimple removers, voice changers, magic eye sparkle—all were particularly fascinating because I had the sneaking idea even then that, though I would have been hard put to articulate it, those advertisers were breaching "warranties." Remember, this was some thirty years before the Cutter case and my contribution to the making of modern warranty law. (See Chapter 13.)

One day while perusing all the myriad advertisements in a modern magazine the thought struck me, "What a pile of goods would come if only I were to send for all the free samples!" I began a project that, had I put in the hours on my undergraduate studies, I would have gotten straight A's in all my courses for the year. For some two months I assiduously clipped every advertisement in every magazine I found that offered something for nothing. Not even counting those who hawked their goods "free" merely for the price of postage, there must have been a thousand that I selected. I cut out all the coupons and put my return address as "Syd Thaxter, Delta Tau Delta Fraternity, 2324 Hillside Avenue, Berkeley, California." I took the bundle of envelopes—and I had to make two trips to the post office—mailed them, then sat down to wait.

The Western returns came in first. It was only a trickle for the first couple of weeks. Then returns from the Midwest added to the stream. When the Eastern returns came in (and the Canadian, too), the stream became a torrent. At first our regular mailman could handle the load. There were just a few raised eyebrows when Syd Thaxter began to receive advertising mail and free samples from Waifer Reducers, Elixir Cough Syrup, Bust Reducers, Hair Remover, Pimple Eradicators, a device for straightening the hump in one's nose, athlete's foot powder (a sample), bicep developers, corn removers, flat-feet straighteners; but then the big stuff began to arrive, the goods sent "on approval." A mailman was added to our regular run and then a special mail truck began to make a morning and afternoon call.

Since the goods ordered were indiscriminate as to use by man or woman, the senior advisor in the house began to be worried over Syd getting so much mail concerning feminine hygiene. He called Syd on the carpet for an explanation. By this time one could hardly get through the front door of the fraternity house after the delivery of the first morning's mail. Poor Syd disclaimed all knowledge of the source of the mail. But he did move out of the house to live at home for the next six months.

The brothers, always hungry at a fraternity house, then began to open Syd's mail, and they ate any of the edibles, whether they were reducing crackers or cakes, supposedly baked to gain or lose weight. Some used the elixirs as hair tonics and others tried out the Mr. Atlas and such bicep developers. But the day of reckoning came when it was time to return the articles sent "on approval." The ten days for "your inspection" were up. We began to be swamped with demands to "return the goods or our lawyer will call." (This could have been an interesting experience.) One day the representative of an Emeryville manufacturer of washing machines sent on approval came to see the president of the fraternity, a skate manufacturer called, an adding-machine supervisor threatened legal action if his machines weren't returned, a medicine-ball fabricator from Los Angeles made his personal complaints, the inventor of a pair of patented glasses that "enabled one to see in the dark" did have his lawyer call, several publishers of encyclopedias wired saying they had only sent their books to us because they thought we were responsible people (I don't know what ever could have given them that idea), the head salesman for several volumes of "original French poses" (this was the day before pornography as we now know it and the pictures really were mild) put in his complaint.

A special house meeting was called and the question

was put to all the brothers, who had to answer under oath, "Who did it?" Of course, when it was put to me, under the sacred bonds of the brotherhood, I could not lie and I answered, "I did."

First I went into the tub (this was a form of punishment in which one was bound hand and foot, then blindfolded, then immersed in a tub of cold water and held under water until he passed out. Really, it was a barbaric form of punishment and a frightening experience.) Then I was assigned the task of getting all the "on approval" goods back to their senders and cleaning up all the advertisements and literature thrown around the house. It was some three weeks before I was able to really make a dent in the trash and return most of the goods, but for some three years afterward, Syd still received mail from various advertisers throughout the United States (and Canada), "as one of our select group of clients and in appreciation of your valued patronage, we would like to send you our latest model—"

CHAPTER THREE

Bellbottoms

I graduated from Cal in June, 1929. I was twenty-two and I still hadn't made up my mind where I wanted to go. I knew I'd be a lawyer and I was thinking about Harvard, but my friends were taking off on cruises to the Orient and to Europe. I had a yearning to travel, too, and I thought of working my way around the world on a freighter. It wasn't a question of traveling now so I could settle down and work all the time for the rest of my life. I knew I'd always travel, I just wanted to get on with it. I bought my bellbottom denims at the army and navy store in Oakland and a big, heavy navy-blue pea jacket and a pair of heavy, rubber-soled boots. I was ready for a stint as an ordinary seaman on the S.S. *Kentuckian* bound for New York— at twenty-five dollars a month.

"Belly?" said the boatswain, as I climbed the gangway, my denim duffel bag over my shoulder.

"Yup," I said. I was heading into a tough, unfamiliar world and I knew enough not to get off on the wrong foot by correcting the guy who seemed to be in charge. If he wanted to call me Belly, that was okay with me.

The boatswain's name could have been Paddy Brennan. He was lean, superbly muscled, a middle-weight boxer. He had an eagle tattooed on his right forearm and two red dragons writhed up out of the hair on his chest. "Okay, Slim, take your things down to your bunk and then get the fuck back up here," he growled. Brennan was a seagoing cliché, but I wouldn't have wanted him to be anything else. I had been sheltered at home, and even when I was at Cal my mother managed to keep a fairly close watch on me. Now I was free.

I had a hard, dirty bunk instead of a good soft bed with crisp sheets on it. Rough clothes, tasteless food and hard talk. It was a complete antithesis to the life I had always had—and I liked it. I told no one I was a graduate of Cal.

The *Kentuckian* was a filthy scow; its night mess was overrun with cockroaches and the regular chow was worse than the night mess. Breakfast was a big piece of salt pork and a few eggs fried in what seemed to have the color and viscosity of 150 weight Pennzoil. (I realized, as never before, that my mother had been a hell of a good cook.) The john was one long, large plank suspended over a trough of running seawater.

One day—we were tied up near San Diego—the boatswain overheard me talking about Berkeley. "Oh, college boy, huh? Well, Slim, I've got just the job for you. When we weigh anchor tonight, you go down to the chain locker with Ernesto here." I had heard that assignment to the chain locker was the worst job in the merchant marine. And when Ernesto and I got down there, I learned why. A winch up above would wind in the anchor chain, and the chain (along with all the dregs of the harbor bottom) would come tumbling and draining into the chain locker. Our job was to grab the chain with a big steel hook and make sure it lay down in even coils.

As the chain kept coming in, of course, there was less and less room for us in the locker. We ended by trying to stand on the links themselves all covered with the stinking slime of the bay, slipping and getting bruised, grabbing for more links and scared that the winch would slip—and that we'd get tangled in it. There were stories all over the seven seas about guys being mangled by the slipping chain. And my partner Ernesto, a Chilean, didn't make me feel any safer. He was a wild man flailing around in that hot locker with his hook. He scared the hell out of me. After the ordeal was over, Ernesto hugged me and kissed me on the neck. You would think we had just gone over Niagara Falls together in a barrel and survived. Now, apparently, we were blood brothers.

It got much warmer as we moved down the coast of Baja California. I found I couldn't sleep in the stuffy bunks below, so I took my mattress to the poop deck, spread it out and just lay there naked, watching the stars and the moon and smelling the sweet, maroon-colored smoke drifting back from the stacks. I could hear the "pug pug pug" of the engines and feel the vibrations of the screws. I was watching the dolphins play in the phosphorescent water when Ernesto stole up and put a heavy hand on my ass. At last, I realized that I was Ernesto's romantic challenge. I belted him.

I'd been waiting to see the Panama Canal, and Brennan, the boatswain, knew it. So he had me painting latrines all through the locks. I never did see the Canal, except through the portholes in the john. But I won a measure of respect from Brennan by not complaining and by doing the work of a half-dozen men when everyone but I got sick in Charleston on some bootleg whiskey. I overheard Brennan telling the second mate, "Jesus, the rest of us are really shit-faced, and the college kid is still standing there belting them down and laughing." As a result, they let me take some turns in the wheelhouse during my off-hours duty. That was fun. It was like steering an elephant.

We docked in Brooklyn in the middle of the night, so I saw nothing but Manhattan's skyline. The next day some of the boys and I took the subway from Brooklyn right into Times Square. Broadway, the Great White Way, more lights than I'd ever seen before, even though it was early in the morning. I just stood there taking it all in: the buildings, the billboards, the theater marquees; God, the people—all kinds of shapes and faces, some of them hurrying along, some taking their time, some extremely pretty girls (actresses, I imagined), some hard-looking hookers, some street types trying to sell everything from mechanical dogs to hot watches, and lots of cops.

What can I say about New York in July of 1929? The country was exploding with prosperity, and New York must have been the epicenter of it all. In every overheard conversation, people seemed to be talking about hundred-thousand-dollar deals, million-dollar transactions. Huge, shiny limousines circled the hotels in an unending procession; occasionally, one would stop to let out the most elegant young ladies and their handsome elder escorts. The menus, posted outside the hotels' posh restaurants, suggested gustatory delights I'd only read about.

At Yankee Stadium, we saw Babe Ruth beat the Detroit Tigers with a two-run homer in the seventh inning. The crowd went wild as the Babe, smiling, rounded the bases with that distinctive, mincing little step of his. Somehow, Ruth's excellence only affirmed the New Yorkers' own chauvinistic view of themselves as surpassing all other humans on the face of the earth. It was fitting, one fan told me, that the Babe would be getting a higher salary than any other man in the world, more even than the President of the United States. (Later, I heard that Ruth himself agreed with the judgment of the man in the bleachers. "After all," said Ruth, "I've had a better year than Hoover.")

That night, we were back on the Great White Way. We had tickets to the Follies, saw Jimmy Durante * perpetrating some mayhem on the piano, banging it with his elbows and his fists, throwing his hat down and having a roaring good time for himself. We didn't return to the ship but found a flophouse where they only charged fifteen cents a night. We slept standing up, draped over a big, padded rope. That's right: they had this rope about four feet in diameter stretched from one end of this overheated room to the other. I looked up and down the line and saw guys sound asleep just bent over the rope, head hanging off one side and feet off the other, and I said to myself, "Gee, how can I sleep here?" I found it was easy. I just fell over the rope and went to sleep. But I didn't have any temptations to oversleep either. And I kept my hands in my pockets.

* Like everyone in America, I've always loved Jimmy Durante. I met him long after seeing him that first time on Broadway and now I've known him for years and spent some time with him at Las Vegas, when I was visiting there with Mickey Cohen. He was also a good friend of Mickey's. So, years later, when it came time for me to cross-examine him in court in Palm Springs, Jimmy eased up to me out on the sidewalk in front of the courtroom and jokingly said, "Take it easy on an old man, counselor."

I had one of those cases I couldn't get out of—and never should have gotten into. Like the friendly surgeon operating for free on Aunt Rosa's appendix. Jimmy and his wife had been guests of some television stars at their Palm Springs digs over New Year's. The male star had purportedly taken too many aboard and had belted a housekeeper, my client, for no apparent reason, or at least the housekeeper said so. She was rather seriously injured and Danny Jones brought

I wanted to ship out for Europe on the *Leviathan,* but discovered I couldn't get a job unless I had an able-bodied seaman's ticket. The union was putting pressure on the steamship company to keep the college kids out. So I took the straightforward step of applying for a ticket as an able-bodied seaman. "Hey, Slim," someone said, "you can't get a ticket. They make you pass a stiff exam and they make you tie more knots than you've ever imagined."

"We'll see about that," I said. "Come on."

So we went down to the Coast Guard, and I wrote a good exam. I passed the little pieces of rope out the window to my buddies outside and they tied the knots and tossed them back in. I got my A.B. ticket. I went on down to the hiring hall and found a job on the *Amerika* for an A.B. who would go as an ordinary seaman. Anything that would get me overseas. Once there, docked in Bremerhaven, I jumped ship.

I wanted to see Europe and I didn't know when I'd have the chance again (it would turn out to be almost twenty years), so I took a train to Berlin and then bought a motorcycle and was off on a tour of Germany. On the

---

suit against the TV personalities—nothing personal, the insurance company would pay it. I was called in to try it and had to challenge Jimmy Durante as a witness to the fracas.

With show folks against you, sometimes it's difficult to get a juror's mind on the case at hand and give objective justice. The jury unconsciously thinks of the show folk in terms of the roles they play which, unless you've got a villain, are all sweetness and light. Jimmy dropped the bomb on me in answer to the first question and from then on I just couldn't wipe the smiles off the jurors' faces. Starting to cross-examine him, I had asked him, sort of matter-of-factly, "What is your full name?" Jimmy took a long pause, bowed his head, lowered his eyes, profiled his huge nose, as though in mock embarrassment from the complete confession he was about to make, then in a low voice said, "James Aloysius Durante," middle name and all. From then on it was like cross-examining and disbelieving Whistler's mother!

first day, I zipped over to Potsdam and slept in the warm summer garden of the castle, right next to my motorcycle. I felt like some kind of Richard Halliburton. But my dreams of motorcycle mobility came to a sudden end the next day. Back in Berlin, I was cruising along, looking at the city, and then, all of a sudden, I saw one of the wonders of the world, the *Graf Zeppelin,* flying overhead near the Brandenburg *Tor.* The Germans were so proud of the *Graf Zeppelin* they were literally crying in the streets. I couldn't take my eyes off her either. Naturally, I went right off the roadway and into a crowd of weepers. I damn near ran down an old blind beggar, except that he leaped out of the way just in time (which I thought showed rather remarkable presence and agility for a blind man), and crashed into a tree. The German policeman couldn't have been kinder. Instead of locking me up, he found out where I had bought the motorcycle, took me back to the shop and made the owner give me back my money on the grounds that I wasn't a competent motorcyclist. Which I wasn't. I ended up taking trains and buses around Europe. I went as far east as Prague and Budapest.

When I got back to San Francisco late in the summer, the stock market was in a frenzy. Always eager to go where the action was, I promptly got a job as a board marker in a brokerage office. That gave me a ringside seat on the greatest debacle of the decade, the crash of 1929. Transamerica would open at $134 and close at $100 and open the next morning at $50. People who had plunged their savings into the market were wandering about North Beach in a daze and, of course, the stockbrokers weren't feeling too well either. They let me go and—it was too late to get into any law school—I was lucky to find a job with the Dollar Steamship Lines. I shipped out for the Orient as an ordinary seaman on the S.S. *McKinley.*

I was still a naive kid with absolutely no powers of analysis. I hadn't worried myself about Europe's political and economic problems and I was even less able to concern myself with the fate or the feelings of those horrors I saw in Japan or China or the Philippines. Instead, I played the role of irresponsible hell-raiser to the hilt. After an eight-hour tour of duty on the *McKinley,* I'd sneak out of the crew's quarters, make my way through a maze of tunnels, emerge on the first-class deck to duck into an empty first-class bathroom and take a luxurious first-class bath. If anyone knocked, I'd put on a phony English accent overlaid with some German arrogance. "Cahn't you zee I am taking a bath in heah?" They never caught me.

I went ashore in Tokyo with one of the finest guys I'd ever met, a youngster about my age named Herman Kroetzsch, from Massachusetts. In Tokyo, you could buy a bottle of Johnny Walker for fifteen cents. It turned out that it wasn't real Johnny Walker at all but a cheap imitation (copyright or trademark laws either weren't enforced or didn't apply). I never got drunker in my life. I fell down a forward hatchway when I got back to the ship. Herman was almost as drunk as I was and he never had a chance to grab me. I landed on my head and I woke up two days later in a hospital bed in Shanghai. I'd fractured my skull—which frightened me. I was even more frightened when I heard what the guy in the bed next to me was there for: spinal meningitis. I made it pretty clear to the authorities that I wanted to leave that ward before I caught meningitis too. Maybe they thought I was a goner anyway.

But I wasn't. I was out of that hospital in no time. The *McKinley* was still in port, and Herman Kroetzsch had already learned how a sailor ought to live in Shanghai. The Palace Hotel on the Bund in Shanghai was a pleasure palace. Real Johnny Walker in the bar there for ten cents, a plate of oysters for fifteen cents, quality goods in the hotel shops, silks and leathers and brocades and perfumes and gold and silver and diamonds and jade for practically nothing.

In the midst of all this cornucopia, I couldn't help but notice the poverty of the populace: little children scrounging through garbage cans and begging in the streets at all hours of the day and night, kids who had been taught the same spiel in three languages: "Me poor little son-of-a-bitch, me no got father, no got mother, you give me money?" In some remote way, I figured there was a connection between all this poverty and the only people around who looked as if they were enjoying any affluence: the well-heeled English and French businessmen who passed us by in their rickshaws, and the members of the military, American, British and French officers, who seemed to be very much present here in Shanghai. The Chinese would bow and actually get off the sidewalk to let them pass.

One night, we went up to the Astor Hotel for dinner. The finest: caviar, oysters, lobster, crab, venison, guinea hen, pheasant, steak, crepe suzettes, fine wine, champagne, music. All for two dollars a head. The maitre d' told us, as matter-of-factly as if he were telling us about the chief's special desert for the evening, that the management could throw in a beautiful woman as well, worth every penny of the extra five dollars. Herman and I looked at each other for a moment and, trying to be as matter-of-fact as the waiter, said yes we'd like some feminine company for dinner.

Ludmila and Natasha were White Russians; they were almost too much for us. Beautifully coifed and dressed in long, white gowns, full-breasted and long-legged, accomplished during dinner in the art of good conversation, inventive later in the art of love. Much later, Natasha suggested that I might commemorate this occasion by getting a tattoo artist on Bubbling Well Road to stencil a rose on my flank. That, apparently, was part of the sex trip in the Orient—hence, I guess, the expression, "Screwed, blewed [that is, blowed] and tattooed." I didn't get tattooed.

We sailed back through Japan, to the Aleutians, Seattle, Portland and then San Francisco, the Golden Gate. What had I gained by my travel? I wish I could say I acquired a general broadening of outlook, a new world view, a deeper tolerance of the world's diversity, but I knew I hadn't. That would take years more. It would take all my life; indeed, the process still goes on. But I did gain a good friend in Herman Kroetzsch. We sat in the rigging for long hours talking about the places we had seen— and those we hoped to see. I, for one, wanted to visit Russia where, I thought then, a most noble experiment was underway. Herman argued with me. He believed news stories about filth and poverty in the Soviet Union, the country's poor and overcrowded transportation and its police state. I was inclined to disbelieve. I wanted to see for myself. And while we were in the Orient, I had tried to prevail upon Herman to go "on the beach" with me and take the Trans-Siberian Railroad from Vladivostok to the Baltic. We didn't make the adventure together. It would be forty years before I would take that journey. When we docked in San Francisco, I headed for Berkeley, he for Dorchester, Massachusetts, and I would never see him again.

CHAPTER FOUR

Smoky Levis

Travel was good for me to this extent: I had poured myself out on the sights, the sounds, the smells, the tastes and the feel of the world, but I couldn't completely grasp what the hell it was all about. I was empty. I was ready, therefore (and at last), to sit down quietly and learn. In the fall of 1930, I applied to law school, and, though my grades at Cal were only average, Boalt Hall, the University of California's blue-ribbon law school, took me in. It was a lot easier then to get in.

Boalt was the best law school in the country then, and it gave me a classic education. Boalt emphasized legal history and legal theory and legal philosophy (which provided me with an understanding of why we do the things we do in the law). Boalt did not emphasize the mechanics of writing a brief or drawing up a will or avoiding taxation (which is what many students get when they go to a legal trade school). For those of us who didn't come to Boalt to fool around, Boalt made us all better-thinking lawyers, better-reading lawyers, better-sounding lawyers. And here, in the first year of the Great Depression, my classmates were not there to fool around, they were an earnest lot who came to study. That made it easier for me—for the first time in my life—to do the same.

From the very first weekend, I started busting the books. I worked from eight in the morning until the library closed at 11 P.M. I worked Saturdays and holidays and right straight through the summers. Law, particularly its history, fascinated me. Why hadn't someone pointed me this way before, so I could have read? So much time already wasted. I took every course they offered, even though I knew I'd never use many of them. One summer, I studied something called Bills and Notes and another time International Law. Someone once defined genius as the application of the seat of the pants to the seat of the chair. If that's true, then we had 150 geniuses in my class because we all had iron pants.

At first, I didn't know how to write an exam and drew an early C in Torts and another C in Contracts. Those two C's kept me off Law Review, but by the end of the third year I was number thirteen in my class, with straight A's in Criminal Law, Property and the toughest courses. By then, I had no doubts about whether I'd make a lawyer. I knew I would. And though I was still relatively tongue-tied in those early years, I felt confident I would not be one of those attorneys who spent all his time in the office or the library or on the telephone. But the incongruity was that despite this feeling of confidence I had no desire to see a trial or haunt the courtrooms. I spent my spare time in the stacks, perusing old books on common law history, Roman law and oddities of the law. I still love a well-turned legal expression from medieval times—when the profession was classical and esoteric.

We had a great faculty. Radin on Common Law, Ferriter on Real Property and Wills, Ballantine on Torts, Costigan on Contracts, McBain on Evidence, Kidd on

Crimes, McGovney on Perpetuities.

I learned ethics, too, at Boalt Hall. Not the formal kind but the real-life principles that I hope have stuck with me. Max Radin was up for appointment to the California Supreme Court, a court that would soon become the best state Supreme Court in the land. A few days after Professor Radin's appointment had been rumored, two itinerant "Communist" workers had been arrested for vagrancy in Stockton. Without funds, they insisted that the trial court appoint California's best lawyer to represent them. They demanded Max Radin. Everyone told Max if he took the appointment in Stockton, he'd lose the appointment on the court. Max would have loved to have been a Supreme Court justice, but he didn't hesitate for a moment. He said he taught legal ethics, now it was time to practice them. His fellow professor, Roger Traynor, was appointed in his place and went on to become the finest state Supreme Court chief justice in the nation.

Crusty old A. M. Kidd (we called him "Captain Kidd") was the best of them. He was small in stature but a giant in the law. Kidd intimidated the entire class. When he stalked into the classroom, you could hear everyone sucking in his breath. Some days, apparently, he wouldn't feel like teaching. He would start the class with a deadly question: "There is an uprising and the President has declared martial law. Does the writ of habeas corpus still apply? Belli?"

"Yyy-yes," I'd stammer.

Then he would stare at me for a moment with the bluest, coldest eyes I had ever seen, throw down the eyeshade he invariably wore on top of the few white hairs he had on his head and cry: "You numbskull! You're all numbskulls. It's a crime your parents are keeping you in school." Then he would assign about five hundred pages of a particular text that we had to read before the next class, pick up his books and float out of the room on his thick crepe soles.

Some days, I was lucky; I'd have the right response. The Captain would pause, and I wouldn't know what reaction was coming. Then he'd say quietly, "Good answer. That required some thought." Then I'd relax a bit and lean back, but the next pitch was fast in coming: "But now, Mr. Belli, I put this to you . . ." Of course, more likely than not, I wouldn't know the answer to that one. He'd blow me out of the water.

Despite Captain Kidd's behavior in class, he was the kindest, most approachable guy on the faculty when you went to him in his office. He taught Criminal Law and Demonstrative Evidence, and what he taught me stuck. At the end of the year, I got a straight 100 percent on his final exam. Though he didn't like giving A's, he wrote an A on my report, and in parentheses after the A he scribbled "reluctantly." But he was a sweet guy and for several years he used to come to my parties in the City. I wonder if he would have come had he known that on a five-dollar bet I balled a waitress from the Variety late one night on the rolltop desk in his office.

During law school some of my classmates and I accepted several invitations to visit President Herbert Hoover at his home in Palo Alto. The President was seeking to know what we thought about the country. But what could the President get from us but an elitist opinion? And anyway, he ended up doing most of the talking, or, I should say, mumbling, as he tossed two silver dollars in his hand, like Captain Queeg in *The Caine Mutiny*. Toward the end of one session the President turned to one of his aides and said, "Now, Sexton, give the boys a little something to drink." We brightened considerably. Christ, we were going to have a little belt with the President of the United States. We wondered what brand the old man would serve and can you believe what came out on the next tray? A glass of fresh orange juice for each of us. But it was freshly squeezed.

I really liked Hoover. He was as square as they come, but the very fact that he invited me to his home—his politics and his leadership aside—made me lean toward voting for him against Franklin D. Roosevelt (though I had voted for Al Smith in my first presidential ballot). Hoover seemed rock-ribbed honest and determined, like my dad. Then I saw Hoover on one of the last days of his campaign. He was standing on the back end of a railroad car in Berkeley and waving to the crowd, and I pushed up closer to see him, maybe to catch his eye. But then I shrank back. He looked like a beaten man. He had the look on his face of a fighter in the ring when he knows he's beaten.

I graduated from the law school in the spring of 1933. I was twenty-five. It was the middle of the Great Depression. I was imbued with high ideals, but there weren't many places I could exercise them. There were no fellowships then for poverty lawyers, no public-interest law firms. There were a few jobs in private firms. All the lawyers were doing their own research; no one needed a law clerk as much as he needed the few dollars he would have to shell out for a salary. People were begging in the streets. Roosevelt was declaring bank holidays, and my father, the financial wizard, had nothing saved for this rainy day. I didn't know what I would do. Prepare for the Bar exam in August? Hell, I *was* prepared. Or so I thought. I really should have taken one of those cram courses designed for the sole purpose of teaching the would-be lawyer how to answer those tormenting examination questions. But I didn't.

Warren Ollney, one of my classmates, came to me and said he had a line on jobs for the two of us. The job involved a little bit of travel, but it was work and paid seventy-five dollars a week. That was about sixty dollars more than I had in my pocket at the moment.

"What is it, Bill?" I asked.

"Bums," he said. "We're going to be bums for the NRA."

"NRA?"

"The National Recovery Administration. It's one of those new agencies in Washington. Roosevelt says we've got nothing to fear but fear itself. But the NRA is scared of a revolution in this country, and they need more information."

I said I didn't have any information. There were a few Communists on campus, but nobody paid much attention to them.

"That's the point," Ollney said. "They want us to go out and get information. We'll have to ride the rods with the bums and the hobos and see what's up. If there's trouble brewing, they want to know about it."

"A government spy?" I said with a frown.

"Seventy-five dollars a week?"

"Well, shit," I said, "if there's a revolution, I might just join up. But what the hell, let's take the seventy-five dollars a week."

We hopped the first freight headed south. For disguises, we wore new names and old clothes. Warren would be Bill Brucker and I would be Louis Bacigalupi, Slim for short. We both wore high-top army shoes, faded Levis and Levi jackets, stuff we could wash out almost anywhere.

We weren't alone on that first trip, nor on any other. There would always be a crowd of hobos on every train, never fewer than fifty, sometimes as many as three hundred. We were standing in the railroad yard in Oakland wondering which train we ought to take, when this freight started up and all of a sudden a bunch of guys came out of nowhere. Some headed for the few open boxcars, some went for the closest car they could grab, because they didn't care to ride inside anyway; they rode up on top of the cars where they could better see what was up ahead.

The NRA guys had told us to watch out for railroad bulls, the sadistic bastards who were being paid to keep the hobos off the trains. It was up to us to stay out of their way. If we ever got into any real trouble, we had a "secret" telephone number to call the NRA. We never used it.

The bulls looked like a lot of the hobos. Most of us were in our late teens and early twenties. We were all in the same boat. We couldn't get jobs and we were doing the best we could. The bulls had family connections with the railroad. The hobos didn't—and that was the only difference between them and us. Oh, there were some bulls who seemed to enjoy the work a little too much. They were the toughs who didn't just chase the 'bos off the train but beat them to a bloody pulp, too.

Riding an empty boxcar wasn't much fun. It rattled your backbone and shook the fillings right out of your teeth. Our car was filled with straw that made us sneeze. Three or four guys in there stared at us with suspicion. Maybe we were too clean-looking. Bill and I climbed on top of the car where we got dirty enough. The smoke from the train just covered us with soot, our faces became black, our Levi's turned kind of dark gray and we began to look like real 'bos.

Our train took us near San Jose the first night. As it slowed down, all of the 'bos started jumping off and tumbling over and over alongside the grapefields. We guessed they knew what they were doing and we jumped, too. After we got back on our feet, we looked ahead on the track and sure enough we saw a whole phalanx of men with clubs. We followed the hobos to a clump of cotton-woods. There was a creek in among the trees, and a whole camp, a hobo jungle, small fires burning, guys just stand-ing around talking, some drinking coffee out of tin cans, others eating beans or chewing on a crust of bread. Bill and I had a couple of candy bars for supper and looked around without seeming to be too nosy.

We were shocked to find entire families there, little kids and even nursing mothers. We joined one knot of young men and we fit right in; they talked just like us. One guy turned out to be a stockbroker and another said he'd had to drop out of college. We heard a rumor that they'd arrested Herbert Hoover and he was a prisoner in the Chrysler Tower in New York. No one seemed to know who "they" were.

In the morning, we hopped another freight. We didn't care where it was going. We weren't heading anywhere in particular, we were just riding and looking and trying to talk to as many bums as we could. The next night, we got picked up in the Manteca stockyards and put in jail for "vagrancy."

In the morning, the judge gave us what amounted to a warning and let us go. What else could he do? There wasn't room in the jails for all the people wandering around California. Those were the days John Steinbeck wrote about so vividly in *Grapes of Wrath,* but it wasn't only the Okies who were on the move. It seemed like the whole country was either sunk in apathy or just wan-dering about, hoping something good might happen. Some of the nation's "leaders" tried to look the other way. Henry Ford said, "Why, it's the best education in the world for those boys, that traveling around."

These were still the days, however, when the authorities could throw you in jail for "traveling around"—and did.

They called it "vagrancy" and it meant you were in jail because you couldn't get a job and didn't have any money in your pockets. (Thirty years later, the Supreme Court would declare this "status crime" unconstitutional.) If you didn't have any money, chances were that you'd do anything to get some. And that wasn't a wild assumption then. I think ethicians say that if you're starving and there's nothing else you can do but steal a loaf of bread, you steal in good conscience. But of course most towns couldn't have bums coming in and taking the bread off the shelves—so they locked us up and then escorted us back to the railroad yards and saw to it that we moved along.

Down the San Joaquin Valley it was pretty much the same story: Modesto, Merced, Madera. Some of the richest farmland in the world. The ranchers were producing rice, beans, grapes, turkeys, walnuts, melons, peaches, every damn thing—and we were starving. We'd go to the towns and beg. I got pretty good at that. I learned how to go into a bakery and ask for yesterday's bread or into a grocery store and ask for a butt of bacon or some old vegetables, which we'd take back to the hobo jungle and toss into the community pot.

In Fresno, we went to the Salvation Army. They had us chop wood in the back and then say some prayers before we got anything to eat. I guess the Salvation Army needed all the prayers it could get: it was having a hard time too, watering the milk and the soup to make it go around. I can still tell when milk is watered. It's blue.

And then we found a hobo hotel right in the middle of town. It was an old warehouse that served as a meeting place for all the 'bos on the road. You could go there to pick up mail, meet people, get news, leave messages, get a bowl of Mulligan stew for fifteen cents, curl up in a corner and go to sleep. I have forgotten the name of the guy who ran the place. He had a beard and a derby and wore a pair of suspenders that had once been red. Based on reliable sources, he'd post warnings on his bulletin board: "Watch out for the sheriff's deputies in Barstow, they're beating people up pretty bad. Deputies are turning people back at the L.A. County line."

The night we were there, Franklin Roosevelt came on the radio for one of his fireside chats, and it was amazing to see what an effect that aristocratic voice had on these bums. Everybody stopped whatever he was doing and hung on his every word. The President said:

> The American people will pull themselves out of this depression. They will if they want to. I have no sympathy with the professional economists who insist that things must run their course and that human agencies can have no influence on economic ills. I do have faith, and retain faith, in the strength of the common purpose, and in the strength of unified action taken by the American people.

And after that, everybody just kind of sighed and said there was hope after all. But nothing got better. Hope was okay for breakfast, but it made a pretty poor supper. Still, things weren't so bad for Bill and me. We didn't have a care in the world. We knew that this was only a temporary lark for us, that we had law degrees from Boalt Hall, that we'd be taking the Bar exam in August.

When we got to Bakersfield, we had a close call. The bulls were beating people up with some kind of clubs and we ran like hell. We skirted the town and found some 'bos on the other side of town who warned us about trying to get into L.A. County.

The prevailing opinion was to hop a freight through the Tehachapis into the Antelope Valley and then, maybe, get into San Bernardino and then the Imperial Valley, where everything grew and you were sure you wouldn't starve.

The trip over the Tehachapis was cold. I stuffed newspapers in my pants to keep warm. "Thank God for the press," I said, "friend of the poor." And the trip was rough, especially on the downgrade. With the brakes on, the empty boxcar stuttered so much and shook us so violently we almost wet our pants. As soon as we could, we sneaked to the back of the engine. That was the best place to ride. The engine was so heavy it just seemed to sink down into the rails, a smooth ride like snowshoes on oil. That's the way we came into Palm Springs—clinging to the back of the engine. Palm Springs was just a sleepy little town then, mostly Indians on the streets and only one golf course, dried out except for the greens, which were in good shape and provided a nice place for us to sleep the night with only the bright stars for a blanket.

Bill and I would sleep back to back as a precaution against anyone coming up and hitting us over the head. But we had nothing to steal. We saw no real crimes and very few fights and no talk of revolution. No one wanted to march on city hall. Everyone was underfed and undervitaminized and minding his own affairs. People were listless and what they looked for most of all was some kind of leadership on the national level, which they thought Roosevelt might be able to provide.

We were walking down the street in San Diego, looking like bums, when a cruising police car stopped at the curb. "All right, get in, you sons-a-bitches," said the righteous Voice of the Law. The jail was worse than anything we'd seen up to then. You couldn't even sit or lie down in the crowded holding room. If you wanted to sleep, you leaned against the guy next to you. If anyone had to go, they just pissed on the concrete floor and it ran down to the drain in the middle of the room. Some men shit in their pants, and one guy started having an epileptic fit and the jailer did nothing to help him. Then one prisoner vomited, and that started a chain reaction of guys throwing up. It was a scene out of Dante's *Inferno*.

When they served us breakfast of acorn coffee and moldy bread in that shitty room, I got mad. What the hell had any of us done to be treated like this? I resolved to fight back, and by the time we got to court I was ready to take my case all the way to the Supreme Court of the United States. Everyone pleaded guilty, but when my turn came I said in a loud, clear, angry voice, "Not guilty, your Honor. The only thing I'm guilty of is being caught in this Depression and not being able to work."

"Oh," said the judge with a grimace. "We've got one who pleads not guilty, huh? A Communist. And what is your name again?"

"Louie Bacigalupi—sir."

"Well," said the judge, turning to his bailiff, "let's see if we can get a jury trial date set for Mr. Bacigalupi. December? December tenth? Six months from now? Is that the first open date you have? Oh." Then he turned to me. "All right, Mr. Bacigalupi, trial on December tenth. I suppose you would like to fix bail?"

I looked around in a panic. I didn't have any money and wasn't supposed to be able to get any. But I was still mad. "I can wait, I can wait." So they took me back and put me in the stinking cage again. Then I started to think. Was I going to sit in this hole for six months? Why? Just so I could go to trial and try to defend myself against a charge of vagrancy, that is, of not having any money? Obviously, I didn't have any money, otherwise I wouldn't be in jail in the first place. So I would be found guilty.

Hopeless. I looked up to find the bailiff standing next to the bars, waving me over.

"Look, kid, I'd like to help you out," he said. "If you'll plead guilty, you can go right now." I just looked at him. I had heard about plea bargaining. It was one of the dirty little secrets in law school. But now I was seeing it first-hand. "And we know your name ain't Bacigalupi," he added, "because you can't even spell it right. You spelled it B-A-C-H, and that ain't the way to spell Bacigalupi. Now maybe a 'make' will come down on your real name and you could be in a lot more trouble than simple vag."

So I ended up back in the courtroom before the judge and I pleaded guilty while the judge smiled his sardonic smile. "Okay, Bacigalupi," he said. "You get out of this town and if you ever come back, I'll throw your ass in jail and tell 'em to lose the key." * I guess that might have been the time when I started identifying with the underdog and the outcast in a real way. Criminals are everywhere. Many of the worst criminals are precisely the ones who claim to be the most upstanding citizens in town. And everyone says the other guy is the crook. Hell, most of us break a law sooner or later, and it's only the unlucky and the unloved who manage to make it to prison. Ever notice who filled up the cells on Death Row in San Quentin? Ninety percent of them were blacks and Chicanos, no friends, no money. (It's not that bad now.)

Bill was waiting for me when I got out. We hopped the next freight we could find going north toward Los Angeles. I wanted to see my cousin Del in L.A., so I

---

* I did come back, years later, and tried a suit against the Santa Fe Railroad on behalf of a client who had lost a leg as he was crossing the railroad tracks. The jury gave him $100,000, the highest personal injury award up to that time in all San Diego County!

could bathe and get my clothes washed and have a beer or two.

The train was almost empty of bums when we pulled out of the San Diego railroad yards. But then we got to a hill. The train had to slow down going upgrade and that was where this whole field just seemed to sprout people, running for the train and climbing on. This one kid with a cap was sprinting alongside our car and almost made it up when he ran into one of those low-lying switches and stumbled. He would have gone under the train—but I grabbed him and pulled him up. He was grateful and I said it was nothing, and then he began to tremble and cry.

He turned out to be a she, with pretty yellow hair under that big cap, and, gee, I didn't know what to say. I made some sympathetic noises, and pretty soon she stopped crying and talked to Bill and me all the way up to Long Beach. There was never any question of romance here. I'd heard of girls taking on all the guys in a freight car one by one but I'd never seen that happen and I'd have been repelled by it. Then again, we weren't thinking about sex, we were thinking about survival. And when you're thinking along those lines, sex comes way down on the list of priorities.

We got to a drugstore in Long Beach. I phoned Del to come and get us. I felt real guilty because I had a way out of this squalor and the girl—I never even asked her her name—quite obviously didn't. She stayed with us until my cousin Del came by in his old Model T and I said, my voice croaking a bit, "Uh, we gotta go." And we went.

We drank beer with Del all weekend, but I still felt guilty when, on Sunday night, Del took us down to the railroad yards in East L.A. and Bill and I resumed our charade.

I was still pretty angry when I got back to Berkeley but I wrote a good report for the bureaucrats. They told me they used the report in designing measures to help this vagabond army of wandering youth. That's how I described the 'bos of 1933. I had no hopes that the authorities would ever do anything good, anything concrete. But the next year the State of California started something like a youth corps to live out in the Sierras, carve out trails, build bridges and the like. And the year after that, the U.S. Government began the same thing on a national scale, calling it the Civilian Conservation Corps, the CCC. Still, my mood was pretty grim when I took the Bar exam in August. What good will anything do? I said to myself. Then, just to show how despairing I was about life, I turned to Betty Ballantine, a Kappa Alpha Theta I had been dating for about a year, and told her—I was the soul of inconsistency—that we were going to drive to Reno and get married.

CHAPTER FIVE

Hangman's Hood

I almost flunked the Bar exam. I couldn't figure out how I'd done so badly, particularly since I was so damn smart and didn't have to study. I found out that a lot of guys fail to pass the first time out.

Betty and I drove to Reno in my Model T and got married before a justice of the peace, then came back and set up housekeeping in a little cottage in Berkeley not far from my mother's—which gave her a chance to continue to do my shirts.

My first job was doing legal research for Leo Hone in San Francisco. He gave me about twenty-five dollars a month and I worked for him about three months. Then along came Upton Sinclair. In 1934 and 1935, he ran for governor of California on some kind of give-the-wealth-back-to-the-people campaign and scared the bejesus out of the business establishment in California. They collected a million-dollar war chest and lots more from Wall Street to keep him from becoming governor. They paid me three hundred dollars a month, a great salary in those days, to give speeches for his opponent,

Republican Frank Merriam, and decry the bolshevism that was coming into the state.

I don't think I did Merriam much good. It was hypocritical for me to campaign for him anyway. I was a young fellow just out of law school now living the good life. How could *I* persuade people to vote for Merriam? I'm sure that every speech I gave for him meant more votes for Sinclair. Merriam won—but that's only because I didn't talk to enough people.

Betty made twenty-five dollars a month as a secretary at Traveler's Aid and so, together, we had enough to scrape through. I think we even bought a used Model A Ford. Those were not unhappy years. We lived nicely on tongue and canned spinach. We had each other. I had no clerks, no responsibilities. I didn't have to meet a payroll. (Payroll: the hangman's noose to any trial lawyer.)

And I felt a lot luckier than Harry Cobden, who had flunked the Bar exam and then precluded his ever taking it again by pulling a dumb trick. He asked to see his exam papers, then went off to check them and came back a couple of hours later wondering how he could have failed. They went back over his exam and, lo and behold, they had an almost-perfect test in their hands! But it didn't take them long to prove (with ink dispersal tests and x-rays) that Cobden had doctored it, and the Bar simply couldn't countenance that. They wouldn't give Cobden another chance. They disbarred him even before he was barred.

Cobden made a good career in sales, however, and did so well he could afford to spend a lot of time each summer up in the mountains. In the summer of 1936 he served as a guide and wrangler for this priest who'd come all the way from Rome to climb Mount Dana in the Sierras. He was a lean fellow, Cobden said, with almost transparent skin and long, delicate fingers. "But he was a good mountaineer," said Cobden. "Carried more than his weight and never complained a bit." In 1939 Harry asked me if I remembered his taking the priest hiking in the Sierras. "He just became Pope," Harry said. "Pope Pius the twelfth."

"Sure, Harry," I said laughing, disbelieving.

I worked then for a sorry old son-of-a-bitch whom I'll call Winston. Winston had a little firm and he paid me fifty dollars a month. The bread and butter came from three or four insurance companies, and he needed each of them to survive—which put him in Dutch with old lady justice from the start, because he'd do almost anything to keep the insurance-company business. Anytime he lost a case, I could see the fear gnawing at his innards. He was afraid the company would get themselves another boy. Someone from Connecticut phoned him once when I was there and said, "Winston, you've got to win your next one. We don't care what the facts are, you've got to win. Understand?" Winston understood. If he lost the next case, he would lose all that company's business in San Francisco.

"Yes sir, yes sir, yes sir," he said. Then he phoned Dr. Burns, the doctor who was working with him. "About this report of yours, Doc, goddammit, we've got to win this. Where it says six months' disability, put three. Instead of saying muscle spasms, put 'feigned' muscle spasms. Where you say the woman had some pain, say she 'simulated' pain and then add our old clincher: when you watched her put on her coat after the examination, 'she showed no evidence of pain.' We lose this one and *you* lose *your* job." Old Dr. Burns, a very distinguished, amply larded professional, couldn't honestly tell an asshole from a gunshot wound. He needed the insurance-company business as much as Winston did. He did what Winston told him.

Winston wasn't a bad guy, it was just that he knew nothing else. If he didn't practice this type of law, what could he do? One day, he got a pleading, and puzzled over some of the language, so I went to the dictionary and looked up a couple of words. He was astounded. Jesus, he'd never thought of doing that. And I was astounded that he was astounded. I saw the difference between the law training he'd had and the academic education I'd received. In three years at Boalt Hall, I never walked into a courtroom, but I had all the background to understand what was facing me in the law.

What Boalt never taught me was how to chase or not to chase a case. In addition to everything else, Boalt Hall was very proper; according to the canons of the Bar, you don't advertise. That was all very nice in theory and it helped the solemn image of the profession, young lawyers just sitting back in their offices all dignity, waiting for clients to come walking in the door. But it didn't happen that way. At least, not to me.

In 1936, when I was twenty-nine, I was occupying some free office space with Harding McGuire at the California Racing Board. I had two orange crates for a desk with a plank between them and an old campstool for a chair—and no one to represent. (Years later I would give a talk on trial tactics to the black members of the Federal Bar Association. When I'd finished, one member rose and said, "Mr. Belli, you just told us how to try cases. Now tell us how to get them." I told them it was easy to get business, once they were well known or famous. And how did they become well known or famous? By having a lot of business. After the laughter had died down I got serious. I told them the trick was to work very, very hard on their first case. Their meticulous preparation would be apparent to everyone; if not then, then surely on their second, third or fourth cases. Word would get around. They'd be on their way—though it might take some time before news editors started calling them "famed.")*

How did I first get work as a lawyer? I was ready and willing enough. My father took a common-sense approach to the problem; he figured that I wouldn't get any business until I could prove myself—gratis, if necessary. So he persuaded a couple who had been charged with murder that his son, a bright fellow just graduated from law school, would take the case for free.

Those first clients were real sweethearts. Hazel Terman was a profane slattern of thirty-four and David Pike was her scruffy lover. Together, they had plotted the murder of her husband, a rancher in Healdsburg. Hazel and David hired a guy named "Happy Ed" Williams to do him in—and he did, with a 30-30. When I walked into jail to talk with Hazel and David, I knew they'd done what they were charged with. I wasn't scared a bit by that. (And I've never been since—it is the jury's problem to determine the degree of legal guilt—not mine.) Anything I got for Hazel short of the death penalty would be a victory for her. As for David, he had to be nuts to fall in love with Hazel, so I had a psychiatrist give him some tests. The doctor (and the jury) agreed with me.

* There are really only a few lawyers in the United States who are "well known," whose names are "household words." Of course, everybody remembers Abraham Lincoln, the lawyer. And then there was Clarence Darrow, who was not only a hell of a great lawyer, cross-examiner and arguer, but lecturer and idealist as well. Sam Liebowitz, before he became a judge, was known nationally for one case, the Scottsborough Boys. Generally, a lawyer has to rise gradually. First, he's "prominent," then he becomes "well known," then "famed." After that, comes a kind of Order of the Legal Garter: "celebrated." Lee Bailey says he became "famed" as a

They found David insane and sent him off to Mendocino State Hospital. So I won my first one.

I had a little more trouble in Hazel's case. I thought I had taken a good deal of care picking her jury—taking particular pains to get an enormously fat lady on the panel because old Captain Kidd back at Boalt Hall used to say that fat people—particularly fat ladies—in their emotional way, usually go for the defendant. Well, I was pretty pleased with myself when I got up to argue, because the fat lady immediately started to weep and kept on through my entire argument. If I wasn't moving any of the others, she at least was with me. The jury came in eleven to one for acquittal—with the fat lady the only one voting guilty.

"Pardon me, madam," I said, catching her before she left the courthouse. "But may I ask why you were weeping such copious tears during my argument?"

"I have a son in law school," she said. "And as you got up to speak, I realized what a hard time *he* was going to have when *he* got out and started practicing law." So much for Captain Kidd's lessons in jury psychology.

The prosecutors tried Hazel again and won a conviction for second-degree murder. Hazel got a five-year sentence in Tehachapi Women's Prison, and I thought she might have at least thanked me. She didn't. She shouldered right past me and shouted at a couple of

---

result of one case, the Sam Shepard case. Edward Bennett Williams earned his "famed" gradually—as did Percy Foreman and Louis Nizer. I got the "celebrated-lawyer" treatment first from the wire services and out-of-town papers, only later at home. In some papers I am the "famed international lawyer." In Germany, they call me *"Star anwalt."* Whatever the press chooses to believe, however, there are many, many trial lawyers in this country who have as much ability as those few of us who are "celebrated." Some of these make their entries quietly in a bankbook rather than in the public press—but we have more fun!

members of the press, "Dave was just as guilty as I was."

Indeed he was, but we have a tradition in California of sending the guilty ones who are nutty to one kind of institution and the guilty ones who aren't nutty to another. There was little difference between Tehachapi and Mendocino. Neither was exactly a country club.

My father got me another case. No fee involved, so it wasn't chasing. It was in Martinez, where I cleared a young man named Donald Streeter of a murder charge in a trial that set some sort of record there. The jury took three minutes to deliberate and came up with a "not guilty by reason of insanity." Streeter had spent eight years at Napa State Hospital for the insane. The hospital authorities said he wasn't insane any more, and the jury thought he ought to go free now. The case drew newspaper attention and the notice of Father George O'Meara, the Catholic chaplain at San Quentin, who phoned and asked me to come over for a chat.

San Quentin was an ugly mustard color even then, situated on a mud flat up near San Rafael. I had to take a ferryboat to get across the Bay and then drive up inside the prison gates, where the guards had my name and let me through. "I've been noticing some of your work, son," said Father O'Meara. "Apparently, you don't mind working for nothing?"

I shrugged and said it beat sitting around waiting for business to drop out of the heavens.

"There are a lot of men here at San Quentin who can use your help," Father O'Meara continued. "They're here because nobody ever loved 'em in the first place. Now they've got Father O'Meara to love 'em, but they need more than love. They need lawyers. And, from time to time, I want to be calling on you, okay?"

Father O'Meara was a tough guy who could use words like *love* without losing any of his manliness. He put up a sign once at Quentin: Four Tenors Needed for the Choir. No Fairies Need Apply.

I smiled. I'd seen the courts of San Francisco and they were filled with expectant young lawyers like myself—and a lot of expectant old lawyers, too. Sometimes, you couldn't tell the lawyers from the drunks and petty felons, all waiting around for something to drop in their lap.

San Francisco was a tough seaport town with one of the sleaziest skid rows in the world. Its courts in the late 1930's were bedlam. On any morning you visited the barred holding tank near the front of the courtroom, you could see some epileptic drooling and shaking, one drunk going through the dry heaves and another in a fit of delirium tremens yelling about bats. Finally, the judge would pound his gavel and turn to the bailiff and say, "Now, let's have some order in this court." But there was only disorder. Once, a Deputy District Attorney appeared before Judge Matt Brady for a sentencing with a crystal ball in his hand. Both the D.A. and the judge were drunk. The judge said, "What do you recommend?" And the D.A. looked into his crystal ball and muttered some incantations, then announced, "I see thirty days." Judge Brady said, "Thirty days it is." The Bar Association was horrified. They brought both the D.A. and the judge up on charges—though they were hard put to cite the specific Bar canon violated.

Many of the judges themselves drank a lot. No wonder. It was the only way they could get through their day, for they were the administrators of a criminal-justice system which was far from perfect. They presided over a people's court, in the sense that it was a court for the poor and downtrodden and the dispossessed. Once, Judge O'Brien, who looked like a poodle dog with his wild, white, stained-yellow hair, tipsily set bail on a little Filipino for $200,000. But the Filipino was overjoyed. "Imagine," he seemed to be saying to himself, "two hundred thousand dollars! Only in America could it happen." But later, the clerks, the real powers in the courts, reduced the bail to twenty dollars and let the poor guy go. Working with Father O'Meara would give me a different kind of experience.

"I'm your man," I said.

"Sure and why not?" replied Father O'Meara, his blue eyes twinkling. Then, almost as if he were reading my mind, he added, "Some of the cases you'll likely get here will help make your name known, maybe bring you some business, who knows? To get the people into the church, you've got to ring the bell."

My chance for a little bell-ringing came soon enough. A half-dozen convicts mounted a big prison break at San Quentin. They had some guns smuggled in and they overpowered the guards. Then they all stood around with their fingers up their ass wondering what to do next. Two of them, Alexander McKay and Joe Kristy, cursed and screamed and told the leaders of this caper that they were idiots to start a jail break without the vaguest plans about a getaway. So they took matters into their own hands. McKay and Kristy went to Warden Holohan's house, where he was having a luncheon meeting of the parole board, cracked the warden in the skull and took him and two members of the parole board back down to the yard as hostages. They commandeered one of the prison cars, tossed their hostages in the back seat and sped off—without their cretinous compatriots.

But they didn't know where they were going; McKay was from Scotland and Kristy from Cleveland. Several hundred assorted Marin County police officers chased them into an old farmhouse not far from San Quentin, where they gave up without a shot and without harming their hostages. I was reading all about it in an extra edition of *The Examiner* when I got a call from Father O'Meara. "Here's your first case from Quentin, kid. McKay and Kristy want you."

They want me? My pulse pounded. This was a big one. The papers were full of the story, and it led all the radio newscasts.

I appeared at Quentin bright and early the next morning with Father O'Meara. The guards were fairly friendly —considering the fact that their warden was nursing a fractured skull—as they ushered us into a four-by-six conference room painted a bilious green. McKay and Kristy couldn't have been much impressed by this rookie lawyer and his brand-new briefcase with nothing in it but his lunch. But they didn't have much choice. They told me their stories and hoped for the best. They did seem to like me personally, however, and I carried on a hell of a detailed, impressive interview—my first one. What was more important to them: I could see their side of it.

As we left the prison in Father O'Meara's Ford, the padre said, "Mel, they don't have much of a chance and sure as the Pope's in Rome they'll hang. But you'll fight for 'em, hear? You're their lawyer, and that's your job."

I fought. The trial was a quick one. The State had a good case, and the prosecutor in Marin County, a friendly young fellow named Harold Haley,* made the most of it.

I did what I could, challenging wherever I had the chance, arguing for other possible interpretations of the facts. During one of my cross-examinations, however, Judge Butler rose from the bench and started to pace back and forth behind his chair. I paused, turned to the

---

* Harold Haley later became a Superior Court judge in Marin County and was himself taken hostage in a dramatic armed escape from his courtroom in August 1971, by the Soledad Brothers. He was killed with a blast from a shotgun held to his head by one of the escapees before the police overcame them.

judge and, summoning all my courage, addressed him. "Very respectfully, your Honor, this is very disconcerting to me and the jury. I know you may be uncomfortable during this cross-examination, but it is very distracting to me, a young lawyer trying to do his best."

Well, I could hear my watch ticking in my vest pocket. The court froze. The bailiff's eyes bulged. The court reporter sat there staring first at me then at the judge, who was the absolute ogre of the Marin bench. The judge gulped, grumbled a bit—and sat down. Everyone sighed, then caught his breath again when the judge, who seemed tall and gaunt even when he was seated, said, "Uhhh, Mr. Belli, would you please see me in chambers after we adjourn?"

As I faced him alone, he began, in a gruff way, "Mr. Belli, of all the young men who've been before me in the past twenty years—" He paused, slipped his robe over the top of his head, hung it up on a beautifully carved wooden hatrack, and turned back, smiling. "You, Mr. Belli, have the makings of a great trial lawyer." I was relieved. But I did not smile. I simply thanked the judge and returned to my clients, who said they also had liked my approach.

Not that it helped. The jury found McKay and Kristy guilty on several counts; the penalty was death. I'd learned another costly jury lesson: The foreman of the death-dealing jury was named Cheda. When I came out of court that day I happened to look across the street from the courthouse. "THE CHEDA BUILDING." It was *his* building. He was *establishment*. He was the man who'd make his community, *his property,* safe by killing anyone who remotely threatened the law and order that protected it.

Father O'Meara and I both felt pretty low as we drove back to the parish house in San Rafael. We didn't believe in capital punishment. There was already too much brutality in the world: over in the Orient, where thousands of Chinese and Japanese were killing each other off; in Spain, where brother was killing brother; in Germany, where, even then, Jews were being rounded up and tossed into concentration camps; and in Quentin itself, where brutality—of guards toward prisoners, of prisoners toward one another—was the order of the day. Punishment and vengeance were the air everyone breathed. "Ah, Mel, Mel. What's the world coming to?" Father O'Meara asked.

I could only shrug. If the good padre didn't know how to explain all the evil in the world, what could I say?

But what about McKay and Kristy? What could I do to stop the authorities from springing the trapdoor? I filed all the usual writs and appeals. Not an appellate ripple. So I tried some unusual channels. I brashly phoned the British Foreign Minister, Anthony Eden, in London, and persuaded him to ask Governor Merriam to grant executive clemency to McKay, a British subject.

That made headlines in London, where some of its enterprising daily newspapers printed interviews they'd gotten with McKay, courtesy of Warden Holohan, who was leaning over backward to be fair to the man who had bashed his skull. Headlines in San Francisco, too. The idea of a young whippersnapper phoning the British Foreign Minister and persuading him to ask for executive clemency! The San Francisco papers wanted interviews with me, and I didn't see why not, so I called my first press conference in my sumptuous offices at the California Racing Board, sitting there on a campstool with my feet up on an orange-crate desk. I liked the reporters who came over. They were a bright bunch who asked good questions. I didn't bob and weave and throw them a lot of legal bullshit. It was the beginning of a long, warm relationship I have always enjoyed with the press.

Governor Merriam turned down Anthony Eden for a second reprieve and finally set a date in May for the hanging of McKay and Kristy. I went to San Quentin on a gusty, rainy Thursday night with Father O'Meara and, together, we clanked up the outside iron stairs to the top of the old sash-and-door factory where they put the gallows. The two prisoners were in the middle of a huge room, held in separate, slatted wooden cages. They'd already had their last meal, and the guards were watching them. Some men on Death Row had tried to cheat the executioner by taking their own lives with ingenious, brutal devices when their time drew near. The guards were here to see these cons didn't cheat.

While Father O'Meara talked with each of the men, I moved on down the room. They used it for more than executions; there was a lot of lumber lying around and half-made doors, and the air was heavy with sawdust. You could see the sawdust suspended in the air and tumbling around in the light of some blue bulbs that hung on long cords. It gave the whole atmosphere a cloudy, unreal aura. I looked up at the gallows all ready for the double hanging on the morrow and shuddered, and shuddered again when I noticed three new manila ropes tied with hangman's knots that were being stretched by weights over in a corner. There would be other executions, and they were getting the ropes ready by prestretching them so they'd fall exactly so far and break a neck— no stretch. And I shuddered once again when I saw two simple wooden coffins set right out there in front of the gallows for men still alive a few feet away. The rain continued to beat down on the galvanized iron roof, and I cannot hear rain on a roof to this day without thinking of McKay and Kristy sitting there waiting to die.

"You want to talk to 'em?" asked Father O'Meara.

"What can I say?" I was beginning to choke up at the thought of the cold-blooded official double-killing that I would see in the morning. But I went over to the men. For twenty minutes, we talked about a lot of things in life. No one mentioned the hereafter. Both men wanted to be sure I'd be there tomorrow. They said they wanted a friend in the official, precisely numbered audience. Father O'Meara and I hunched our raincoats up over our ears, clanged down the outside iron stairs and drove back to the parish house. Early in the morning, Father O'Meara said mass and I served it. Then we went back for the hanging.

There was a big crowd, mostly law-enforcement officers there for the show. No women. I guess it was some kind of emotional payoff for them—they'd worked to put these guys on the gallows; now they were going to be in on the kill. There was a smell of death and sweat and un-eaten last meals in the air. The rain was still beating on the roof and an old scratchy phonograph played "Clair de Lune," one of the last requests of the condemned. Suddenly, they rushed McKay and Kristy out in their denim prison garb and cotton slippers and marched them up the narrow stairs. "So long, Mac. So long, Joe." I said in a croaking voice. One of the guards bawled at me, "Quiet! There'll be silence in here."

The two of them fell through the trapdoor simul-taneously without a cry and with hoods over their heads. Thank God the executioners knew their business, because the fall broke their necks. They stopped the music, the coroner rushed over with a stethoscope, ripped their shirts open to expose their knotted blood vessels and listened first to one heart and then another. In that dead and silent room, torn shirt buttons bouncing on the floor sounded like manhole covers rolling down a deserted city street at midnight. One sweaty deputy sheriff fainted right on the spot, and the coroner intoned something for the record.

Father O'Meara blessed himself as we bolted down the iron stairs again and headed for his car. The padre was furious. He gunned the motor and sped straight for the gates, as if he were going to knock them open. The guards swung the gates apart just in time for the father to roar out. He had no intention of waiting for them to search the car. They did not want to deal with the priest's wrath. He drove back to the parish house in silence. There he opened a bottle of Vat 69 and the two of us drained it without saying a word.

I was no good after that. I woke up in a sweat each morning for three days in a row; it wasn't until Betty awakened me in the middle of a scream that I realized I was on the gallows myself with one of those new manila ropes around my neck. It was a nightmare I would have again and again for years to come. It was my own personal fight with established society.

The next week, I was introducing Earl Warren to the Press Club in San Francisco. He was District Attorney of Alameda County then, but running for Attorney General of the State of California. Warren publicly thanked me and said I was a real comer, a young lawyer who, when the trap had sprung at San Quentin last week, "had half his practice wiped out."

My dad, who was in the audience, was horrified at my rejoinder. I got up and said, "Mr. District Attorney isn't telling the truth. I had my *whole* practice wiped out."

CHAPTER SIX

Death's Gray

I could laugh (on the outside) with Earl Warren, but inside I was in a turmoil. I couldn't abide a system that would put a couple of misfits like McKay and Kristy to death and wink so much of the time at the white-collar and corporate crime going on all around us.

The criminal-justice system was lopsided; the system, from the cops to the judges, had already determined in advance which criminals would be vacationing in Acapulco and which would be spending time in San Quentin, Folsom or Alcatraz. The police were adequately equipped to handle the guy who stole a rutabaga from a Third Street supermarket, but they didn't have the smarts to do anything about the Stanford grad who was floating a phony stock scheme, swindling not one but hundreds. State and federal prosecutors barely lifted a finger against the corporate plunderers who stole from the people at large on the grandest scale. And they were the principal speakers at the Thursday morning prayer breakfasts.

As far as I could see, the courts were trampling on the rights of the accused in a way that didn't square with the Constitutional law I had learned at Boalt Hall. These were the days before a number of combative attorneys took the Bill of Rights and fought cases through the U.S. Supreme Court (the Warren Court) and helped us all realize that the Constitution wasn't just a piece of parchment but the very instrument that would make our country the land of the free—in fact as well as in theory. Judges in those days generally ignored the Bill of Rights because it was (and is) a profoundly antigovernment document. Antigovernment sentiments found approval during the days of the American Revolution. But, as Richard Harris has written, "Once that [antigovernment] sentiment was embodied in written sanctions against *all* government, as it was in the Bill of Rights, the new government was expected to interpret, implement and enforce these sanctions against itself. That was too much to expect . . . because all governments in all places at all times try to increase their power, at the expense of the individual."

For most of the nation's history, then, it has been far too easy for local, state and federal officers to ignore Constitutional guarantees. And almost as easy for the courts to go along with them, for the judges were only human; they were on the side of the law and against those who broke it, never mind the niceties of the Constitution. The Constitutional freedom against self-incrimination? The Constitutional right to a fair trial? They meant nothing in my next big cases, the case of the Black-Gloved Rapist and the Louis Gosden murder case.

No one knew the identity of the rapist, but all the papers in San Francisco made circulation gains for weeks with breathless stories about the guy's midnight raids on the mansions of Pacific Heights and the inability of the police to catch him. The newspapers dubbed him "The Black-Gloved Rapist" because police accounts said the man dressed in black, including his leather gloves. Furthermore, he purportedly could leap over twenty-foot walls with the ease of a comic-book character then making his appearance for the first time, Superman.

The cops finally caught the rapist, who underestimated a thirty-foot wall with a twenty-foot leap. His name was Frank Avilez. He was big and lean and as muscled as the victims had claimed, twenty-four years old, an immigrant from Jamaica with a father, mother, sister—and a seventeen-year-old bride. The police squeezed a quick confession out of Avilez, then they turned him over to Gerald Kenny, the most placid of public defenders. Kenny took one look at Avilez's confession and pleaded him guilty to thirty-two counts of rape, robbery and assault, which were worth about four hundred and forty years in the slammer.

Frank's parents called me. I hustled over to Judge Melvyn Cronin's court the next day to ask for a delay in sentencing. I maintained the guy didn't even remember some of the crimes he was supposed to have admitted, that he hadn't stolen anything, that everything he had taken (cigarette lighters and bits of jewelry) were gifts, tokens of appreciation from the women he'd "raped." If anything, I maintained, the charge should have been "assault with a friendly weapon." Why, some of his "victims" had even invited him back.

"Let me get him a psychiatric exam," I told Judge Cronin, and when the judge nodded his assent, Frank's wife burst into tears. The psychiatric examiners found Avilez "psychoneurotic." Jesus, to these guys, everybody was psychoneurotic, so that wasn't any help to me. Judge Cronin sent Avilez to San Quentin, and I wrote a brief protesting that the authorities had applied undue haste in getting Avilez to trial, denied him the counsel of his choice and failed to give him the opportunity of changing his plea. The District Court of Appeals agreed with me, reversed the kid's conviction and ordered a new trial. It was one of the first in a line of new decisional concepts.

But I couldn't really put on a new trial, not one that would end up with any different verdict. The community was up in arms. Herb Caen, a bright young newspaperman with an acid penchant for the distaff twist, pointed out at the top of his column one morning that the rapist had made one of his house calls a block away from my own home. More important, the cops had five good witnesses who had identified Avilez in a lineup. Assistant District Attorney Tom Lynch let me plead him guilty to half the counts, and I figured I could do no better than that.

Big deal. I got his sentence reduced from four hundred forty years to two hundred twenty. But Avilez was grateful and sent me a telegram from San Quentin: THANK YOU FOR CUTTING MY SENTENCE IN HALF.

Frank Avilez, in fact, became one of my fans over in San Quentin. He used to talk good about me. Father O'Meara liked that because O'Meara had picked me out of the crowd himself and now here I was, a young lawyer getting a big rep in the yard. "Never be without a case in jail," Father O'Meara had told me, and he always did his best to see that I had one at San Quentin.

In the Louis Gosden murder case, I had to contend with an overzealous judge. He ignored Gosden's Constitutional right to a fair trial by making gratuitous comments to the jury on the evidence, and Earl Warren, who was prosecuting this case, urged him on. I could understand why any judge might be tempted to do this. Louis Gosden was a plumber with the foulest mouth I've ever had to listen to, and he had poisoned his wife with strychnine. But Gosden's moral credentials were not the issue here. If Constitutional guarantees are to protect us all, they have to protect even the worst of us.

The authorities made a good case against Gosden and there was nothing I could do about that. He was guilty, all right. But I might have saved him from the death penalty if the judge, Frank Ogden, hadn't told the jury in his final charge, "In the event of your finding the defendant guilty of murder in the first degree, you should consider all the evidence to determine whether any circumstances or reasons exist for the exercise of your discretion in relieving the defendant from the extreme penalty. *I have been unable to find any.*"

A comment like that would be grounds for reversal today, and that's exactly the course I insisted the Supreme Court should take when I wrote my appeal brief. Never mind the judge's final words—"I have been unable to find any"—which were clearly improper. The jury didn't *have* to find any. I maintained that the law on capital punishment provided that a jury did not have to find *any* mitigating circumstances in order to spare a man from execution at the hands of the state. A jury could simply decide to spare a man's life for no reason at all—or because he had red hair and the jury liked red hair. But the Supreme Court affirmed Gosden's conviction—then reversed itself fifteen years later in *People v. Friend.* By then, of course, Gosden was dead. Louis had lived—and killed his wife—just fifteen years too early! I wrote Earl Warren, then making a great reputation as a liberal jurist, reminding him of the case—but he'd forgotten Gosden.

Louis's passing may have been no great loss to society, but it was a life and it was his. I was asked to his execution, too. This time, San Quentin had gone modern. They had built themselves a gas chamber. Father O'Meara and I proceeded through the same ritual. On execution eve, we went in to see Louis. He ordered his last meal and it was some order: oysters, Caesar salad, pressed duck, champagne, banana split. Father O'Meara grimly smiled when Louis told him what he had asked for and shook his head. "It's not to your weddin' that you're goin', Louis." And then the food came and Louis couldn't eat it, not a bite. He just started to cry. I clenched my fists. Yes, I knew what he had done. But I was furious with the system.

We returned at dawn. They brought Louis into this octagonal glass enclosure, strapped him in a chair and took off his shirt. Father O'Meara gave him absolution, then left the room. Someone punched a button and cyanide pellets rolled into a container of acid. The fumes started filling up the chamber. Louis's features began to contort until his face no longer looked human. Moments before, his arms and his chest and his face were ruddy and warm. Now his skin was absolutely gray. I remembered Ruben's *Descent from the Cross* at the Cathedral in Antwerp. Same effect. Death comes in all colors. But in executions, it wears gray.

My father died around Christmastime, 1938. He was fifty-eight. I was thirty-one. Christmas had been the traditional high point of my year, but it was a sad time now. My dad caught pneumonia somewhere out on the road— he was selling mutual funds—and then went back to Santa Rosa, where he and my mother had moved a few years before. I sat through the holiday with him. I remember the doctor coming to visit him, shaking his head and telling me, "Well, a drinking man's a bad risk." And my rejoinder, "Dad's not a drinking man."

The doctor had a quizzical look on his face and said nothing. Then I knew. My dad *was* a drinking man. Funny I wouldn't have known that (maybe I didn't want to know), but by then, my dad and I weren't very close. I had run into him on the street in the City one day shortly after I got out of law school. He was with a woman.

I stopped and talked with him for a minute. He seemed embarrassed. We never talked about that meeting afterward. We never talked about much of anything. I was standing there at his bedside when he went. He looked at me, then turned his head to the wall and he was gone.

My father died because the goddamned drugstore had made a mistake on the goddamned prescription. The doctor prescribed the new drug, sulfanilamide, and the drugstore sent out the wrong dosage. Knowing what I know now, I should have sued. But I did what most people did then: *I let them get away with it.* I wasn't even sure at this point whether being a lawyer was worth all the trouble or whether anything else was either, for that matter. It was a low point in my life, and I sunk even lower when my doctor told me it was a duodenal ulcer that was causing my stomachaches—and that he didn't know *what* was causing my headaches.

My dad died with no insurance, no estate, but he did have a lot of clients. I wrote to King Merritt of Investors Syndicate to see whether I could take over my dad's district. Only recently I found a copy of the letter I sent to Mr. Merritt—an indication to me now that despite my early ambition, my petty successes and notoriety, I was still so unsure of myself and my career after almost five years of law practice that I may have considered leaving the law to sell mutual funds.

I considered anything to help drum up some law business. I thought of joining some of the clubs in town, but any club that wanted me to be a member I didn't want to be a member of. There were several establishments in the city, one centered around the Bohemian Club. This was real upper crust, captains of industry and all that. There was another called the Union League Club, once about as stuffy as the Bohemian Club. And then there was the Olympic Club—mostly Irish Catholics, including a lot of judges who had gone to the old St. Ignatius College. Later I was to join both the Olympic Club and the Union League-Press Club.

I did join another, unofficial, club instead. At the end of the day, I would hie myself down to the back of an old warehouse off Bryant Street and have a few shots of whiskey with some of San Francisco's political bosses. Tom Finn, one of the top guys, told me to stand off to the side while the heavies drank and told their stories. I wasn't to say anything until the boys got to know me. In the meantime, Finn said he'd throw some little legal work in my direction. He did. I was taken under the wing of the number one boss in San Francisco, Murphy Hirshberg, years later. I guess I can say now that I drank a lot with him.

I've often said that I never really worked a day in my life, but when I said that, I was feeling too proud to remember those dark days when I was working my ass off and seemingly getting nowhere. It was then that I told myself I'd better look for some new direction in the law—otherwise I was not only going to make a poor living, I'd end up in the slammer myself. Criminal law in those days was as risky a game for lawyers as it was for the felons they were defending. The idea hit home one night when I was sitting in a car near Fisherman's Wharf, waiting for two cops. For a price, they were going to tell me all they knew about the District Attorney's strategy in a case I was about to try. "Hell," I said to myself, "this is no way to go." I knew that everybody was doing it. But it was not for me.

I really wanted to get into the civil side, specifically into the field of personal injury. I felt that our economic system (like our criminal system) was stacked against the little man. The insurance companies, for example, took in unbelievable amounts of the public's money—

billions of dollars each year. Ostensibly, the public was buying protection. But the insurance-company executives seemed to forget they were holding other people's money in trust. They had come to regard that money as theirs and they would be damned if they'd give it up without a struggle, or even account for it. They still won't—and don't.

The insurance companies had entire firms of lawyers to help them in their struggle. But the people-at-large had damn few attorneys ready to fight on the other side. It just didn't pay. In personal-injury cases, the lawyer got one-third if he won the case and nothing if he lost— a real gamble, in which the payoffs were low and late in coming.

But maybe I could make these cases pay. And then maybe the poor man in America could have as much justice as the rich man. Once I began to see the struggle in those terms, I was on my way. All I had to do (as Judge Ike Harris had told me sometime before, only it hadn't sunk in) was make a good beginning.

Just exactly *how* would I make the right start? I had to find a different approach, discover a new way of vividly making my case to a jury. If I could do that, then the awards would be more adequate for the victims—and hurt the victimizers to such an extent that they would mend their ways. I found the right way in the middle of a criminal case—the Ernie Smith case—by discovering for myself the real impact on a jury of something I'd heard about in law school but rarely seen: the use of demonstrative evidence. Shortly, I found a way to apply demonstrative evidence on the civil side.

Ernie Smith was a black, a convict at San Quentin who had kicked another convict in the head in the prison yard and killed him. He looked like a killer to me.

I didn't know what a killer "looked like"—I guess my

stereotype was one formed by books and the movies—but, whatever, this guy fit the stereotype: glowering eyes, overworked maxillaries, pouty lips. I thought I could see R-A-G-E in every pore of his being, but when he spoke to me he couldn't have been sweeter. I liked Ernie Smith. In fact, I took a liking to most of my clients and I soon made their cause my own. (Good for enthusiasm but bad for objectivity. If there's a common fault among the new breed of lawyers. I believe this is their problem, too.)

"What happened?" I asked. I wanted Smith to tell me the whole story in his own words. I was learning that the way I saw a client on the first interview was probably the way a jury would see him.

Smith told me he'd been in a fight with a con named Artie. "I knocked him down," Smith said, "but then he had a knife and he was going to throw it at me. So I stomped him."

"Whoa," I said. "What?"

"I stomped him."

"No, not that. You said he had a knife?"

"Yeah. Every con in here carries a knife."

" 'Every con in here carries a knife?' That's crap, and you know it. Now we better find something sensible to hang a murder rap on or, brother, we've had it."

Ernie Smith insisted. "You ask me how come I had a knife. I tell you. You don't want to believe it."

I shrugged, heard him ramble on some more and then left the cell. I wanted to talk to the captain of the guard, Ralph New.

"Ralph," I asked, "was it possible for Arthur Ruis to have had a knife out there in the yard?"

"Possible?" he said. "Here are some of the weapons we've found." And with that, he opened a great, big, deep drawer, full of the most evil collection of weapons I'd ever seen: broken saw blades, files, tire irons that had been sharpened down, bedsprings made into twisted daggers, villainous-looking things, all made right there by the cons in San Quentin. That did it for me. Ernie Smith's defense suddenly became dramatically plausible.

The trial deputy in the D.A.'s office, Harold Haley, thought he had the case all wrapped up. He asked for first-degree murder, which meant the gallows. I could see the skepticism in the jurors' faces when I made my opening statement, that I thought this was a matter of "self-defense." *

Haley put his case on first. Then I came up with mine, and one of my first witnesses was Ralph New, the captain of the guard. In my subpoena duces tecum I had ordered New to bring the whole goddamn drawer full of knives with him, and when he arrived before the morning session with the drawer of contraband, the bailiff told Judge Butler. The judge called me into chambers. He wanted to know what the knives were all about.

"I didn't think anybody had knives inside the prison," I said. "I think the jurors need some education on this little point."

Judge Butler hesitated, then gave me the benefit of the doubt. "I think you may have something here," he said.

I put New on the stand and got him to tell me about the knives. Then I went over to the counsel table and picked up the entire drawer and started back toward New, asking the judge's permission to introduce the drawer's contents into evidence.

To this day, I don't remember if I made my next move

* Vin Hallinan once told me, "A good opening statement is one that makes the jurors want to go out and vote for your client right now and not wait until the evidence is in." Another attorney once told a jury, "I'm going to make an opening statement. Listen carefully. This is the only time and place you'll hear this—because the judge won't allow this later on into the trial."

deliberately or whether it was an accident, but I really did stumble. I spilled the knives right there on the floor in front of the jury. I looked up at the judge, and he had a little smile on his face. He was shaking his head. I couldn't have found a better way of bringing home a point to the jury. So I made the most of it. I took my time picking up the knives, one by one, and as I would grab one, I would look at it and shake my head and put it back in the drawer.

Harold Haley put on a rebuttal witness, another con who said the victim, Arthur Ruis, did *not* have a knife in the yard. But this guy's mere word that there was no knife was hardly enough to counteract the searing images of the real knives in the minds of the jury. In their view,

poor Ernie Smith had been defending himself against an arsenal. They came back with an "acquittal" for my client.

I had learned a valuable lesson, one taught by Captain Kidd at Boalt, but only half realized: that jurors learn through *all* their senses, and if you can tell them and show them, too, let them see and feel and even taste or smell the evidence, then you will reach the jury. "A good trial attorney," said Captain Kidd, "is a good teacher. He doesn't overestimate the jury's knowledge, either. He has to show them." A lot of lawyers knew this, of course, and some of those who did were even using the knowledge in court. But, for some reason, they only saw it as a tool in criminal trials—when someone was accused of breaking a law, murder or robbery or rape. The D.A. would bring in the lethal weapon, the autopsy picture, even the aborted fetus, the blood-spattered scene of the crime. All would be admitted, no matter how grisly. But they weren't using demonstrative evidence nearly enough in *civil* cases. (It would be years before I could get a picture of the deceased admitted in a civil case.) It didn't take long before I would step into the breach. Today even *more* demonstrative evidence is being used in civil than in criminal cases, as I was to advocate in my six-volume *Modern Trials*.

I found my chance one day when my good friend, the newly elected District Attorney of San Francisco, later governor of California, Edmund G. Brown, and father of California's present great governor, Jerry Brown, asked me if I would take the case of Chester Bryant. I had helped campaign for Pat Brown, so he owed me a little something—and that's what he threw me, a little something. The Bryant case was a tough one, which Brown had already booted before the Workmen's Compensation Commission.

Pat Brown thought I might try to take the case to the Superior Court. I said I would, but the first thing I would do was hope to God I didn't get Judge Dan Deasy sitting on the case and the second would be to raise the claim from $15,000 to $50,000. Dan Deasy's sympathies were with the local street-railway companies, or so it seemed. If anyone was ever lucky enough to win a case against one of the streetcar companies, Judge Deasy would automatically grant the defense a new trial. In fact, when he died, lawyers all over town claimed that the streetcar companies flew their flags at half-mast.

My prayers worked. I didn't get Deasy and I gave thanks, because the Bryant case gave me a chance to show what I could do on a personal-injury case—with demonstrative evidence.

Bryant was a gripman on the Market Street Railway Company. One day, as his cablecar was entering the O'Farrell-Powell intersection, the grip shot back inexplicably and hit him such a severe blow in the midsection that he was suffering what appeared to be permanent palsy.

The problem in the Bryant case was this: no one could understand how the accident happened and, therefore, no one could decide whose fault it was. By rights, the grip should not have snapped back and hit Bryant in the belly. But it did. I found this wasn't Bryant's fault, nor his company's fault; it was the fault of the gripman on the Powell line—then operated by another company. The ancient San Francisco cablecars are powered by a steel cable running under the street. On each car, a gripman manipulates a pair of iron grips that reach down and hitch onto the moving cable. At the Powell-O'Farrell intersection, however, trouble came if the gripman on the Powell car didn't drop his grip as an O'Farrell car approached. Otherwise, the cables got fouled and the gripman on the O'Farrell car got hit in the stomach—and that's what happened to Chester Bryant.

But how would I demonstrate this to a jury? According to the rules of the trial court, I could only bring in expert witnesses, in this case, the gripmen themselves, to explain the situation—and these gripmen had no special training in communicating the intricacies of the cable system to a group of ordinary laymen. I had to find another way.

I spent three hundred dollars (a lot of money in 1938) to have a craftsman build a big scale mockup of the Powell-O'Farrell intersection, cablecars and all. The model was bigger than a king-sized bed, but I brought it into the courtroom—and a full-size gearbox, too.

The defense lawyers cried, "Foul!" Lawyers had brought models into courtrooms before, but they usually did it in criminal trials, hardly ever in civil actions for personal injury.

Logically, of course, there was no reason for this. Judge Griffin, one of our best evidence judges, agreed with me. If the jury was going to weigh the facts, they had to understand the facts, and that was the only reason for the model. When I saw the jurors leave the jury box and pore over the model and examine the gearbox and the grips, I saw frowns turn into smiles of understanding. The light dawned on me, too. Now I saw how demonstrative evidence in a personal-injury case could turn the tide in favor of the injured. It was something I would get better at as time went on. *

All the jurors needed then was a proper instruction from the judge on the law; they found that Bryant's injuries were not his fault, but the railway's. I brought a blackboard into the courtroom to help the jury compute my client's award. No one had ever brought a blackboard into court before for such a reason. This, too, was a new wrinkle that made the railroad lawyers unhappy. (I began calling the defense lawyers thereafter "the railroad lawyers." This always brought an objection with its own built-in implications of shame.) But I was just trying to be a good teacher, why not use a blackboard? There, I chalked up a breakdown of my client's medical expenses and added up his current and future pain and suffering in terms of dollars. It wasn't a very big figure. Chester Bryant's pain and suffering came to far less than a dollar a day over his life expectancy.

The jurors awarded Bryant $31,883.25, a big award in those days. In this case, however, what then happened was also instructive. I was not to get the $10,000-plus contingency fee for myself. I had to divide that with Pat Brown (who gave me the case) and with two other law-

---

* And so would everyone else. During a recent court trial in Mount Clemens, Michigan, one fellow approached me with a business card and brochure. He had a company that did nothing else but make courtroom models and exhibits for lawyers. The guy was trying to sell me something I had discovered thirty years before!

yers who helped on the appeal—because the insurance-company lawyers took the verdict to the California Court of Appeals. (And that continued to happen over the years. I made a lot of money—for *other* lawyers.)

When insurance-company lawyers lose in a trial court, they almost always appeal. Indeed, why shouldn't they appeal? It gives them more legal work, which they bill by the hour. And their client goes along. The insurance company can afford it, because it really isn't the company's money, it's money that belongs to the people who pay for the protection they're supposedly getting. The winning plaintiff gets a legal 7 percent interest, the appealing insurance company can get 10 or 12 if they lend out the money during the time of appeal.

The appellate judges affirmed my victory in the lower court. They didn't think the award was excessive. In my high-court brief, I had brought in statistics on the going prices for injuries all over the U.S. I had found that juries and judges everywhere were stuck on terribly low levels, amounts that hadn't kept up with the times and changes in the value of the dollar. If a person lost a leg in an accident in any Southern state or in New England, he or she might be awarded as little as $10,000. Some states even put limits on the award that could be given the heirs of a man who lost his life: $5,000.

If I could just list these awards and compare one with the other all over the country, I thought I might be able to publish the analysis in a prestigious law journal. This might help other lawyers to start thinking about asking for more adequate awards. And give trial judges and appellate justices some food for thought, too.

There were those who criticized the "high" award in the Bryant case. There are those who criticize high awards even today. In 1973, an editorial writer in the Tucson *Star* attacked a colleague of mine who had given a seminar to trial lawyers at Arizona State University—on the grounds that he was teaching them how to ask for "more adequate awards" (my phrase). "Even the argument that money is an inadequate substitute for an arm, a leg or pain and suffering, but it is the best we have," he wrote, "does not make sense. . . . [It's] a value that reveres money in lieu of life and punishes human beings for being inevitably and humanly flawed, imperfect."

But I wonder. What else can we offer a personal-injury victim but money? We have nothing that will make the man or woman who is permanently injured whole again, nothing that will help him walk without a limp, nothing but drugs to let him sleep without pain. For some, inevitably, not even drugs will ease their suffering, and the only alternative left is a chordotomy, the severing of the spinal cord to halt the journey of the pain impulses to the brain. Some may say they would be better off dead, but the law forbids them to choose death; they have no legal choice but to go on living—and suffering. Those responsible, I felt, should pay—in the only coin of the realm.

"The Adequate Award and Demonstrative Evidence" appeared in 1944 in the *California Law Review.* I've been told by judges and other trial lawyers everywhere it has made more of an impression on civil trial law than any other law review article in the last fifty years.

CHAPTER SEVEN

"Torpedoed Again"

Whenever I try a case, I suffer all the ailments, pains and agony, all the ridicule, humiliation and embarrassment of my client. I have been a sick pregnant woman, a man with one leg, a blind man, a woman about to be committed to Bedlam, a man with a burst appendix, a woman with quadriplegia, a chorus girl with diarrhea, but my most acute suffering is when I represent a small child. I don't know how I could do the wonderful work that pediatricians do, or more particularly, pediatric surgeons. They seem to be so gentle, so patient and so happy, in spite of all the suffering of the little ones they see daily.

I've seen the poliomyelitis cases, diseases of every kind, head injuries and blindness of young children, terrible birth defects caused in some cases by mother nature, in others by the malpractice of the obstetrician. But I guess meningitis scares me the most. (I remember we landed in Brasilia a year or so ago, Caesar, Lia and I, and the bellboy told us there weren't many people in the hotel; there was a spinal meningitis epidemic. We left, but quick.)

Spinal meningitis is diagnosed one way. With the analysis of the fluid taken by spinal tap. If the doctor doesn't do a spinal tap, he guesses. A doctor in Sacramento guessed. Negligently, he let a little child go through all tortures and sufferings for a week without doing the spinal tap that would have made the diagnosis that would have led to curative therapy that my doctors were ready to testify would have prevented the ravages of the disease.

We sued. I'd seen the child, he crawled on the floor; he was three years of age. He couldn't raise his head, he had that terrible, vacuous look of someone who has had serious brain damage. He croaked unintelligible words. The boy's parents were taking exquisite care of him. They were beautiful people. One doesn't realize just how much care and work he can do in taking care of an injured family member until he tries it. It becomes so all-consuming that minutes fade into hours and night into day without one really knowing how much time has been expended.

We have a doctor in our office, or rather he's both a doctor and a lawyer, Tom Collins, and Tom did a herculean job of workup on this case, so great in fact, that when we came to the time of trial the defendants called me and wanted to settle. They were willing to pay us $1,000,000, but we were to do something new. Medical malpractice insurance companies were complaining that "huge awards" were sometimes "windfalls"—the person who gets the award is so badly injured that he only lives a year or two and then the award goes to the family, his heirs. Philosophically, I suppose it's a question of whether there is anything wrong with this. But, without debating the philosophical issue, we took the $1,000,000 in settlement but in the form of an annuity whereby the child would get some $30,000 a year and if he were alive at the end of seven years, all of it would go to him. If not, the balance remaining would revert to the insurance company.

But adults can "suffer," too: Captain Mineo Egawa was to fly Japan Air Lines flagship 747 out of Los Angeles airport bound, nonstop, for Tokyo, flight number 61 at 10:30 A.M. He'd awakened after a good night's sleep, put on his well-pressed, dark blue captain's uniform with the four gold stripes, shined his shoes to military brightness, then looked at his Seiko wristwatch and determined that he had time for a long, leisurely breakfast. All packed, he left his gear, with the exception of his flight bag, which he carried with him, at the motel desk counter and went into Sambo's Restaurant for breakfast with the rest of his crew.

He didn't make flight number 61 on that day and indeed, he's never flown a 747 again.

He finished a leisurely breakfast, then ordered a second cup of coffee. As the busboy was cleaning off the table in front of him the boy dropped a cup. It fell on the parqueted floor at the feet of Captain Egawa and shattered, but worse, a small fragment flew up and hit the captain in his right eye.

The accident didn't seem serious at first, more embarrassing, with all the solicitations for help for the captain. But when the captain went to the washroom he began to notice a blurring in his right eye, and after he had put some wet towels on his eye his vision remained blurred. He had to call Japan Air Lines crew dispatchers and tell them that he was reporting disabled for the first time.

The captain then went to an eye doctor and into the hospital. The accident was more serious than it had first seemed. The retina had been torn by the jagged edge of the particle. The captain was hospitalized in Los Angeles for several weeks, then flew, "dead-head," back to Japan.

There his company furnished him the best of medical care, but after some six months the prognosis came down: a very slight but *permanent* diminution of vision. For you or me it would have hardly been noticeable. It wouldn't interfere with his driving an automobile or renewing his driver's license. Indeed, the captain could still fly a 707 or any other equipment for Japan Air Lines, but for just that little bit more perfection required for a captain of a 747, he was grounded.

I'd represented Japan Air Lines since their first inaugural flight and had handled a number of cases for them and their personnel. Not only did Captain Egawa come to me, but I got telephone calls and letters from the top personnel in the airline: Captain Egawa was one of their best pilots. He wanted to fly 747's. He could no longer fly 747's. Did I realize how much "loss of face" this meant to him?

I wasn't sure I did. There would be very little, if ány, loss of salary for the captain because of his seniority, and there would be no loss of pension rights. Indeed, the total loss to the captain would be this "loss of face" concept which is so typically Oriental and which is sometimes hard for the Occidental to understand. At least I'd never before presented it to an American jury for dollar evaluation.

When it came time to go to trial in Santa Barbara, Japan Air Lines sent from Japan a vice president, an economist, a doctor, two 747 captains and a general observer to report back the progress and the result of the trial—and my performance and understanding of "loss of face."

I had sued Sambo's Restaurant as the prime defendant, negligence for dropping the cup, and the manufacturer of the cup as the second defendant, for being negligent in not supplying a "bounceable" cup. Well, I didn't exactly sue for not having a "bounceable" cup, but I did suggest that injuries such as these must have happened before (though I'd never heard of one), and the state of the art of china making must have come to appreciate that a broken cup flying into pieces might go into someone's eye and damage it.

Representing Sambo's was the Bronson office, one of the largest defense firms in San Francisco and good friends of mine over the years. Larry Driscoll was their assigned trial lawyer and he was a particularly good friend of mine. This was going to be his last case. He intended to retire, and I tried to help him in a retirement gesture by loading the liability (cause of the accident) onto the cup manufacturer.

We broke a couple of hundred cups in trial preparation and took slow moving pictures, fast moving pictures, colored moving pictures, every kind of moving picture, to show that these cups were particularly prone to shatter. What we really came up with was that all cups break in about the same manner unless the floor is rubberized or soft. And to claim that the floor should have been rubberized would only have put the blame back on Sambo's —not on the cup manufacturer.

In an opening statement I explained, as best I could, what loss of face meant to a Japanese. But Captain Egawa was beautiful. He portrayed to a jury what it meant to sit up in the little seat in that big airplane and have control over that huge flying machine and all its passengers. What it really meant to be a "Captain" and how he could never again sit in the left-hand seat but would always, always, thereafter be relegated to the copilot right-hand seat. The jury sat on the edge of their seats while Captain Egawa gestured and explained his responsibility over the huge machine, the entire crew. How he was in complete command to alter course for smoother flying weather, altitude, how he personally rechecked fuel and fuel consumption, how everyone looked up to him—and how he had lost face.

He was more eloquent than I, and the jury rewarded him with a verdict of $251,435, against Sambo's only.

Then there was Captain "Andy."

Captain Andy had been a seafarer for many years, in peace and war. Indeed, twice, as a captain of a merchant cargo ship, he'd had his deck shot out from under him and had been rescued from the cold waters of the North Sea, shivering and half frozen, only to go back to his beloved captaincy again. He particularly liked the North Sea run, even though stories were being circulated about him that he spent more time swimming in its frigid waters than on the deck of his command.

Only one thing Captain Andy liked as much as the sea. That was hard drinking. And while he never drank on duty, he more than made up for it ashore.

One week's furlough in San Francisco he had really been making up for it. He was rooming, alone, on the top floor of a third-class seaman's hotel. Late one evening he staggered from his room along a dimly lit corridor to the single elevator. The door seemed open, so he opened it farther and stepped in. That first step was a long one. About three floors. As so often happens in my business, safety locks and safety devices fail. The elevator was above his level on the roof floor. I only see the ones that fail, so consequently I suppose I think more fail than really do; but over some forty years of trial practice I've seen some safety devices on almost any kind of equipment, from airplanes to tractors, elevators to automobiles, fail so miserably that the devices seem somehow to have been made by an inventor planning wholesale destruction. Indeed, I particularly like, on cross-examination, to ask the expert who is always called from General Motors or General Electric, or one of the Generals, "Are you the expert who is usually called by your defendant company to testify that the accident that happened couldn't happen?" This interrogation is particularly effective when the same expert has to fess up that he has, over his lifetime with the company, testified in some seventy similar cases that the accident "couldn't happen." Most big companies do have in the back room one such well-fed, dignified-appearing expert.

Captain Andy landed at the bottom of the elevator shaft. He crashed into some four feet of oily water. Why he did not kill himself, except that he had been drinking and was probably thus protected, he'll never know. He did receive some serious back injuries.

Captain Andy hobbled in to see me and I filed suit for him.

In the trial, of course, defendant elevator maintenance company and the hotel tried to prove that Captain Andy was drunk, therefore "contributorily" negligent, that he didn't look before he stepped, and that his negligence was the sole cause of the accident. That he shouldn't have assumed that the elevator would be there just because the outside door was open. I was relying on an old California case in which a drunken man was injured stumbling into a hole in a street in broad daylight (*Roginson v. Pioche*). Said the California Supreme Court, in that case, to a plea of contributory negligence by the defendant: "A drunken man is as much entitled to a safe street as a sober one, and indeed, twice as much in need of it!"

The insurance lawyer should have left well enough alone. Instead, he went after Captain Andy. He didn't understand that Captain Andy, despite his alcoholism (maybe in San Francisco, *because* of it), was a sympathetic figure, a character who'd be sure to win over jurors the more he talked. When you have a character on the stand in an adversary position, you don't draw him out; you spend as little time with him as possible. But, on cross examination, this lawyer thought he'd get Captain Andy to make some damaging admissions. "How many steps did you take?" he asked Captain Andy.

"When?"

"When you came out of your room?"

"I took one last step," said Captain Andy, "the last one ever on this earth on my own two feet."

Some jurors were obviously moved by this and shifted uncomfortably in their seats.

"And then," persisted my opponent, "what happened?"

"I don't know."

"Surely something happened."

"I was out cold. I didn't know."

"What did you think?"

"When?"

"When you woke up."

"Right then when I was lying down there in the dark, in the oily water?"

"Yes," said this donkey, hoping perhaps that Captain Andy would say something like, "I'll never take another drink as long as I live."

Andy didn't say that. He said, "Goddamn it, torpedoed again!"

That brought out all the pent-up feelings of the jurors. They exploded with laughter. With that, the insurance company instructed the lawyer to settle with us—for $261,000. I persuaded Captain Andy to let me give the money to a trustee who kept Andy from spending all that money in one place.

But the heart of all trial practice is cross-examination, and it can make or break a case, raise or lower an award.

Cross-examination searches the innermost recesses of the closet of the mind, selects and sweeps it clean. And everybody has some sort of a skeleton in his own personal closet. That's why he's afraid of cross-examination. If his lawyer would only tell him that cross-examination can search only the *relevant* matters, the prospective litigant or witness might not be so terrified of "going to court" or even being a witness. Still, with only "relevant matters" being fair game for the cross-examiner, the layman still fears that somehow an adroit lawyer may get into that innermost secret chamber wherein his deepest immorality resides.

A witness fairly warned will not "volunteer" because, as soon as he does he will be led out to the end of the branch, then the limb sawed off behind him. A yes or no should suffice wherever possible.

A nurse in Salt Lake City should have been told this, and particularly not to "volunteer": The nurse had received a back sprain, rather severe and for which she should have been compensated in an automobile accident in downtown Salt Lake City. She'd left the hospital early one evening with an intern, and on a harmless and innocuous drive downtown she'd been "rear-ended." Old Holy Grail Insurance Company wouldn't pay what the case was worth, so her lawyer took her to trial. She told her story, but the defense lawyer had nothing to lose so he fished about for any extraneous material that might permit an opening for prejudicial material. He asked about the drive downtown. He suggested that maybe the nurse and the intern were out for a romantic evening, which of itself might even have been perfectly legitimate, but which he hoped might offend one of the spinster jurors.

Then the nurse volunteered, "I'll have you know, I'm

a good girl and I had no thought of any romantic interlude with Dr.——. In fact, I'm a *virgin!*"

The "I'm a virgin" did it! No one had claimed, up to then, that she was or was not a virgin, and indeed, it was completely irrelevant to her back injury, but *she* brought it into the case. It was too late for her own lawyer to strike it.

Counsel for the insurance company asked for a recess and then did the gracious thing. He called the nurse's lawyer aside and showed him an X-ray that had been taken after the nurse had gotten back to the hospital to determine whether she had had any broken bones. There, right in the middle of the X-ray, squarely placed in the X-rayed pelvic area, showed a rubber diaphragm—something a "virgin lady" would certainly not be wearing on an evening's drive into Salt Lake City! The case was settled at one-half its value, not because the nurse wasn't injured or because she didn't tell the truth about her accident, but because she *volunteered* and she wasn't quite truthful about that *collateral* skeleton in her closet.

I've got the X-ray in a shadow box on my wall in my office. It reminds me to tell all of my clients and witnesses not to "volunteer"—and particularly about collateral matters.

Some witnesses after a searing cross-examination almost believe lawyers practice black magic. Do trial lawyers believe in the occult, ESP, and the like more than "ordinary folk"? I think so. I had one vivid experience in the extraordinary—I can't tell whether it was ESP or occult or what. It had to do with my life-long friend, Sooey Ng. It was July, 1960, and Sooey was alive and well in San Francisco. He and his family were living in "Chinatown" in a well-furnished and maintained apartment, and Sooey was a very respected teacher of English in our public schools. He frequently dropped by for lunch, and whenever a new Chinese restaurant opened, Sooey and I, *en famille,* were there to break the first fortune cookie—and dinner—for free, of course.

One day I got a telephone call from Miller's undertaking parlor in Oakland, across the Bay from San Francisco, and indeed, I logged it in my daily journal. I was told that my friend Sooey Ng had died and he was to be buried "next Thursday at ten" from that undertaking parlor. It was a usual undertaker's call inviting guests and pallbearers. I was asked to be the latter.

That "next Thursday" I drove over to the undertaking parlor to pay my last respects and to attend the funeral. I went into the gloomy building to the front room. It was empty. There was no funeral scheduled for that day. Somewhat mystified, I asked, "Where is the funeral of Sooey Ng?" The undertaker answered quizzically, "We don't have any Sooey Ng, maybe you've made a mistake, I'll look and see if any other undertaking parlors have a Sooey Ng." He looked, they didn't.

I drove back to San Francisco and rather gingerly picked up the phone and called Sooey's number. Sooey answered. I was somewhat shocked but didn't tell him about my experience. I checked my ledger. There was the phone call. I guess it was good I didn't tell him because the next Thursday, exactly at 10:00 A.M. Sooey did have his funeral at Miller's undertaking parlor! He had suddenly and unexpectedly died between the two Thursdays. When I showed up at the undertaking parlor I startled the same undertaker out of his wits by my presence. I did a silly thing. I couldn't help it. I winked at him! No doubt he's wondering about it to this day.

Then there was the time my dad saved my life—*after* he was dead. I was driving down to Los Angeles in a new red Thunderbird convertible with the top down, just having come from a visit at San Quentin with Caryl

Chessman, who had been fighting for eleven years to stay out of the gas chamber. I was furious with the people who thought that the system needed this man's life to preserve itself. Perhaps I was abstracted by this and not paying as much attention as I should have been to my driving. I was on a curving mountain road between Paso Robles and U.S. 101, not far from the spot where the actor James Dean had lost his life in an auto accident. Now my car started to skid, unaccountably. It ran smack into an earth bank, fetched back and threw me out. I am sure that everything happened very fast. But to me it was a slow-motion picture sequence in a bad dream. I was lying on the road, but my car hadn't yet come to rest. I started to scramble to the other side of the road. Then I heard an admonition, unmistakably the voice of my father, now dead for some years. "You sit still!" he commanded. I obeyed. I sat still—and watched as my car, still in motion, landed right on the spot I'd been headed for. It would have squashed me, like a run-over squirrel. I know *what* happened. But who, how, why? I do not know.

CHAPTER EIGHT

Butcher Paper and Gingham

My careful preparation on the Bryant case led to talk around town. Fame, I discovered, is a grass that grows in any dirt when no one's looking. And fame had its advantages: it would bring in cash by bringing in more cases. Often enough, if I did my homework, I wouldn't have to go to trial at all; the insurance-company lawyers would simply settle out of court.

Once, a man came into my office with a sad story about an L-iron that had crashed into the windshield of his pickup truck as he drove up U.S. 101, fracturing his wife's skull. Three lawyers had told him he had no case—they couldn't figure out whom to sue. But I could. The man had one clue: he still had the offending L-iron. It took me a good deal of time, but I finally traced that L-iron. I checked the truck weighing station's records for the day of the accident and inquired about more than a hundred trucks that could have lost L-irons. Most of the trucks didn't carry hardware of this particular type. We found that the iron was specifically manufactured to hold lumber on a truck. Finally I narrowed my search down to three lumber trucks that did carry this iron, then at last to the single truck that passed the scene of the accident at precisely the time the "mysterious" L-iron came crashing into my client's windshield. The company paid policy limits with hardly a protest.

When I did go to trial, however, I enjoyed the challenge of persuading a jury to see things my way, with ever-new kinds of demonstrative evidence—and beating the lawyers on the other side, who, though they individually might be good guys, were working for cruel and heartless companies. I had one client, Katherine Jeffers, a wholesome, slightly plump young mother with pigtails, who stepped off a San Francisco trolley on Market Street one day in 1941 (when four trolleys ran there side by side) and got knocked down by another passing streetcar. The car ground through her right leg, just below the knee. It seemed clear that the Municipal Railroad was responsible for the traumatic amputation. I sued, and the jury awarded her $65,000. Incredibly, the railroad attorneys moved for a new trial. The $65,000, they said, was too much. Nobody had ever gotten that much for the loss of a leg. And anyway, they added, doctors were now able to do remarkable things with artificial limbs. On those grounds, the judge set aside the verdict as excessive. (Verdicts for amputations nowadays go for over $300,000.)

We went to trial again. This time, however, I was glad I had a second chance. I came to court with more than a silver-tongued argument. I brought an exhibit. Along with my briefcase and my law books, I carried an L-shaped package wrapped in cheap yellow paper and tied with soft white string. The judge and the opposing attorney, John Moran, stared at it and wondered where they had seen that sort of paper before. It was butcher's paper.

Moran and the judge knew I was capable of doing

almost anything in court. After the Bryant case, I had seen the value of good exhibits, and bringing a part of a skeleton or someone's brain preserved in alcohol into a courtroom wasn't beyond me. They continued to look at this package with more than ordinary curiosity. I didn't open it, but I did have occasion to move it from place to place on the top of the counsel table. On the second day of the trial, I brought the package into court once more and ignored it. On the third day, I knew that the package was drawing more attention. I could see the jurors sizing up my client, dressed in demure gingham, her one good leg in a black stocking, and then shifting their gaze to the L-shaped package and whispering among themselves.

John Moran gave the argument I had expected he would make. With one of these wonderful new artificial limbs, my client could do almost anything she could before: drive cars; play with her kids; swim; dance with her husband, a navy commander; make love. Then I moved to the package.

I took my time. I plucked at the knots in the string. I might have snipped the string with the scissors offered by the bailiff. I was strong enough to simply break the string. But I carefully undid each knot, then slowly peeled off the butcher paper, crumpled it and let it fall to the floor. Underneath, another layer of the same paper. I took a half-minute to loosen that. When I had milked the moment for all it was worth, I turned to the jury and with a sudden, almost violent move, I held what I had aloft.

The defense attorney started to cry out his objection, then fell silent. I was holding up Katherine's artificial limb, with all its lacings, glistening metal joints, straps, suction cups and new plastic shaft.

"Ladies and gentlemen of the jury," I said, moving

over to the jury box, "this is what my pretty young client will wear for the rest of her life. Take it." I dumped it in the lap of the first juror. "Feel the warmth of life in the soft tissues of its flesh, feel the pulse of the blood as it flows through the veins, feel the marvelous smooth articulation at the new joint and touch the rippling muscles of the calf."

The first juror gingerly passed on the prosthesis to the next juror and he to the next, and as he did so, I continued to talk. "Don't be alarmed by all the harnesses and straps and the creaking of the metal. My client is no longer frightened. She will wear this artificial leg for the rest of her life in exchange for that limb which God gave her as she started life and which she should have worn for the rest of her days."

It took the jurors twenty minutes to examine that artificial leg, and I could see their verdict sealed in the looks on their faces as they passed the limb along. Then I gave it to the judge. I doubt if he had ever seen a prosthesis. He examined it, too. This time the jury came back with a verdict of $100,000. John again asked for a new trial. The grounds: excessive verdict. The judge denied the motion. Ten years before, loss of a leg below the knee might have been worth $1,000, $5,000, maybe $10,000. Now I'd asked $100,000—and got it. The times, they were changing, and I was helping make the change. Indeed, why not? The cost of everything else was going up, but the courts were still computing the cost of human pain and suffering based on figures that were almost half a century old.

My next three cases—Gluckstein, Sullivan and Duvall— helped me see even more clearly the intimate link between the best kind of demonstrative evidence and a more adequate award. In the Gluckstein case, the demonstrative evidence was obvious, but if I (or my client) had worried about proprieties, we never would have used the best evidence at hand.

Jeanette Gluckstein was a handsome woman dressed in high style with a wispy scarf that matched her shoes and bag when she first came to my office. Maybe it was her English accent that gave me a feeling that here was a woman of quality and maybe it was the way she moved that gave me the feeling that here, too, was a woman of passion. I liked her at one. She told me she was a dress designer and that she'd been working in San Francisco for eleven years. "And what is your problem?" I asked.

Her eyes brimmed with tears. "I had plastic surgery on my, on my breasts, and they're—ruined." Once she communicated this information, the ramrod of her spine softened, and she sagged in her chair like a sack of sugar. I called in my secretary to stand by while Miss Gluckstein showed me her scars. She unbuttoned her blouse and removed her padded bra. I thought that I'd seen some surgical errancies, but nothing like this. She looked like a Picasso nude. Both breasts were almost square. One was obviously larger than the other, the nipples had been sliced off and transposed inches higher than they should have been and the nipples looked inward. In addition, she had a large gash running from her breast to her pubes. "Did the good doctor do that, too?" I asked. She nodded.

We sued for $250,000, and that's why we didn't settle with the insurance company's attorneys. One of them was a wonderful guy who represented Lloyd's of London in San Francisco, Bob Lamb. Lamb said he might be able to get Lloyd's to come up with a tenth of that, so he said, why didn't we go to trial and see what award a judge and jury might make?

Lamb (who was later to represent *me* in one of my many trials before the State Bar) took a considerably longer, more honest view of things than many of his game-playing colleagues. For a number of reasons the insurance companies were raising their premiums, but rather than tell people what those reasons really were (simply the higher cost of doing business, higher salaries and higher expense accounts for the insurance executives, in addition to higher and higher claims) they were welcoming my presence on the scene as a convenient scapegoat to help them in their public relations. Actually, the greater the claims (or the jury awards), the more they could charge on premiums and the more money they'd make. Insurance companies don't ladle up all the money they collect in premiums—they put 7 percent of it in reserve and then they turn around and invest the reserve —millions of dollars. The insurance people should have thought of me as a friend. In fact, Lamb did.

In the trial, I presented the only doctor I could get to testify. I called him "Clean Him Up" Smith, because I used to clean and sober him up before I could take him to trial. He'd been a pariah in his own profession for years because he was the only doctor around who dared testify against another physician. Other doctors followed the unwritten law (and in some cases the canons of their particular medical societies) never to so testify. Dr. Smith had never joined any of the medical societies and was proud of it. (On cross-examination, defense lawyers would usually ask him a single question—and sometimes to an unsophisticated jury, it was enough: "Doctor, when did you get off probation?") He told the court that the defendant, Dr. Phillip J. Lipsett, had "cut too much fat away,' that he cut the fat away instead of "tearing it" and that this cutting process had created minute adhesions, perhaps as many as five hundred. "It was simply not good plastic surgery on the abdomen," he said, "and as for the breasts, nothing was accomplished. Right now all this woman has is a couple bags of degenerative tissue and the cutting has shut off the circulation of the nervous system."

"What does that mean?" I asked.

"Sir?"

"What effect does that have on Miss Gluckstein?"

Doc Smith was a crusty old guy, as unhappy as I with the medical profession's ordinary circumlocutions. "It means there's no more titillation in the tits," he said.

"Thank you, Doctor," I said. "No further questions."

On cross-examination, Bob Lamb went ad hominem with Dr. Smith. He asked the doctor if it wasn't a fact that he'd been testifying in malpractice cases against doctors for twenty-eight years. "Brain cases, legs, most everything that comes along. Is that correct?"

Doctor Smith wouldn't allow himself to be browbeaten. He hadn't done anything wrong. The physicians who had been guilty of malpractice and those who covered up for them were the guilty ones. Dr. Smith told Lamb, "Yes, we had one case in Stockton a little while ago—twenty-seven doctors in Stockton and the poor boy that lost his arm, and they couldn't get one doctor to say a good word for him—not one doctor. They were all told that if they testified their insurance would be cut off."

Lamb protested to the judge. "I assign that as prejudicial misconduct, your Honor, and not responsive."

Doc Smith was ready to fight. "You accuse me of—"

The judge cut him off. "Wait a minute, wait a minute."

Lamb decided to forget it. He said, "Doctor, I am just asking you a few questions." And then, without asking the judge to have Dr. Smith's reference to the doctors' insurance stricken from the record, he went ahead with his cross-examination. And got nowhere with Dr. Smith.

So far, so good. But how could I demonstrate Jeanette's condition to the jury? I'd had some black-and-white, color and infrared pictures taken (to show the distortion of the blood vessels below the skin), but Lamb and Dr. Lipsett told the judge that "Jeanette's fully recovered now, and she looks a lot better than these pictures." Lamb said, "Why don't you just put your client on the stand and have her tell the jury what she suffers?"

I almost choked laughing. I was making my reputation winning what I thought were almost adequate awards precisely because I wasn't content to "tell" a jury anything that I could show them instead. But how could I use demonstrative evidence in this case and stay within the bounds of acceptable taste? I couldn't ask Jeanette to strip. But in the judge's chambers I could threaten to do so. "Your Honor, I want your permission to have my client strip right down in open court."

"Impossible," Lamb said.

"Why?" I asked. "A person has the right to show a jury what she suffers."

"A jury maybe," Judge Franklin A. Griffin said. "But not an entire courtroom."

I looked at the judge. "Okay. Just the jury then. In chambers."

The judge hesitated.

"One by one," I said. He ummed a bit. "With a lady bailiff in attendance."

The judge sighed, "Well, Mr. Lamb, what do you think? I think Mr. Belli's client has a right to show herself to the jury if she wants to."

Lamb said that would be more inflammatory than the pictures. The judge said he had ruled against the color pictures, because the defendant said they didn't represent the woman she really was. "Obviously," he said, "the jury ought to see the woman as she is. She had the operation because she wanted her breasts to look better, not to a doctor but to the average layman. The jury is composed of average laymen, and they have a duty to look at her breasts. I'd like to see 'em, too," he added.

So Jeanette disrobed completely in the judge's chambers, and the bailiff covered her with a sheet. Then the jurors filed into the judge's chambers one by one, the bailiff pulling down the sheet for each one to see, then covering Jeanette again until the next juror came by to stand in front of her. Jeanette stood there like a statue, face scarlet, head down, her eyes filling with tears and the tears running down onto the scars on her breasts.

And the jury awarded her $115,000. Today, that would have been half a million or more.

The Frank Sullivan case was another half-million-dollar case in today's dollars. My old friend Bob Callahan, the firehouse politician, brought Frank Sullivan, Jr., into my office for the simple reason that he knew I could help Frank. He'd been badly hurt in a streetcar accident on the Fillmore line. Crushed pelvis, fractured vertebrae and a ruptured urethra. That ruptured urethra was the biggest problem. Every ten days for the rest of his life he had to have a doctor pass a sound (a thin plastic rod) through his penis and into his bladder to keep scar tissue from forming at the point of the ruptured urethra—thereby preventing the guy from taking a normal leak like almost every man who's ever lived. Worse: The sound was not only painful and caused bleeding and acute prostatitis, it made Sullivan impotent—and Sullivan was only twenty-one, just married, an ex-sailor with a pretty and very pregnant wife.

Young Sullivan had been standing near the rear door of the streetcar when the streetcar came upon a parked truck jutting out into the street. Could the car squeeze by? It crept up on this truck, and when the front of the car had cleared the truck, the motorman figured everything was okay and proceeded up the street. But the back door of the streetcar hooked the back of the truck and somehow young Sullivan got pulled out of the streetcar and mangled between the streetcar and the truck.

"He had a badge that entitled him to ride on the city streetcars free," argued the defense attorneys. "Therefore, he must have been riding free, and if so, young Sullivan shouldn't be suing the City in Superior Court for fifty thousand dollars. He should be filing a claim with Workmen's Compensation for an injury suffered on the job."

They would have been right—*if* Sullivan was riding free. But he wasn't. At least he said he wasn't. He was a temporary noncivil-service fireman with a badge but no uniform; he thought he didn't have the right to ride the streetcars free and he so testified in court. He didn't even have his badge with him on the day he was hurt. The City's attorneys grumbled about that. They said they couldn't imagine a worldly-wise young mick in San Francisco who didn't know what he could boost and what he couldn't. They said they'd heard a rumor that one of the guys in the firemen's union (my friend the firehouse politician?) had slipped up to Sullivan's hospital room and taken the badge before they could send an investigator around to take an inventory of his effects. But they couldn't prove a thing. The attorneys had rejected my claim for $50,000, contending it was the fault of the driver who had parked his truck so badly. So I filed suit for $150,000 and included the truck driver and the owner of the truck, then, during the trial, let them out of the case and got a jury verdict against the city alone for $125,000.

I had been doing my homework, medically speaking. By now, I was able to talk to a jury like one of the Brothers Mayo. "Assuming also, Doctor," I said as I examined my expert witness, the doctor who had been treating Sullivan, "assuming with the rupture of the prostatic urethral membrane near the neck of the bladder, he has become impotent, that he will remain impotent, not sterile but impotent, for the rest of his life. . . ." That helped. Again, I used demonstrative evidence. I brought into court the thin plastic rod that Frank Sullivan would have to pass through his penis every ten days for the rest of his life. That helped, too.

The judge, George Schonfeld, also helped, unwittingly, by getting himself involved in my blackboard computations. "If Mr. Sullivan's earning power were only reduced one hundred and fifty dollars a month for forty-four years," I told the jury (the actuary said Sullivan had a life expectancy of forty-four years), "that would amount to sixty-six thousand dollars in lost income as a result of these injuries, which have rendered him crippled." I was hoping that some numbers freak on the jury would catch my deliberate mistake and feel so proud of his discovery that he might become an advocate for this number inside the jury room. The judge himself became my advocate, which was even better.

"Wait a minute, Mr. Belli," said the judge, standing beside me at the blackboard. "You've made a mistake in your mathematics. I think if you take forty-four times one hundred fifty a month, you will get the sum of seventy-nine thousand two hundred dollars instead of sixty-six thousand dollars. Forty-four times eighteen hundred a year comes to seventy-nine thousand two hundred dollars. The young man should get seventy-nine thousand two hundred dollars."

"Yes, your Honor, he should." I could barely keep from clapping him on the back.

The City's attorneys were furious, and in their appeal they protested that the judge had in effect told the jury what they "ought to allow." "No such thing," said Peters, the justice who wrote the appeals decision. "It is not beyond the realm of expectation that a trial judge can add and add properly. It is his duty to do so."

But the thing that gave me the biggest boot was the way Justice Peters dealt with the City's contention that $125,000 was an excessive verdict. Judge Peters wrote, "While $125,000 is a large sum of money and while it perhaps represents the largest verdict that has heretofore come before an appellate court in this state . . . we may interfere only if it appears as a matter of law that the award was the result of passion or prejudice." And then he quoted the law that had been made in a recent case where the jury made a similarly large award: my case, *Gluckstein v. Lipsett!* And again, the court took "Judicial notice" of the shrinking American dollar.

Was an award of $125,000 for Frank Sullivan "too high"? I think not. Two years later, I saw the boy again, and what I had feared within myself had happened. His wife had divorced him, his home was gone, he had nothing left but the remainder of the award money. Would anyone swap places with him for $125,000? For a million?

I was building legal victories (and a legal reputation) on precedents I had created myself. It was like hitting a seven at the crap tables in Harrah's Club in Reno and letting my winnings ride while I threw another seven. And I felt good because I had elevated the injured little guy to the economic level of stocks and bonds, a prize Hereford, a yacht, old paintings and prized violins. Why shouldn't a man or a woman be worth as much as a Stradivarius?

I threw another seven in my next case in the same way. I sued TWA on behalf of Whitney Duvall, a young baker, and his wife, Alberta, after a huge gasoline tank truck near the San Francisco airport plowed into their car and crippled them both, she certainly for life, and he for a good long time. I brought mockups into the court of the roadways and intersections near the airport and models of the tank truck and car (and displayed the injuries to the Duvalls, of course) so the jurors could see for themselves. After all the testimony, they didn't think that Duvall was negligent in any contributory way, and they were appalled at the couple's injuries. Mrs. Duvall, then twenty-eight, could never have children, her right leg would always be one and a half inches shorter than her left and during the eight months in the hospital on the critical list, she developed jaundice, thrombophlebitis and a pulmonary embolus. The jury awarded the Duvalls $120,000, perhaps the equivalent now of more than $500,000, tax-free.

Again, the attorneys protested in their appeal at "the excessive verdict." Again, the California Court of Appeals repeated the same rule. There was no showing that the jury acted out of passion or prejudice. The trial judge —a thirteenth juror, in effect—denied a new trial and didn't reduce the size of the verdict. And then the court cited two recent cases that seemed to establish the law on excessive verdicts pretty clearly: *Gluckstein v. Lipsett* and *Sullivan v. City and County of San Francisco,* both mine.

CHAPTER NINE

Fireman's Red

Up until now, each of my attempts to make evidence vivid to a jury involved bringing something into a courtroom that jurors could see with their own eyes. In my next case, I had a different challenge. I had to find a way of making visible to a jury evidence no one had actually *seen*. It was a case that began in Vallejo, a town on the northeast edge of the San Francisco Bay, when a twelve-ton tractor-trailer smashed into a ten-ton fire engine. The crash put a fireman into an institution for life. It gave me the biggest case of my career up to that time, one that would get ink in most of the newspapers in the world and be written up with alarm by *The Reader's Digest,* as if I were some new kind of disease.

At 7:15 in the morning of May 2, 1944, Captain Fred Reckenbeil had almost finished his twenty-four-hour shift and was phoning his wife to ask her to have his breakfast ready at 7:45 so he could go off on a little fishing trip with his boys. At 7:16, an alarm came in and Fred Reckenbeil began the last run of his life with Engine Company Number 2.

Driver Richard F. Lee climbed into the front seat with

the stationhouse's Dalmatian beside him. Lee started the engine and threw the switch that started the red warning lights blinking on and off. Lieutenant Carl Winters got in next to the Dalmatian, pressed his foot on the siren button on the floor and held it down. Captain Reckenbeil climbed onto the back of the truck and remained standing on a rear step, his normal post.

The fire wasn't far away—about a mile up Benecia Road, just past State Highway 40—and when the fire truck lumbered into the intersection of Benecia and Highway 40, driver Richard Lee noted that the speedometer needle was exactly on twenty-three.

At the same moment, a man named George Silveria was barreling along State Highway 40 toward the Benecia intersection in a twelve-ton tractor-trailer. He rolled right through the intersection, and when he rammed the fire truck, people heard the crash for a mile around. "I hope that's not Freddie," said his wife Maxine, home cooking the captain's breakfast when she heard the boom. The fire truck flew seventy-five feet into the air, and so did Fred Reckenbeil, who had been standing very close to the point of impact.

Driver Lee was hurt but he could still walk, and when he got to Captain Reckenbeil he found him standing on his own tongue. Blood was oozing from his ears, nose, mouth and temples. In the Vallejo Community Hospital, Captain Gerald Smith, a navy doctor stationed at Mare Island and an expert in neuropsychiatry, examined Reckenbeil and threw up his hands. The man's entire skull was crisscrossed with stellate fractures, reticulated like a cracked eggshell. Smith gave him a couple of hours to live.

Reckenbeil did live, if you could call his existence life. He was breathing but he was almost a basket case. When Mrs. Reckenbeil asked the firemen what she should do, they told her to get Melvin Belli. I filed suit against the Taylor-Wolcott Company, the firm that owned the truck, and asked general damages of $250,000 plus unspecified special damages and court costs. There was no real legal problem here. According to the law then, a fire engine had the right of way, even through a red light, as long as its siren was blowing and it was going to a fire. That pretty much summed up the legal status of Engine Company Number 2 there and then on May 2, 1944. But, of course, I had the burden of proof. It seemed to me that all I had to do was prove Reckenbeil's injuries and prove that the siren had been blowing. Then there would be complete liability, and only the question of how much in damages would remain.

I had the word of Reckenbeil's fellows on the truck: they turned on the siren and it was screeching away when they hit the intersection. But that wasn't enough. How could I prove it? How could I show it to a jury? A sound leaves no mark. You can't catch it and take it into court in your hands or in a briefcase, and nobody was standing on the street corner with a tape recorder. It doesn't come in pints or quarts.

While I was mulling that over, the insurance carrier for Taylor-Wolcott had put their own attorney on the case, an excellent lawyer named Paul Dana. Dana wondered what figure I'd settle for. I asked for $90,000. Dana rejected it; the Taylor-Wolcott Company would take a chance on the trial.

So I went out and hired an unusual chap as my investigator. Not an ex-cop, who would go around scaring people, but a fellow who used to be a vaudeville comedian, Vince Silk. Vince's job called for tact in dealing with people, and Vince had plenty of that. I put him to work circulating through the neighborhood around the Benecia Road-Highway 40 intersection, finding witnesses who could swear that they had heard the siren blowing clearly, loudly and without stopping from the moment the engine left the firehouse to the moment of the crash. Silk talked to hundreds of people, subjected those who remembered the crash to close interrogation and persuaded the best of them to become our witnesses at the trial. In some cases, this wasn't easy. One of our potential witnesses was a prostitute who conducted business in a trailer park near the intersection. "All right," she said to Silk at last, "I know what trouble is. If I can help, go ahead and call me." Some witnesses had moved out of the neighborhood. Silk chased them all over California and into Nevada and Arizona. He finally came up with thirty-five witnesses who could swear they had heard the siren blowing loudly and continuously up to the moment of the crash.

With thirty-five witnesses I could *show* sound to the jury. I chartered a plane and had an aerial photographer take scores of shots of that intersection, selected the best one and had it blown up and mounted on a stiff six-by-eight-foot cardboard. When I started to put on my case, I brought each one of these thirty-five witnesses into court, had them identify where they were standing, sitting or lying when they heard the siren (and the crash).

"Mr. Jones, where were you on the morning of May second?"

"I was at home."

"Would you please look at this photograph, Mr. Jones, and locate your home for me?"

Then Mr. Jones would peer at the photo, orient himself. "Oh yes, here's Benecia—uh, lessee, our house is two blocks over—here!" He would find his home and smile triumphantly at me and the judge.

"Thank you, Mr. Jones. Now please hold your finger on the spot on your house while I paste this piece of paper beside it." Then I'd put a pennant-shaped slip of paper on the spot and continue with my questions establishing the relevant details—that he had heard the siren and the crash. When I had finished with the examination of all thirty-five witnesses I had a graphic illustration every juror could not only understand but see with his own eyes. About halfway through the tedious process, Paul Dana tried to object—"How many witnesses do we need, your Honor?"—but this only gave me a chance to tell the judge (and the jury) what I was attempting to show. "When I'm finished, your Honor, the cumulative testimony will demonstrate—graphically, I hope—that this truck driver had to burst through barriers of sound, the sound of a screaming siren, in order to get to that intersection at all." And when I had finished with the examination of all thirty-five witnesses I had succeeded in doing just that: I chalked a series of concentric rings around the intersection, each ring passing through several bits of paper on the photo, making the jurors actually "see sound."

Paul Dana made no further objections to the photo nor to what I had done with it, and it rested there in front of the jury for the duration of the trial so the jurors could see it—and listen to it, too: When it got warm in the courtroom, the bailiff opened the windows; the breeze came and rustled those little slips of paper, each whispering slip a symbolic witness.

Dana let me go ahead. I introduced witnesses who said the Taylor-Wolcott truck was going "at least fifty." I introduced the doctors who treated Captain Reckenbeil and described his bloody, comatose condition after the crash, his high temperature for a month afterward, his delirium while he was in the hospital. I introduced attendants from the Livermore Sanitarium to detail the man's irrationality when he was taken there. And then there was my summation. Several years later, Paul Dana told *Life* writer Robert Wallace what he, my opponent, thought of my final remarks to the jury. "I felt the hair on the back of my head rise as I heard Belli's description of this man and his suffering. Belli actually became Reckenbeil. At some time, in some way, Belli had suffered in his own vivid imagination whatever Reckenbeil had suffered." It must have been the way I said it: the cold transcript demonstrates that I used no rhetorical tricks.

I used no rhetoric but I was unable to resist using another bit of demonstrative evidence during my summation. When I began the speech, Bob Callahan, a fireman * who has been my great friend for thirty-six years, went out to a pay phone and called his buddies at a nearby engine company. "This is it," he said, "Belli's on now. If you get an alarm in the next half hour, be sure and go down McAllister with your siren on. If you don't get a call in the next half hour, make a run anyway—with your siren *on.*"

I do not know (and don't care to know) if there was a real fire, a false alarm or what, but halfway through

* Callahan and I had a marvelous election forecasting service for several elections running. We figured we could predict the results of an election by midday if only we could get a look at a good number of sample ballots (which voters took with them to the polls and discarded after they had finished voting). Callahan, a firehouse politician, merely put out the word to his firefighters, scattered all over the city. They scooped up the sample ballots for us outside the voting booths, counted the votes in key races and phoned them in. Callahan and I hocked everything we owned and went down to Breen, the bookie, and bet—big. We won big and kept winning until the mother of one of our firemen saw him rummaging through a garbage can near a polling booth and raised hell with the town's political boss, Tom Finn, on the grounds that firemen shouldn't have to go through garbage cans. Tom agreed with her, and that was the end of our "garbageman's poll."

my argument I had to stop speaking until the fire truck with the screaming siren had passed. Otherwise the jurors wouldn't have heard me. I didn't even have to ask the jurors: How come this truck driver couldn't hear a fire siren?

I had no wish to wait around for the jury's decision. Those were "ulcer hours" for me. I had prepared the case as well as I could, advanced thousands of dollars on aerial photographs and investigators and additional thousands in my own time, making hospital visits, taking depositions, preparing exhibits—and I still could not bet that the jury would decide in favor of my client or, if they did, how much money they'd give him.

Anyway, I was needed elsewhere. Now, after years of genteel poverty and dreams that someday I'd make it, I was hot. Everyone wanted me. While the Reckenbeil jury was out, I was over in a federal courtroom picking a jury on another case.

I'd barely gotten started when Bob Callahan burst into the courtroom with a frenzied look in his eye and shouted, "Mel, you won, you won, and the jury made it two hundred and twenty-five thousand!" George Harris, the federal judge, was ready to cite me for contempt of court, but he was as dumbfounded as I over the size of the verdict and called an immediate recess. In fact, $225,000 was the highest ever given to a single plaintiff in any personal-injury case in the history of the world.

On that basis alone, Dana argued for a new trial. The award, he said, was simply excessive. No jury had ever gone that high. But the judge said simply, "This one did, Mr. Dana." And he let the verdict stand. Emboldened by that, I told the press that there'd be higher verdicts still. "Soon," I said, "we'll see a million-dollar verdict." Dana told the press he would appeal. He had to. He'd advised Taylor-Wolcott not to settle for $90,000. Now they had to dig up the $90,000—and a lot more besides.

A few weeks later, I got a phone call from Paul Dana. His voice was as wrinkled and scratchy as an old piece of sandpaper, and I asked him what was wrong. "Where you calling from, Paul?"

"Livermore Sanitarium," he said. He explained that he didn't think—necessarily—that Captain Reckenbeil was faking or anything, but he owed a duty to his clients, I guess he meant the boys at old Holy Grail Insurance Company, to *make sure* that Reckenbeil was really sick. So he had one of the insurance adjusters committed to Livermore with instructions to befriend Reckenbeil and see whether and how the captain was deceiving old Holy Grail.

"*Is* he faking?" I asked icily.

Dana strangled and choked a bit. "No."

"So?" I said. "Why are you calling me?"

"Well," said Dana, his words coming in a rush now, "once my adjuster learned that Captain Reckenbeil was on the level, he found the superintendent at an inmate softball game and asked to get out. 'Yes,' the superintendent said, '*most* people in here would like to get out.' 'No, I'm an insurance adjuster,' he said, and the super said, 'Sure, we've got a lot of insurance adjusters here. Matter of fact, we've got Napoleon over there in left field and George Washington is coming up to bat and that's Abraham Lincoln having the conference there in the bleachers.' And he wouldn't let my investigator out. Still won't let him out until you tell him I'm on the up and up."

"*You* on the up and up?" I said. "Why would I tell him that, Paul?"

"Come on, Mel," he pleaded.

I toyed with Dana for a while, put him on "hold" a few times while I attended to some nonexistent calls on another line and finally agreed to talk to the superintendent.

Paul Dana was indeed humbled. To add to his humiliation, he had to come to my office a couple of days later and tell me that the Taylor-Wolcott Company could go on the rocks if they had to pay the whole $225,000. I had no choice but to believe him. "How much can they pay?" I asked. "One hundred eighty-seven thousand five hundred dollars," he said.

I had no business settling for $187,500 if the jury said $225,000 and the judge affirmed it. But the case was on appeal, and I had found a technical flaw in one of the judge's instructions to the jury which, if Dana pushed, might overturn the verdict entirely. So I took the $187,500 to be done with it, which made the award even less "excessive" for the Reckenbeils than before.

That insurance company then spread one of the first canards about my verdicts, the likes of which continue to this day. They told their employees there would be no Christmas bonuses that year. "You can thank Belli for that. He took all your money!"

Whatever the insurance companies said, however, I was a winner and I began to enjoy the love and affection that the world bestows on winners. And I tried to look the part. I had tailors doing variations on the standard lawyer's charcoal gray. They made me suits with a slightly rakish Western cut, all the jackets lined in red silk, high slash pockets on the trousers, no pleats and spare all the way down to my boots, which were not Texas cowboy boots, but Congress gaiters, calf-high black boots molded from a plaster cast of my foot by Peal's of London. Sometimes I wore a black homburg.

It was thus attired that I went up to Sacramento one day on behalf of the Association of Chinese Herbalists of North America. Practicing an art that is thousands of years old, the herbalists in the City produced medicinal potions from dried roots, plants, fish, lizards and the like. Other Chinese bought them, they injured no one and maybe did some good. Nevertheless, the California Pharmacological Association thought it could put the herbalists out of business by getting a bill drafted in Sacramento forcing them to pass a stringent pharmacology exam.

In Sacramento my clients and I sat in the subcommittee's chambers for hours, listening to arguments for and against a half dozen other bills and then to arguments in favor of the bill directed against my clients. When I finally got up to speak I could see my clients expected me to talk for at least two hours and destroy the bill for all time. I didn't speak for two hours. I didn't even speak for two minutes. After addressing the distinguished lawmakers I said, "Gentlemen, the time is short. These are distinguished, hard-working gentlemen. They have been in our great state for a long, long time. All they want is a Chinaman's chance of making a living." Then I sat down. After hours of bullshit, my speech was a refreshing change of pace. And the lawmakers tabled the legislation on the spot. They could just as well have voted against me, saying I didn't even make an argument! But that's the chance a trial lawyer takes in his daily business. Is it any wonder we don't gamble for *recreation* in our off hours?

CHAPTER TEN

White Suit and Homburg

As a memento of the Reckenbeil case, Bob Callahan sent me a parrot. I dubbed the bird "Captain John Silver," bought him a cage and taught him how to drink Kentucky bourbon. That bird became famous around town. Jack Rosenbaum wrote him up in his column: "Captain John Silver, the drinkingest bird in town, is also the fussiest. His keeper, Barrister Melvin Belli, insists that the only thing he'll drink is Jim Beam, Black Label. Neat." The president of Jim Beam wrote asking if I could bring Captain John back to talk to a meeting of the board of directors in Kentucky. When Captain John and I refused, he sent us a free case of Jim Beam anyway. Captain John and I went on the biggest binge ever experienced by man and bird. And in the flush of my recent successes, I was on some other kind of emotional binge as well.

"Goddamn it, Mel," said Lou Ashe, "Look at you. You don't go home at night. You sleep in your clothes here in the office. You're killing Captain John with that damn booze. Have you ever smelled the breath of a drunken parrot? And swilling it as you do, you aren't doing yourself any favor either. Why don't you get a shave and go home and spend some time with your wife and kids? If I had a family that's where I'd be."

Lou Ashe was my partner and my very best friend. Not many months before, in 1947, I found him waiting to see me in the reception room of my old office on Union Square. I noted his white shoes. We don't wear them in San Francisco. I assumed he was an outlander, probably a recent arrival, possibly an impoverished law student looking for a job. I ignored him and found out from my secretary that he had graduated from Boston University Law School with highest honors and struggled through the 1930's like the rest of us, working as an M.C. and light comedian in nightclubs just to get by. Then he went into the Air Corps, passed through San Francisco on his way to the South Pacific and decided this was where he wanted to live. "Bernie Witkin sent him to see you," said my secretary. Bernie Witkin was a classmate at Boalt and one of the country's leading legal scholars.

I didn't give Ashe so much as a nod, but he came back the next day. And the next. "Gee," I thought, "this guy is really serious about going to work here." On the fourth day, I was headed to a hearing and said, "Come on, let's go to court." Ashe got up and followed me and ended up taking over the case, a probate matter that he handled with dispatch—even got the judge to award him some extraordinary fees in the case, "How'd you get two hundred fifty-two bucks out of that chicken-shit case?" I asked Ashe. Ashe only smiled.

Ashe worked in my office for months and I never paid him a dime. He generated his own income, and at that time that was enough for him. One day, I went in and said, "What do you use for money?"

He said, "None of yours, I'm sure."

"Well," I said, "what kind of money are you thinking about?"

He said he could make it just fine on the work he was doing. "I just want a chance to be associated with the best," he said. "That's enough for me."

I asked Ashe to stick around. Ashe became a stabilizing force in the office, my best friend and most outspoken critic. He was to become one of the most respected lawyers in the land. I listened to his advice, particularly his admonitions about my family. I knew I should spend more time with Betty and my four children—Rick, Johnny, Jean and Suzie. I loved them deeply. I ended up taking them on an extended trip to Europe in 1949, even put the children in Swiss schools for a semester, then beat it down to Rome so we could have an audience with Pope Pius XII. The Pope was receiving a lot of travelers then, right after the war, and we met a monsignor from Sonora, California, who said he'd try to get us into a semiprivate audience. That very afternoon a messenger from the Vatican, knee breeches, buckles and all, arrived and presented us with an engraved invitation, sealed in wax, to meet the Pope. Betty and I were awed by the frescoes in the Sistine Chapel and the Michelangelo ceiling and by the Pope himslf, who looked so lean and ascetic next to the gang of overstuffed topers and tosspots who stood in attendance upon him. The Pope had a word or two for each of the two dozen in our group. He'd been briefed on each of us, I guess, but I was absolutely flabbergasted when it came our turn and he smiled at me and said, "How is Harry Cobden?"

"Porco Dio!" I whispered to Betty after I told His Holiness Harry was fine. In all this time I'd thought Cobden was telling me one of his tall tales. I'd never believed Cobden's story that he'd really taken the future Pope climbing in the Sierras. Now I believed.

Betty and I were no sooner settled into our suite at the Hassler in Rome, after our audience, than Lou Ashe was on the phone, insisting that I had to fly back, to Cleveland.

"Hell," I said, "I just got to Rome."

Ashe pleaded with me. "Would you at least give Sam Horovitz a call?" Horovitz was the founder of a new kind of legal organization, the National Association of Claimants Compensation Attorneys (NACCA), a group as anti-establishment as Thomas Jefferson, and Ashe thought we ought to be a part of it. Ashe was beginning to understand my style, my flair for the unusual and the unexpected, and he knew that the last thing in the world that Horovitz expected was a phone call from Rome. So I phoned him.

"Look, Sam," I said, "I want to join NACCA, but I don't want to fly all the way back from Europe for a convention in Cleveland."

Sam didn't understand. "Where are you?" he said.

"I'm in Rome."

"In Rome?"

"Yes."

Sam's silence told me he was mulling that one over. I might as well have been phoning him from the moon. Finally, he recovered enough to tell me, "Look, you're the guy we need in Cleveland. For years this personal-injury stuff has been a chicken-shit affair. They've been robbing cripples and widows. In 1927, the Massachusetts Bar tried to disbar me on the grounds that I couldn't be doing all the claimant's work I was doing for thirty-five dollars a week. They thought I had to be on the take."

There was something likable about Sam Horovitz as he argued with me on the phone. I was inclined to hop a plane and go to his convention in Cleveland but I wanted him to beg me a little more. "Goddamn it," I said, "I've gotta be with Errol Flynn in Paris."

Horovitz laughed. "I don't believe you, Belli, but you've got class, making this transatlantic telephone call and all—which is just why this organization needs you—to give it some class."

That did it. I gave Betty a pocketful of traveler's checks and told her to enjoy Europe. Then I hopped the next plane to New York and from there caught a connecting flight to Cleveland.

Sam Horovitz turned out to be a lean, Lincolnesque figure who looked something like Pope Pius XII: prominent nose, deepset eyes, very expressive hands. Sam was the real founder of NACCA. Since 1927, he'd been specializing in personal-injury work, had become an expert in workmen's compensation. He knew attorneys like Perry Nichols in Florida, Nate Richter in Philadelphia, Jim Dooley in Chicago and Melvin Belli in California were winning big personal-injury awards and he could see that a whole new field of law was opening up. The establishment lawyers had their Bar—the ABA and its affiliates in each state. Now, we who opposed these lawyers (though we were also members, albeit second-class members, of the ABA) would have *our* Bar. We were, most of us, total individualists, but we would band together, Saint Georges slaying dragons together, helping one another with information: who was getting the big awards and how we were winning them. Horovitz said he'd edit the *NACCA Law Journal* and forty of us or so who were there said we would help him fill it.

Lou Ashe was at the Holland Hotel in Cleveland for the NACCA convention, too, and he had all kinds of good news for me, new cases coming in, big checks. Lou was okay, and with him minding the office, I could go back to Europe. "Lou," I said, "how much would it cost me to give you twenty thousand dollars?"

"In your tax bracket?" he asked. I nodded. He diddled a moment with a pencil and said, "About six thousand dollars."

"Okay," I said, "write yourself out a check for twenty thousand. I'm going to Paris."

I planned to pick up Betty and the kids. But I also wanted to see Errol Flynn. I had met Flynn not long before when I had had to take a deposition from him on the Warner Brothers lot in Hollywood. I had appeared on the set in a white linen suit, my homburg at a rakish tilt. At first, Flynn wouldn't see me. I had been retained by a young man, Wallace Beery's son, who had been harpooned in an accident while crewing on Flynn's yacht, the *Zaca*, and given no medical treatment for days. Flynn wanted no part of any lawyer who was suing him. But when he saw me, he threw back his head and laughed. "Now that's the way a lawyer ought to look," he said, and my beautiful secretary, Nancy, and I ended up having dinner that night with Flynn and his wife, Nora, at their palatial home in the Hollywood Hills. I took Flynn's deposition the next day, and the lawsuit was eventually settled in my young man's favor. But the money didn't come out of Flynn's pocket, it came from the insurance company. We remained friends and soon we would become very good friends indeed.

I saw Flynn in Paris at the George V and spent about three days there with him and his friends. Then I rendezvoused with Betty in Switzerland, visited the kids in school and made arrangements to spend some time at Kitzbühel. In 1949, Alpine skiing wasn't much in the U.S., but Kitzbühel and Saint Anton had been pioneering exciting new techniques for years, and it wasn't long before I was schussing and yodeling with the best of the Austrians. The kids joined us for Christmas. Then we all flew back to England and sailed for New York on the *Queen Mary*.

Soon as I got home, Lou had a couple of big cases for me. I tried them, then flew back to Paris to help Errol Flynn in a legal fight with his coproducer William Marshall over his participation in the profits on the film Flynn was then making, *The Adventures of Captain Fabian*, with a leading lady named Micheline Presle (who happened to be Marshall's wife) and also starring Vincent Price and Agnes Moorehead.

I thought I'd stay two days. I ended up staying two months, going on location in Nice, drinking and falling in love with Franka Faldini. Franka was only eighteen, olive-skinned, full-breasted, teeth that shone, eyes that flashed.

"What's the matter, dear boy?" Flynn asked when he saw me worshiping the child with my eyes as she lay on the deck of Flynn's sailboat in a flimsy bit of nothing. I could only mutter.

"You're slow, dear boy, you're slow," said Flynn.

"You son-of-a-bitch," I said, but Flynn soon made things happen. He sent us both off to orange-blossom-scented Sicily to scout out some locations. It may have been the temples, the moonlight or the Marsala wine, but when we returned to Nice, Franka and I were the closest of friends.

When we finished shooting in Nice, we returned to Paris for more legal harangues, this time with the French government. That was just fine with Flynn. This picture was just another swashbuckling epic, and he was bored with almost everything except with new people who happened along with his two bottles of vodka a day—which he poured from a clear water pitcher.

When we landed in Paris, we were met by a French *avocat*, a man I had asked to join the case because he knew his way around the Paris courts: "We can't lose," he told me proudly after we had gotten into his car. "I have given the judge one hundred thousand francs."

That gave me some pause. It wasn't quite the way we did legal business in California. "Uhh," I said, "what about the other side? What did the other side give him?"

My colleague was shocked. "Mr. Belli," he cooed, "we

are dealing with a respectable judge. He is a man of honor. He would not think of taking from *both* sides."

Flynn and I were inseparable. We spent weeks gourmandizing in Parisian restaurants and sipping calvados in the sidewalk cafés. One night, we drove over to Les Halles in Flynn's big Cadillac and tried to eat all the oysters in the market district and then walked up and down through the market singing and drinking and telling stories.

It was 5 A.M., and on the way back to the Hotel Prince DeGaulle, we stopped for every hooker on the Champs-Elysées. By the time we got to the hotel, we had about a dozen streetwalkers piled in and on the car. We went into the bar and ordered champagne for all of them, but, before the party could really get going, Flynn excused himself and went up to bed. The girls were disappointed. They wanted to see more of Flynn and appealed to me for help. See more of Flynn? That gave me an idea. I picked up some unused bar chits, asked the bartender for a pair of scissors, cut them up and wrote a bunch of "Flynn tickets." I sold each girl a ticket for fifty francs apiece, went out on the Champs-Elysées and found a dozen more girls still on the street and sold them tickets, too. Then I took all the girls to Flynn's suite and paraded them through to "see more of Flynn"—which they did—because he was lying there sound asleep on top of his bed, balls-ass naked.

I had told them to keep quiet—that they could look but they couldn't touch—and as I was ushering them through the room and out the other door, the last of the girls, a sexy broad with breasts that stuck out like two toy cannons, rushed over to Flynn and cried, "Fleen, Fleen!" He woke to find this girl leaning over him and distinctly "touching" him. When he looked past her to see me standing there with a handful of francs ushering the others out of the room, he got the picture immediately and cried, "I'll take half the change, dear boy—for my friend here."

He had the girl giggling and moaning before we could all get out of the room.

Which gave me ideas of my own: I selected two of the prettiest girls (French hookers looked like high-fashion models in those days), gave them some francs and popped off with them. I couldn't get rid of them until late the next day—time enough for Franka to find out what a rascal I'd been. She locked her own door against me and said she would remain absolutely incommunicado.

"But Franka," I pleaded, "you must let me explain." She wouldn't listen, and maybe it's a good thing, because I didn't know what kind of an explanation I could have come up with. The bottle and the brothel are good friends, and that's the short and the long of it for me. I didn't feel guilty, just a bit embarrassed about being caught.

I don't know whom Flynn and I dined with that night, but Franka wasn't part of the crowd. After everyone had gone to bed, Flynn and I sat in the bar of the Prince DeGaulle wondering what I could do to propitiate Franka. We dismissed flowers and champagne as too unimaginative, the boutiques were all closed and the only thing that was open were the fruit and vegetable stalls at Les Halles. So we took a taxi there and loaded it up with beautiful vegetables—cabbages, celery, lettuce, turnips, potatoes, rutabagas, carrots, eggplant, squashes of all kinds, cauliflower, radishes, onions, leeks and lots of beautiful ripe tomatoes, all the extravagant bounty of the French countryside. There was a little room left in the cab, so we tossed in all the oranges and apples and grapes we could and told the cab driver to take us to Franka's hotel. He looked at us with great amusement (we assured him that we'd reward him handsomely for all his trouble) and he told us to climb on the runningboards of his cab—and then he crept through the predawn darkness so the two drunks hanging on wouldn't end up on the streets of Paris. At the hotel, with the help of a few bellboys who were still on duty, we piled Franka's door high with all the fruit and vegetables, then got the bell captain to rouse her. When the half-ton of produce tumbled into the room, her laughter rang up and down the hotel corridor. Naturally, she forgave me. Good women always forgive.

This was 1950, in the days before the pill had liberated half of womankind, but the sexual revolution had already hit Europe's upper classes. Strangely enough, however, this lover's paradise only frustrated Flynn the more. One day, we were sitting on a sidewalk café on the Champs-Elysées and seven striking beauties sailed by, one right after another, before we could make a move. Flynn began to weep. I ignored him. I hate to see a grown man cry. But finally, when the tears kept rolling down his cheeks, I demanded to know what was the matter. He didn't reply. "Look here," I said, "you've got everything a man could ask for—good looks, a surfeit of the world's goods, a name, a career and all the women you want."

"That's just the trouble, dear boy," said Flynn, grabbing my lapel. "Think of all the beautiful women in the world that could be mine for the asking! I'll never have the time. I'll die before I can get around to *all* of them!"

"Goddamn it, Flynn," I said, "you're absolutely right. We'll just have to step up our activity."

And we did. Flynn deserved some kicks; he wasn't getting them from the movie he was making. It was one of the dullest stories ever put on film, and the government people who had helped to finance the effort were so embarrassed that they waived the usual requirements that the film be dubbed in French. *The Adventures of Captain Fabian* was finally released by Republic Pictures in the U.S. and died a quick, merciful death at the box office. I had a piece of the profits. A piece of nothing.

In August, 1950, I was settling down with Franka. I opened a Rome office and was running my San Francisco law business via long distance. I would phone Ashe from time to time; I would conduct my business on a Dictaphone and mail the recordings to my secretary in San Francisco. Notes that I've saved from the period indicate that the office was getting a lot of new cases, that I had a pumping oil well near Galveston, Texas, and a couple of hot movie deals besides. Franka and I had found this documentary on Mussolini that we thought we might sell to the "March of Time." And I had invested $10,000 in a spy story that was being shot in Japan called *Tokyo File 212*, one of the first postwar films to be made in Japan.

Then one of my investigators sent me a note saying he thought Betty was considering a divorce.

I returned to San Francisco and tried to effect a reconciliation. It didn't work. Betty filed for a divorce on January 8, 1951, and got custody of our four children. Rick was then fourteen, Johnny twelve, Jean nine and Suzie six. That's when I lost them. Lou Ashe did his best to save my family for me. I didn't listen to him. I wish I had. But I'll never forgive Betty—or the children—for changing their last name from Belli to Ballantine.

My own career was accelerating fast in 1951. Sam Horovitz had me booked to speak at Princeton, Yale, Cornell, Columbia and the Boston University Law School. When I got to Boston, he introduced me to the dean of the Harvard Law School, Roscoe Pound, perhaps the most eminent legal scholar of the day, who took a big liking to me. He told me that I was helping fill a much-neglected gap in the law and invited me to lecture in February to his Torts and Evidence classes. Maybe he'd even have me teaching at Harvard during the summer.

I became president of NACCA, and in March, 1951,

the editors at Boalt Hall published my article, "The Adequate Award," in the *California Law Review*. To write my winning briefs on Gluckstein, Sullivan, Duvall and Reckenbeil, I'd gathered material which would show the court why the jury awards, considered excessive by my learned opponents, ought to stand. In this article, I brought together all the facts and figures that demonstrated how verdicts had risen over the past fifty years—but not nearly enough, not proportionately to the cost of living—and that lawyers, juries and appellate courts had placed far too low a value upon a man's life, his mind and his limbs. I pointed out that a baseball player got $100,000 a year, racehorses sold for $300,000 and paintings and violins for $500,000, yet judges and juries were awarding far less than $100,000 to human beings who were so seriously injured they could never work again. The dignity of man, I wrote, had long since been heralded in the arts, literature, painting and music. Now, I said, the courts should be ready to acclaim in law the dignity of man with adequate awards for personal-injury losses to those with humble as well as with gifted hands.

The program committees of bar associations all over the country began asking me to become a speaker. They could read my article in the *California Law Review* (in fact, their requests for reprints forced the review into an extra press run), but they wanted more than that. They wanted to know how they could obtain big awards, too. Their invitations came at precisely the right time in my life. I wanted to get the hell out of town anyway—and my partners were only too eager to pay my expenses. I didn't want any fees. I was a missionary giving these lawyers a new gospel.

I visited thirty-five legal groups—bar associations and law schools—barnstorming all over the U.S. I felt as good as a Maryknoller bringing hybrid wheat and hospitals to southeastern Brazil. If awards were low in some states, by God, I'd help bring them up. "The highest verdict that has ever been sustained in Oregon," I told the assembled delegates to the Oregon State Bar Association, "is a mere thirty-two thousand dollars. Yet the price of bread, of milk, of butter, of gasoline, is the same in Oregon as in California . . . Certainly the threshold of pain is as high in Oregon, the value of human life should be as great, tears and pain as brutal and lost laughter as gay and clear in Oregon as it is California." *

And I'd show them how I did it, too. My secret was demonstrative evidence. I told them about the drawerful of knives. I told them about the leg and the butcher paper. I told them about the concentric barriers of sound which that truck driver had crashed through to make Captain Reckenbeil into a basket case. But what they wanted to hear most of all was the money part. I told the assembled delegates of the Mississippi State Bar Association at Jackson:

> A doctor may bind up the physical wounds after personal injury, but it is only the plaintiff's lawyer who rehabilitates economically the client, his widow, his children. Let us speak frankly. Under our system of jurisprudence, compensation can *only* be allowed in terms of dollars. We've no system whereby man, after personal injury, can be made whole again, can walk without a limb, sleep without pain.

* I liked doing missionary work in Oregon, a great but stingy state where jury awards were too low and judicial discretion much too high. A few years later I gave a major address to Oregon's judges. I tried to persuade them that they could blaze a new Oregon trail by simply letting the jury verdicts in personal-injury cases stand.

I pointed out that according to the language of the U.S. Constitution and the precedents of the common law, no judge

I quoted one of the great jurists of the West Coast, Judge Mathes, in *Maxi v. Southern Pacific Company*. The award was $165,000. Two legs had been amputated above the knee.

> "Assuming that Maxi, instead of being a railroad worker, was a bum, was one of those thousands of human beings who are sort of peculiar, at least to us they are peculiar—maybe we are peculiar to them— who do not work. They just walk up and down the railroad tracks and the highways—wanderers, hobos. He comes into court. His legs have been cut off through the negligence of the defendant. He says, 'My legs are cut off. I want to be whole the rest of my life with my legs on. I enjoy it. I have no earning power. All I do is live.'"
>
> Gentlemen, all *any* of us do—is live! We are guaranteed by the United States Constitution the right to live out our lives with our right of privacy and pursuit of happiness—free from pain and suffering. When the terrible catastrophe of personal injury comes down upon us, the award must be—adequate!

Erle Stanley Gardner was on the same program with me in Jackson, Mississippi. The delegates gave us both standing ovations, and we stayed up with some of the Mississippians until dawn, sipping their finest bourbon and talking about the law. Erle and I became fast friends.

---

should dare cut a jury verdict unless the damages must be "so excessive as to strike mankind, at first blush, as being beyond all measure, unreasonable and outrageous." And *how* would these judges know if the verdict were outrageous? I suggested they not follow their own feelings—as did one judge in California not long before, who heard the jury foreman announce a verdict for my client of $200,000 and spontaneously cried, "Jeeeee-sus Chriiiiist!"

The talks I gave were not simply money talks. I loved the law and I was grateful to God for giving me the chance to practice the kind of law where I could help the poor and down-trodden. I remember telling members of the Dade County Bar Association in Miami, "You've read of the great cases in our jurisprudence, the landmarks in our law. These cases didn't come into the lawyers' offices with signs on the clients' backs saying 'I am the *Dartmouth College case,* I am *Pennoyer v. Neff,* I am *Marbury v. Madison.'* These cases will come into your office only as humble human beings, perhaps some of them even incapable of adequate expression. These men will be great cases only as you're able to interpret their human rights to legal remedies before a jury and as a plaintiff's lawyer makes them great." And then I told them about Charlie Simon.

Charlie Simon wasn't much when he came into my office. His clothes reeked, he hadn't shaved in weeks, his eyes bulged, he had a harelip. I wondered to myself, "What do we have here?" I was glad I took the trouble to find out. I took him into my office, got his story (he'd been knocked unconscious for two months by a San Francisco streetcar whose motorman didn't even slow down when he thought he saw something near the track ahead) and took his case to court. I lost the case in the trial court but won it before the California Court of Appeals. The reversal isn't important here, nor even the reasons for the reversal. But the court's reaction to tricky tactics by the other side was important, because the court's language set some new trial standards in California:

> The trial of a lawsuit is not a game [declared the court] where the spoils of victory go to the clever and technical regardless of the merits, but a method devised by a civilized society to settle peaceably and justly disputes between litigants. The rules of the

contest are not an end in themselves. Unless the rules tend to accomplish justice, strict compliance is not always required.

Home from my lecture tour, I found a crowd of reporters waiting for me at the San Francisco Airport—along with Lou Ashe, whose grin told me he was terribly pleased with himself for getting the press out to greet me like a conquering hero. I growled at him. "Goddamn it, Lou, I didn't want this." Lou's face contorted with pain. Of course, I liked having attention, but I didn't want Lou becoming public-relations counsel. The reporters gathered around, and I traded quips with them as we walked toward the baggage claim. They were scribbling down a description of what I was wearing—philodendron red slacks and a matching shirt that I had picked up in Palm Beach.

"You reporters see me when I'm *not* practicing law," I said. "You see me when I'm dressed to relax and then you go away and write about my flamboyance."

One young man—the youngest reporter in the group—took me up on that. "Do you get angry when we write about your flamboyance?"

"Yes," I said. "I'm not flamboyant in court. On trial I've always contributed to the dignity of the courtroom."

"What about when you're *not* on trial?" he said. "Are you flamboyant then?"

"Sometimes."

"Are you angry when we report about you then?"

"I'm not going to give you a blank check 'yes' on that question. What stories are you talking about?"

"Well, the one about your sending thirty-five hundred dollars to your ex-wife's attorney in two sacksful of small change—with some stinking fish inside the sacks?"

"There were no fish in the sacks." I paused and roguishly eyed an attractive photographer who was snapping away at me with a Rollei. "Lou Ashe made me take the fish out of the sacks." Laughter from the other members of the press.

The young reporter continued. "Do stories like that do you any good?"

I became reflective. "Nooooooo."

"Don't they harm you when you appear in court?"

"Stories like that make me work harder," I allowed. "I have to undo my reputation."

"Well, where does Herb Caen get these items?"

"Usually from me."

"That doesn't make sense. He harpoons everyone." -

I shrugged. The kid was right. It didn't make sense but I did it anyway. I didn't want to waste too much time right then thinking about it. I was interested in this photographer. I turned to Ashe. "Lou," I purred. "Who's that girl with the Rollei?" Lou didn't know but he said he'd find out. "Wait." I smiled at the girl. "Where'd you come from? I never saw you before!" She snapped my picture right in the middle of the word "saw." My mouth was open.

She laughed. "I won't print that one."

"Okay, okay, but where *did* you come from?"

"From the *Chronicle*."

"You're new," I said.

"Yes."

"Can I see you?"

"Nope." She started for her car, a Porsche convertible.

"Wait a minute," I said.

"I've only been here for a couple of months," she said, "but the job gets me out and around. Your reputation got to me before you did, Mr. Belli."

I watched her get into the Porsche. She was a pixie with a totally engaging smile and a great little ass. "Lou," I said, "she works at the *Chronicle,* I think, but I still need her name and phone number." Lou's face darkened. Then he smiled and nodded. I turned to the reporters. "Now what case was that you were talking about?" I had a pretty good serious exchange with the reporters. I always liked talking with the guys from the press. They were bright and they did not have time for too much bullshit. Then the redheaded stewardess who was on my flight came strolling by, curious. I stopped her. "What did you say your name was, honey?"

She was embarrassed right there in front of the reporters. But not too embarrassed to reply. "Grace," she laughed.

"I just won a case. Want to help me celebrate tonight?" She did, we celebrated, but I never saw her again.

I did see the girl with the Rollei. In fact I married her on November 27, 1951, in a civil ceremony outside Mexico City. Her name was Toni Nichols, she was a photographer for *Life*, not the *Chronicle,* and she resisted my advances while I made a half-hearted plunge—it didn't last more than six months—into my new bachelorhood.

Many of the lawyers I'd met in my nationwide tour showed up in San Francisco when NACCA held its annual convention there in the summer of 1951. It was a time, naturally, when as president I had to play "host"—a duty I gloried in. There is only one thing I like better than a good party, and that is several good parties. I had Ben Cohen, a lawyer in L.A., bring up about twenty actresses and models. They weren't hookers, just young women a little bit ahead of their time who didn't mind going to parties and getting laid if they chanced to meet the right guy. They certainly dressed up the convention, which we held at the Mark Hopkins Hotel. In August, 1951, an abnormally balmy August in San Francisco, I had lots of parties, most of them in my home on Vallejo Street, some of them aboard my fifty-one foot yacht, the *Warwine,* which had once belonged to the actor Warner Baxter.

I bought the *Warwine* for $17,500, a pretty good deal, I thought, since it cost almost $100,000 when it was brand-new. It slept ten and it had big twin Chrysler engines, and you could go to sea in it. It had a lot of things wrong with it, however, and I had little time to spend tinkering away my weekends on a boat. I ended up selling it—and happily—for $11,000.

My home on Vallejo Street had a commanding view of the Bay and both bridges. Mrs. Ambrose Diehl, a great twenty-two-carat socialite, rented it to me for five hundred dollars per month, furnished, under the mistaken impression that I was always sober as the judge who accompanied me on the day I signed the lease.

I guess the first couple of nights I had invited a few college professors along with a bishop. By the third night, everybody was there. Errol Flynn showed up one night in a cab. I hadn't gotten home yet, and he was trying to get into the house. And then James P. Mozingo, a NACCA buddy of mine, the leader of the senate in South Carolina, pulled up in a cab. He didn't know Flynn from a bar of soap, but the two of them went around the back and opened the window, and Flynn crawled in. "In like Flynn," said Mozingo. Flynn gave Mozingo a searching look, tilted his FDR cigarette holder up in the air and said with some amusement, "I guess I am."

I wanted to introduce Flynn to my San Francisco, so I invited everyone I knew: lawyers, cops, judges, firemen, bookies, some of the city's best hookers. One judge came up to Lou Ashe and said, "Is that Sally Stanford over there?" Sally Stanford was the best madam San Francisco ever had, a grand lady who now serves as mayor of Sausalito and has a restaurant there called Valhalla. Ashe allowed that it was Sally. The judge couldn't have folded any more quickly if Ashe had given him a blow to the solar plexus. "Well, give my respects to Mr. Belli," he said, "and tell him I was here." But not before he had my servingman make up two large sandwiches for himself and his wife. And then he went home, cum sandwiches in a paper bag.

Of course, the judge didn't want to be seen in the same room with Sally Stanford. But he could have talked to Sally and remained a good judge anyway—maybe become even better, more understanding, more compassionate, more fair—and I guess he knew that, too, but he was living up to the expectations of others. He knew that he belonged to that class of people that society needs to put on a pedestal. The Pharisees put Jesus down with the observation that "He dines with publicans and sinners." And this judge was a living proof that the modern Pharisees were ready to stick him with the same charge.

There's a little bit of the Pharisee in all of us. We like to think that someone can keep all the Commandments all the time in order to preserve our sense of law and order and the fitness of things. We need heroes and saints and impeccable public servants, need someone to take up the slack in what we suppose to be that tug-of-war called life, and woe betide the hero or saint, priest or president who turns human on us. But life isn't a tug-of-war or a battle or a forced march. It's more like a dance: sometimes wild, sometimes gentle, often exhilarating. During a dance, of course, people can stumble every so often. No big deal. The beat goes on. But the biggest blasphemy of all is to say to life, "No, I won't join in." I had stumbled and fallen pretty hard and had lost my kids. But for me, life went on.

The convention was not all partytime. Conventions, professional meetings of any kind, are a time for sharing ideas, insights and information which will help make a member a better banker, biologist or bureaucrat.

The trouble was, at these early NACCA gatherings, we had all the top plaintiff attorneys in the country, professional egotists who didn't mind sharing their secrets, but only a limited number of spots on the program; not enough of the delegates were able to get up on their feet during those early meetings. Then, in San Francisco, I stumbled on a device that was just a beautiful thing for a group of articulate trial lawyers who loved thinking on their feet.

It happened like this. We ran out of speakers at the convention and so, to fill the time, I started discussing some recent court decisions and their impact on some of the cases I had in hand. Then as I talked I noticed an attorney from Chicago sitting in the audience and said to myself, Hell, there's Jim Dooley over there and he knows as much about railroad law as anybody in the world. "I wonder, Jim," I blurted, "if you'd care to come up here for five minutes or so and tell us about that case you have on appeal in Illinois?" Well, Jim Dooley was only too happy to tell us about that case and about the one he'd lost earlier in the year. I started asking him questions, and he came right back with some sharp answers. Before we knew it, we had a real good legal rap session going. Lawyers all over the room began adding their two bits' worth, nobody really showing off too much, just standing up and giving us stuff we could really use.

Nobody really showing off but me, because I had the gavel and I played the part of a traffic cop for all these ideas that were zipping back and forth across the hall. I kept things on the track and, when anyone started bogging down, I interrupted and asked him a question that got him to make his point and sit down. Before you knew it, five hours had passed, and someone said, "Hey, this is better than the planned program." And someone else said, "We ought to do this every year." And someone else said,

"Yeah, Mel, how 'bout it?" They all looked to me to take the lead on it, so I began to think about doing the same thing again the next year and calling it my seminar. Horovitz mentioned it in the *NACCA Journal,* and other delegates who'd been there kept writing me for citations of cases mentioned during "The Belli Seminar." When we met the next year in Houston, I did it again, and it was called the Belli Seminar and was the most popular event at the convention. The seminar would become a standard feature of our convention for the next twenty-five years. (Several years later the California Bar Association actually preferred charges against me for referring to it, no matter how deservedly, as "The Famed Belli Seminar"!)

As the years went on, the Belli Seminars became more and more popular with my colleagues, who clamored to get on the program so they could talk about the new law they'd created that year. They were usually scheduled on the day before or the day after the ABA Convention or the NACCA Convention and in the same city and the same hotel.

Naturally enough, some of my brethren in the law grew jealous. They tried to take over the Belli Seminar and, when that failed, they tried to ostracize me. In 1961, I took my Belli Seminar to the ABA Convention in St. Louis, but the boys in the ABA threw me a curve: they spread their convention to different hotels, making it harder for my sideshow to draw a crowd. But I beat them anyway. Three days before the seminar, on the eve of the ABA Convention, I stole space in both St. Louis papers. The *Post-Dispatch* had a story headlined "MAVERICK OF BAR CONDUCTING OWN SEMINAR HERE FOR BORED LAWYERS." And a story in the *Globe-Democrat* reported that Belli and his twenty-man faculty would put on something of a "legal jam session." Reporter Ralph Wagner said we were "traditional camp followers at big bar meetings . . . roosting wherever a lot of lawyers are in one town at the same time." Wagner quoted one ABA staffer who was less than delighted. "Oh, Belli is in town, is he? That blankety-blank. He drives us nuts." I was glad to hear it. In fact, I told reporter Wagner that maybe next time I'd "pitch a Chautauqua tent right in front of their main meeting hall with letters in lights. But Old English letters. Something dignified."

Dignity, of course, was the last thing I wanted at a Belli Seminar. Lawyers had to be dignified in court, but they needed an occasional release. The law, after all, was a living thing. Dignity was for the dead and the dying. So I put on the Belli Seminar in Kiel Auditorium, scene of many a fine circus (not to mention NBA basketball and NHL hockey), and here's how the *Globe-Democrat* reported the event under the headline, "BELLI'S 17-HOUR ABA SHOW BEATS THREE-RING CIRCUS":

A 17-hour session of hypnosis, hooplah and horse sense which topped the best of Barnum & Bailey shook the dignity of Kiel Auditorium Saturday under the skilled guidance of a flamboyant but friendly enemy of the ABA. . . . The highly successful damage suit lawyers offered up a lot of noise, nonsense, and new ideas for more than 200 attorneys and wives who attended the session.

Dressed in his usual black cowboy boots (highly polished but run over at the heels), Mr. Belli pushed and prodded his cast of characters through lively demonstrations of hypnosis, "demonstrative" evidence techniques, trial tactics, medicine and mechanics.

Highlighting this sensational sideshow designed purposefully to compete with the ABA convention was a session with a discussion and demonstration of hypnosis by Dr. William J. Bryan, Jr., a medical doctor from Hollywood. . . . Six volunteers were hypnotized by Dr. Bryan. He stuck needles in the hands of five of them with . . . no pain and no bleeding. The six skeptics became believers.

I usually parade expert witnesses of all specialties, all shapes and sizes before my audience at a Belli Seminar.

The trial judge will instruct a jury that an "expert" witness is one who, because of his learning and proficiency in a specialized area, is entitled to express an *opinion* or *conclusion*. To me, an "expert" is a witness who knows the most about the least and generally sells his knowledge, if it can be called that, to the side that gets to him first with the most. There are experts in almost every field, and each specialty has its own "specialty expert," handwriting, gunshot wounds, automobile reconstruction experts, airplane accidents, medical experts, products experts, experts in as many fields as human activity is varied.

What I've always admired about experts, though, is the great aplomb with which they can appear for one side on Monday and testify with equal sincerity and persuasion for the other side on Tuesday. They "qualify" with a string of degrees and attainments that takes at least a half hour to enumerate. Very often they are "professors of surgery" when they give one lecture to a surgical class at a hospital in the whole year. Some dress in tweeds and affect the homely approach. Others profess really sharp attire with lapel badges, watch fobs, vests and well-shined shoes. But to me the best example of an expert witness I've ever seen is Dr. L. in Los Angeles.

Syd Irmas and I were trying a gunshot-wound case in which we were attempting to prove that our man, fatally shot through the aorta with a shotgun blast, would still have enough life left in him to jerk the steering wheel of a car one way or another. It was important to prove this because the police officer who came up to our man's car and negligently shot him through an open window claimed that our man was trying to flee and pulled the steering wheel to run him over. The reconstruction experts had chalked out the course of the automobile so that the car did pull over at or about the time of the shooting. We claimed that this was *after* the shooting and even though the aorta had been pierced, the man could jerk the wheel.

So one day after court Syd and I went up to see Dr. L. at his sumptuous offices. I said, "Dr. L., I want you to assume that a man is shot through the aorta with a shotgun blast. Will this kill him instantly if the aorta is severed, or would there be enough 'life' left in the man so that he might pull the wheel to the left or the right?"

Dr. L. drummed a bit upon his resplendent desk, then leaned back in his massive leather chair and said, "There's no doubt about it. A shotgun blast through the aorta would terminate life immediately and the man who was so shot would not be able to move volitionally or even in reflex action."

I said, "Thank you, Doctor. I knew we could get a straight answer from you, and I'm not going to put you on the stand because this would destroy our theory."

Dr. L. interrupted, "Wait just a minute, are *you* contending that the man could pull to the left or the right *after* he was shot?"

"Yes, Doctor, that's our contention."

Dr. L. interrupted. "Well, what I have just told you is what the *other* side will contend, and they'll undoubtedly have someone in to testify to it, but *my* opinion is, very conclusively, you're right, the man would have enough life left in him to pull to the left or right!"

We thanked the expert for *his* opinion. But we didn't call him.

CHAPTER ELEVEN

A Crown

But I couldn't be content with national meetings and the short-lived glory of one-day Belli Seminars. Like all lawyers I loved reading books and I had a yen to write them as well. The enthusiasm I'd seen demonstrated for those early seminars told me, moreover, that there was a crying need for one of us, a plaintiff's lawyer, to write a manual for the instruction and edification of the younger brethren in the plaintiffs' bar.

In order to keep up with the demand for copies of my stuff, I had already published some of my talks in pamphlets: "The Adequate Award," "The More Adequate Award," "The Use of Demonstrative Evidence in Achieving the More Adequate Award."

Now I would write a book, a big one, even if I had to work on it all night and weekends. Sometimes, I wouldn't even go home at night. I did it by dictating from my notes or just off the top of my head. I wrote it simply, just as you'd write any kind of how-to book. I began at the beginning—with the moment the client walks into a lawyer's office. Then: how to investigate and prepare the case, how to determine the applicable theory of law, how to file the complaint and pick the jury, how to use demonstrative evidence, how to argue, examine, and cross-examine and sum up. But I didn't want it to be dull. I included a lot of the souvenirs of my life in the law, pictures of blowups I'd used in court, diseased wombs and cancerous penises and hacked-up breasts. I included appropriate jokes when I could remember them and if I happened to run across a good recipe for veal parmigiana, I put that in a footnote to the manuscript, too.

The parrot, Captain John Silver, wasn't around anymore. When I went to Europe my secretary stopped giving him Jim Beam, and he died. They said he died of cirrhosis of the liver, but I think the cause of death was a broken heart. He'd gotten used to the sour-mash bourbon, you see, and when they cut it off, he just figured there was no sense living in a sterile world.

But by then I had a tomcat named Jerry to take John Silver's place. He liked Jim Beam, too. Except for a few rare occasions, he was the soul of moderation and only took enough nips to keep the blood running warm on our cold, foggy San Francisco days. Jerry had a pair of enormous rear accouterments that swung rhythmically back and forth, and I used to love watching, from the rear, that sleek black cat walk up a flight of red-carpeted stairs.

Rattling around all alone with Jerry in that big four-story house, however, wasn't good for me, and I became less and less interested in going home unless I could have some pulchritudinous company—which wasn't always too easy. I had a romance going with Toni Nichols, a free-lance photographer, but she had two children and she couldn't just stay over anytime she felt like it. And I was busy writing *Modern Trials*.

One morning, I was alone in the office hard at work on

the book when the phone rang. "Who the hell is this?" I demanded.

"Happy Thanksgiving, darling." It was Lorraine Fontaine. I'd know her whiskey baritone anywhere.

"Oh hi, hon," I said. I guess I am kindest to drunken parrots, tomcats, little kids, hookers and particularly madams.

"Mel Belli," she said, "you ought to be ashamed of yourself, working on Thanksgiving."

"It's just another day to me." (It had been since my childhood, when it was just the opposite.)

"Well, I'm going to send a car for you about three o'clock."

"What for?"

"For Thanksgiving dinner, that's what!"

"No, no," I pleaded. "I'm going good on the book. I don't need a Thanksgiving dinner." She wouldn't take "no" for an answer. I told her I was unshaven and dirty. I told her I had on an old pair of cords and a turtle-neck.

"Three o'clock," she said. "Be there."

By three, I was pretty well tired. What the hell. Lorraine had her chauffeur down in Union Square. He took me to her place on California Street, and Lorraine had a real old-fashioned Thanksgiving dinner—for just the two of us. Lorraine said she was on the wagon, but she would have a little Fernet Branca. We got a little oiled, and then seven of her girls dressed in their finest gowns served us a turkey with all the trimmings. When the turkey came in, a brown Siamese cat jumped up on the table and started to go at the turkey. Lorraine took a swat at him and mumbled something about the problems of having a cat in a cathouse. And then we started in on the fine cabernet. By the time we got around to our coffee and cognac, Lorraine was overflowing with generosity. "Mel Belli," she said, "I want to give you your Christmas present right now." She called for her girls to come out and line up. "Girls, introduce yourselves to Mel Belli." They did, and then Lorraine said, "Mel, as my Christmas present to you, I want to present you with these seven: one for Friday, one for Saturday, one for Sunday and so on, if you want. Or if you prefer, take one of them home with you for a week."

I circled the group, came back to the table, poured myself another cognac and pointed to a tall redhead who couldn't have been more than nineteen and a callipygous brunette with a turned-up nose. "I'll take these two," I said, "for the weekend."

Lorraine snapped her fingers. "Melody, Mary, you want to go with Mel? Okay, get your things." Lorraine's chauffeur took us back to my digs on Telegraph Hill (after a daring stop at the Fairmont Hotel bar for a drink), and the girls spent the rest of Thanksgiving weekend with me, a real San Francisco Thanksgiving.

But when Monday morning rolled around I took Melody and Mary back to Lorraine's, phoned Toni and told her I wanted to take her to Mexico and get married.

In the summer of 1953, when I was forty-six, I talked my book, *Modern Trials*, into a Dictaphone. I ran my usual Monday-through-Thursday schedule of trial work. I let Lou run the office (which had gotten bigger now, with a couple of other partners and a continually changing lineup of six to ten junior lawyers and researchers). Up at our new home at 1228 Montgomery Street or in the office, close to my law books, I dictated into that damned machine every weekend. The secretaries would type it out during the week and I'd polish it up a bit, and then by Thursday night I'd be ready to plunge ahead with more dictation. It was an exhausting time for me, and I kept myself going on cigarettes (which I gave up soon afterward), Dexedrine and gin.

Toni just did her own photography work in another room (my room was a foot deep in discarded paper; in fact, one of our cats had her kittens without my knowing it in the middle of the mess). Toni would join me from time to time, and we'd talk a bit and then I'd go back to work. I couldn't have gotten more than two or three hours' sleep each night, and Toni began to worry about me. "All right," I said, "I *am* killing myself, but slowly, and anyway, who isn't?" She said that I ought to see a doctor. I went to Doctor Bruck and told him what I was doing and he said, "Well, Toni's right. You're shortening your life with this regime, but just come in every month for a checkup so we'll know what's happening."

Within six months, Toni and I had separated and I had a first draft finished. I'd written some three thousand pages, and Bobbs-Merrill was pleased with what I'd done. They gave me a good contract, 25 percent of the royalties instead of the usual 15, and sent one of their best editors and legal scholars out from Indianapolis to help me lick the thing into final shape for publication. They sent a delightful, gangling fellow named Wibur Furlow, a Hoosier, with sparse, light hair and a twinkle in his eye, who had never been west of Chicago. He loved the week he spent with me. I put him in a room that overlooked the Bay, where he could see the ships coming and going, and he worked away from six every morning till eight at night and then he took the manuscript back with him to Indianapolis.

When all the labor was done, the editors realized that they had themselves a three-volume gold mine. They sell legal books figuratively by the pound: the more they weigh, the more they charge for them, and for these tomes they thought they'd charge fifty dollars. I flew back to add some finishing flourishes. I wanted to dedicate the book "to Dexedrine and Holland gin," but Bobbs-Merrill was an old-time conservative house, and they fought me on that. "This isn't your autobiography, Mel," they said, "This is a law book. This is something that lawyers and law libraries all over the country are going to buy, something that'll go into every law school in the country."

"Well hell," I said, "lawyers like to have a little fun, too, don't they?"

Bobbs-Merrill said yes they did but Bobbs-Merrill had to preserve a certain amount of decorum and most especially since Dean Roscoe Pound of the Harvard Law School had agreed to do the introduction for *Modern Trials*.

"What?" I said "Dean Pound? You didn't tell me that!"

They said that Pound had just seen the galleys. Now he was writing an introduction. In the meantime, they wanted me to get busy coordinating all the pictures and illustrations I'd lined up for inclusion in the book, some four hundred of them, which I did. But we had an argument about pictures, too. Or rather, one picture. I wanted a portrait of myself as a frontispiece, but I didn't want your standard stuffed shirt of a legal portrait, I wanted an X-ray of my head and neck. Impossible, they said. They couldn't do that.

I don't know why they were so stuffy with me. I was turning out reams of extra copy, throwing in huge chunks of material that I had overlooked. I'd taken my efficient— and beautiful—secretary, Norma Roberts, back with me, and she was typing out the stuff just as fast as I was dictating it. The Bobbs-Merrill people gave me a key to their old wooden building, and Norma and I would go down there at four in the morning and work until eight in the evening. They gave me an old Audograph dictating machine to work with, just like the one I had in San

Francisco, but the damned thing didn't function very well. One day I just heaved it over the partition where I was working, and it bounced down the stairs as the Audograph repairman was coming in. With all this swearing and the machine clattering down on top of him, he was so scared that they couldn't even get him into the place after that. Bobbs-Merrill bought me a new machine. And they let me put my own X-ray in the book.

Roscoe Pound called the three-volume work an "indispensable book for the trial lawyer in personal-injury cases." Lord knows that I did not invent demonstrative evidence, but Pound praised my technique so warmly that I might as well have. There were other lawyers, he said, who employed their finely honed skills on behalf of industry and business. Now here was Belli, showing lawyers how they could do the same for people who were the luckless victims of a mechanized age. The book sold about six thousand copies immediately, which brought me $75,000 in royalties, an adequate reward, I thought, for all the days and nights I spent writing it. The book kept on selling (I do not think that anyone has come along yet with a work to supplant it), and I've earned more than $250,000 on it by now.

I didn't write to make money. I could have made much more money trying cases in court. The reasons I wrote and lectured were basic. Like any good actor (or trial lawyer), I liked being noticed. And it was fun out there on the sawdust trail, sharing what I had with others, sharing theirs.

It was a good thing the royalties started coming in, however, because I needed the money for my divorce settlement. Toni and I were separated some eighteen times in the two short years we were married.

After one of the separations, I took Toni to Washoe

County, Nevada, where Judge Harold Taber married us for real. Toni had complained that we'd gotten married in Mexico before my divorce from Betty was final, and she didn't even feel married.

But I'd say that wasn't it at all. She didn't feel married, because I was really married to the law. Most trial lawyers are. Besides, they work under a lot of stress and strain, they put in impossible hours, usually with a secretary who's always there and ready to go out with him for drinks and a late supper and some kind of release. Pretty soon, they're having a romance with their secretary. Then, after that happens, they find it easier to go off with any number of interesting women. Most trial lawyers I know have an extracurricular romance going on the side. At parties, they find they can't just party a little bit. They go to a party and find half their brain is still mulling over the case they're on, and so the only way to enjoy a party is forget the case and get loaded. Trial lawyers are hard drinkers, and most, on the defendant's or plaintiff's side, are pretty damn good guys. But no matter how hard they prepare, there's always the unexpected in that courtroom; that, and the tensions of the battle keep them up on a high wire. They need a release, and if their wives aren't there when they come down, they'll find it elsewhere. If a trial lawyer's wife wants her marriage to last, she has to be there when her husband needs her. She has to come down to the office to get him, go on trips with him, have the midnight supper ready when he comes home.

Toni didn't know what to do with me. She had two kids and a mother who moved into one of the apartments below us at 1228 Montgomery. She had to spend some time with them. She couldn't spend it all with me. Instead of just accepting the situation as it was, however, she kept wondering what was the matter with me. I said I didn't think there was anything the matter at all. She said there

was. Would I agree to go see a shrink? Sure, I said. She
sent me to the best psychiatrist in town, and after a few
sessions with him, he sent me over to some other poor
bastard of a psychiatrist. I ended up converting him. I
recounted my escapades, and he got so fascinated and
horny that he decided to go out and start chasing, too, and
his marriage ended up in a divorce.

I thank God that I was able to give Toni a substantial
cash settlement on the royalties from *Modern Trials*. I
didn't seem to have much else left over from my practice.
The office had a big overhead, and winning a case always
triggered a celebration where I ended up buying drinks
and dinner for everyone in sight. I had other extraordinary expenses. I bought an apartment building on
Telegraph Hill, put a big addition onto the penthouse,
had it all completely remodeled. I did it in Mother Lode,
whorehouse Victorian, with velvet drapes, cut-glass chandeliers and a white carpet that was ankle-deep. I had two
bedrooms enclosed in floor-to-ceiling picture windows
overlooking the City and the Bay and a large open kitchen
done in copper and sandstone. I filled the terrace with
flowers of every kind I could grow in the City: camellias,
begonias, and roses and Burmese honeysuckle and orange
trees that gave off ambrosial perfumes through much of
the year.

In one of the bathrooms, I installed a sunken marble
tub for two and a sauna bath. Over the john, I hung a
colorful framed poster I had picked up in Germany,
advertising something called the "Circus Belli." I had a
fireplace built with bricks from the White House (which
I bought when Harry S. Truman remodeled). Up above
the fireplace on a jutting platform, I installed a full-size
bed with a coverlet made with the fur of white Alaskan
wolves. Up there on that bed, a cunning bit of engineering
surrounded on three sides by plate glass, I could show any

visiting young lady the most romantic city on earth. Years later, in 1972, Mayor John Lindsay of New York came out West campaigning for President of the United States. I threw a fundraiser for him up at the penthouse. Lindsay looked around at the digs and up at the bed over the fireplace and said, "If I lived here, I could get in—a—lot—of—trouble."

Modern Trials wasn't a popular work for the general public, but it got good reviews in the law journals. Dean William Prosser of Boalt Hall did a baroque assessment in the *California Law Review* that didn't hurt me (or the sales) a bit:

> . . . Every good trial lawyer is to some extent an actor, be he artist or ham; and he is also a playwright and a director, who prepares the script, sets the scene and stage—manages the evidence. Mr. Belli is all of that, and more. *He is a Hollywood producer, and his trial is an epic of the supercolossal.*

And then, by God, a review of me and my work did come out in a popular magazine, *Life*. Robert Wallace, one of *Life's* best writers, had spent a few days around town, interviewing me and my partners, and he had a photographer take a few pictures. He was a modest fellow and he said that although he was doing a piece about me, the odds were one hundred to one against it ever appearing in the magazine. "We have the most prosperous magazine of all time," he said, "and probably the biggest and most competent staff. They do enough work each week to fill four *Life* Magazines. They've got files full of stories they've never used and probably never will."

As the days and weeks passed without a spread in *Life*, I put more credence in Wallace's story and forgot all about *Life.* Then in early October, 1954, in an issue that featured pictures from the off-year congressional campaign (including shots of Jacob Javits and Franklin D. Roosevelt, Jr. vying for the U.S. Senate in New York) and the breakup of the storybook romance between Joe DiMaggio and Marilyn Monroe, I found a huge "Close-Up" profile of myself, written by Robert Wallace. It wasn't so much a personality profile as a coronation, a positive fun-filled text piece entitled "The King of Torts."

There were a few pictures; in almost all of them I was clowning around. In one, I was driving my convertible with my skeleton, Elmer, sitting in the front seat. In another (taken from my Christmas card of the previous year) I wore a surgical gown and a head mirror and stood in front of a hundred surgical instruments. Wallace asked the question that must have occurred to *Life's* fifteen million readers: "How can this clown have such a national influence?" Wallace replied that I was colorful and therefore made myself part of the shop talk of every lawyer, that I had spoken in forty-five of the forty-eight states spreading the good word about demonstrative evidence and more adequate awards and that I had just written the ultimate handbook, "the Bible of personal-injury lawyers."

I heard that the stuffy fellows sitting on the boards of the country's leading bar associations didn't like the *Life* piece. Some lawyers wrote and said that they thought it was self-laudation at its worst, but hell, I didn't write it, Wallace did, and who was I to interfere with the freedom of the press? And I didn't see it or ask to see it before the article was published, nor did I ask that the article be done. I think establishment lawyers objected not so much to the substance of the piece as the tone; in the text, anyone could plainly see that I was having fun. Lawyers weren't supposed to have fun, least-ways in public. Wrote

Wallace: "People insist that at the first sound of an emergency vehicle Belli picks up his ears, breaks out all over in large black spots, and barks. His own comment on this is merely 'That's ridiculous. Ambulances can do up to eighty or ninety mph. I can scarcely do ten.' "

Of course, the *Life* article had some serious implications for the general public and for me personally. Wallace ended the article by citing a recent victory by my NACCA colleague, Jim Dooley, who had successfully sued the Milwaukee Railroad for $420,000. Would juries start giving the million-dollar verdicts I had predicted? Wallace clearly believed they would: "The insurance industry, which has been fighting Belli (and NACCA) tooth for claw, must brace for a jolt."

Stories like this might have endeared me to my natural constituents, the little people who possessed enough common sense to see through the shams of society. On the other hand, takeouts in *Life* could only harden my natural adversaries, the insurance companies and the establishment that controlled the Bar Association.

CHAPTER TWELVE

Cloaks of Dignity

I have been jousting with the Bar and many of its leaders for most of my professional life, and the Bar has been trying to tumble me for almost as long. I've won all the battles so far, because the Bar's charges against me have always been ridiculous. The State Bar of California went after me once because my alleged endorsement of a Scotch whisky appeared in *The New York Times*.

The mandarins of the Bar ought to know better. But they keep going after me for speaking my mind. Why? Perhaps they believe that their charges will keep me quiet for a time, at least, and make me an object lesson for other lawyers who might be tempted to be as outspoken as I. Perhaps they only intend to make a nuisance for me; they know it must take time and money for me to keep defending myself in these local and state proceedings. And it is probably for this reason that my partners keep telling me to shut up. But that's just what these people would like. I will not shut up. I think it's only fair that when I am right I continue to make a nuisance for *them*— wherever and whenever I get a forum. And if the Bar keeps going after me for that, I will take it as a continuing clue that I am doing something right.

I know that I am on the right track when I consider the people who run the local, state and national bars. As individuals, they work for the nation's largest establishment law firms and, in that capacity, their main concern is to help predatory corporations screw the people at large, fix prices, challenge the constitutionality of antipollution laws, put together phony bond issues. And, as members of their various bar associations, they have provided retrogressive leadership in the country for more than a century—and continue to do so.

Historically, the American Bar Association has been anti-Catholic and anti-Semitic. They wouldn't let black men or women join their club, they lobbied against child labor laws, against woman suffrage and Social Security. They were the ones who told our crooked corporations how to lie and steal and cheat—and how to get away with it. Now, of course, they make a show of being on the side of civil rights and the black man and the environment. Balderdash. They're still sitting alongside General Motors and General Mills and General Electric and all the other Generals who have feathered their nests at the expense of you and me.

Though the people at large have no voice in their selection, the high priests and Pharisees in the ABA exercise considerable sway over the people. They pass judgment on the appointment of federal judges, they accredit law schools and they have an important, though hidden, influence on the rulings of federal agencies and the substance of national legislation. They exercise this influence largely through their work on various ABA committees, where they help make public policy to benefit the special economic and corporate interests that normally employ them. And they can do so, because as members of the committees, they have private discussions with the makers of public policy at the crucial time—before the policy is formally proposed by the government agency or the congressional committee.

The ABA committees are rife with conflicts of interest. The last time I looked at the purported form book for lawyers, the Martindale-Hubbell *Directory* (1975), I learned that the chairman of the ABA's coal committee, Robert F. Stauffer, was general counsel to the National Coal Association. The vice chairman, Thomas E. Boettger, was counsel for the Eastern Consolidated Coal Association. The chairman of the oil committee, Richard P. Ryan, was general counsel for Exxon Corporation; one vice chairman, George S. Wolbert, Jr., was general counsel for Shell Oil and the other vice chairman, C. Harold Thweatt, was an attorney who represented Getty, APCO and Champlin Petroleum. A vice chairman of the natural gas committee, Paul W. Wright, represented Exxon; the chairman of the hard minerals committee, Clayton Parr, represented the Anaconda Corporation. The vice chairman of public lands and land use committee, Jerry Haggard, represented Southern Pacific and the Arizona Mining Association. The marine resources committee vice chairman, Vincent Brown, is counsel for the National Petroleum Council; his committee came out a few years ago in favor of extending rights to drill for offshore oil and minerals and limiting rights to sue polluters.

According to Martindale-Hubbell, the chairmen of many other ABA committees seemed like nothing so much as foxes in the chicken coop. The head of a committee on health insurance worked for four insurance companies. The head of a committee on forest-resources law worked for Boise Cascade. The head of a committee on beverage law worked for Coca-Cola, of a committee on food law for Swift and Company, of a committee on drug law for Abbott Laboratories. And so on.

The ABA's Martindale-Hubbell *Directory* itself is a symptom of the sickness in the law today. In its four-volume annual set, Martindale-Hubbell lists almost all the lawyers in the U.S. (not me—by express order) and rates them with an arbitrary system designed to give good marks to lawyers from big firms representing banks, insurance companies, mortgage companies and other large corporate defendants. And who does the rating? These very same lawyers.

Martindale-Hubbell is filled with ledger jockeys for corpulent corporations, and under this kind of leadership a noble profession has become more and more an industry —the law industry.

Today, the legal establishment in America is not there to serve the people but to serve itself. I blame all lawyers for this. (Though the younger ones coming up show some hope.) They've abdicated their responsibilities to their local bar associations and let mediocre lawyers from the big law firms come in to fill the vacuum, politicking and "going through the chairs." The layman thinks that the president of the local bar association must be some great shakes as a lawyer. In reality, he may be a fellow who never could distinguish between a tort and a tart, or a felony and a misdemeanor, he may have been just a sycophant, attended all the meetings and ingratiated himself to the point where finally the boys said, "Old Joe's been faithful, and he's been around a long time. He's regular. We've just got to make him a president this time." In local bar meetings you rarely hear anyone ask, "What's good for the people?" Nor do you hear much discussion about improving the administration of justice. Generally, you hear the officers talking over ways of maintaining their own political prestige, of perpetuating those laws and rules and institutions that will secure the lawyers' livelihood and the lawyers' fees. It took the United States Supreme Court to outlaw the minimum-fee schedule—so much for drawing up a deed, so much for a divorce—and heaven help the lawyer who charges less.

Too often, the bar associations have tried to block efforts to maximize the benefits of the law for the general population. The ABA has consistently opposed some of the better no-fault auto-accident insurance plans, plans which would relieve congestion in the courts and compensate all auto-accident victims at substantial cost savings. Their opposition takes many forms. In Texas, for example, the State Bar doubled membership dues to finance a four-year public relations campaign against no-fault and disguised the effort as a fight to save the ancient right of trial by jury. Other bar associations have propagandized against no-fault with "educational seminars" that typically present one spokesman for reform whose speech is prefaced and rebutted by a series of no-fault opponents. And now, some of the same organizations are trying to raise funds for a "war chest" to fight legislative efforts that would lower contingency fees in medical malpractice suits. Again, a case of some lawyers thinking more about themselves than they are of the people they're supposed to serve.

Another example: The profession of law is shot through with inefficiencies for which the people end up paying outrageous sums of money in matters of rank simplicity. Filing a divorce, probating a will and recording a property title all cost far more than they should, considering the amount of work the attorney (or, generally, his more knowledgeable secretary) does for the money. But bar groups oppose any reforms that would correct this thievery and blackmail. When Norman F. Dacey published a bestselling book, *How to Avoid Probate* (which contained do-it-yourself forms for the layman), the New York County Lawyers Association promptly had him prosecuted for the unauthorized practice of law.

The ABA and various state and local bars have entered into "treaties" with a wide variety of potential competitors: accountants, architects, banks with trust functions, claims adjusters, collection agencies, life-insurance companies and underwriters, realtors, social workers, engineers and title-insurance companies and abstractors. These treaties purport to prevent the unauthorized practice of law. In effect, they are agreements to divide the booty in the law market, and their net effect on the law industry is to promote more business for lawyers. Such agreements between industrial competitors would be violations of the Sherman Anti-Trust Act. But lawyers are a privileged class, and anyway, who would prosecute under the Sherman Act but other lawyers?

My first run-in with the mandarins of the ABA came in the mid-fifties. Just exactly how it all started, I'll probably never know. My guess is (and it's not a paranoid guess; you can see how unparanoid I was by my own actions on this occasion) that someone in the ABA with a good deal of clout sent the word to ABA headquarters in Chicago: get Belli. To get me, some staff member of the bureaucracy that runs the ABA concocted a plan. Friendlylike, they asked this flamboyant hick from the wilds of San Francisco to "stop by" sometime when he was passing through Chicago to tell them how I thought lawyers could better handle personal-injury suits of all kinds. I was flattered and proud to tell the ABA what I was doing. And so, the next time I was headed back east, I stopped in Chicago and met at the ABA headquarters with a group (led by a lawyer from Michigan named Brucker, later a very stuffy "Secretary of the Army"), who received me cordially and plied me with questions about my law practice for an entire afternoon. Fully and frankly, I told them everything I could— and referred them to *Modern*

Trials and its sequel, *Modern Damages,* for further details. Nothing I did was ever a secret, and I had spent a good deal of time and money touring the country to tell my brothers in the law how I did it.

Imagine my astonishment when several weeks later I got a letter from the ABA advising me that its *grievance* committee was recommending that I be suspended from the ABA for six months and that my California Bar Association take disciplinary action against me! For what? The letter didn't say. I hadn't seen or heard of any charges lodged against me, but, apparently, I'd already had a "hearing" (that informal afternoon in Chicago) and been convicted to boot.

At first, I laughed. If lawyers knew anything at all, they ought to know about (and cherish) due process of law. If a man's accused, he ought to know what he's accused of and who his accusers are so he can prepare some kind of defense. There was no due process here at all.

Then my mood changed, to disgust and then to anger. I resolved to go after the ABA and retained Abe Freedman of Philadelphia, a good friend and able politician of the Bar who liked to help trial lawyers in trouble, to appeal my case to the House of Delegates, a group including many past presidents of the ABA.

Freedman fixed things for me, but I'm sorry he did. He made a few phone calls and got a concession from Chicago that indeed the so-called proceedings against me lacked due process. The ABA spokesman in Chicago told Freedman they'd simply quash the whole thing. But they, in turn, had a favor to ask. They wouldn't say anything publicly about their change of mind about me, and they'd rather I not say anything either. So the ABA had really buried it. Well, I said, cooled down by this time, what the hell? There'd be other innings. And anyway, the ABA later tried to make atonement by inviting me to present a Belli Seminar at their convention in Miami, which I did.

When I got to that Miami convention, however, I did a naughty thing. I brought along Professor Julian O'Brien of Harvard to talk about tax law. Professor O'Brien gave a pretty good talk, an amusing little pastiche which ended with an altogether fitting peroration. "My parting advice to you guys is, 'Pay your taxes.' "

But "Professor" O'Brien was really a ringer I'd brought in, a friend named Meyer Harris Cohen of Los Angeles, who was currently under indictment for income-tax evasion, because the FBI couldn't get anything else on a man whom the Hearst papers invariably called "Mobster Mickey Cohen." The pompus delegates to the ABA convention hadn't recognized Cohen, of course, and they'd overlooked his "deses," "dems" and "doses" because his talk made much good sense. When they heard in hotel corridors and elevators later that evening how they'd been hornswoggled by Belli, however, they went bananas (in the privacy of their VIP suites) and issued stuffy communiqués to announce they were not amused. The English barristers visiting the convention loved my little joke.

Abe Freedman wrote to tell me he thought I'd spoiled a beautiful seminar "by the introduction of a pug ugly." But Freedman was only speaking as an elder statesman of the ABA who was trying to keep the heat off colorful lawyers.

I was a member of the ABA at this time (in the early 1960's) and probably a second-class member at that, because I opposed most of what the ABA stood for. Even so, the ABA tried to throw me out of the club again in 1964 in the aftermath of the Ruby trial. I managed to block that move—for symbolic reasons (as you will see later in this narrative) rather than substantial ones: to practice law, you didn't have to belong to the ABA, but you do have to be a member of a state bar. Future efforts to fix my wagon, therefore, zeroed in on my good standing with the State Bar of California.

In 1970, when I was on safari in Africa, my then New York lecture agent, Richard Fulton, arranged with some Madison Avenue ad people to feature my endorsement of Glenfiddich Scotch, a relatively recent arrival in American liquor stores. In February, 1970, while I was still in Africa, the ad appeared in *The New York Times*. About three thousand miles away, the State Bar's local San Francisco chapter picked up the ad, focused on my agent's attempts to get me speaking engagements and charged me with "solicitation." For what—speaking engagements? I maintained that there was nothing improper about that. My agent was soliciting lecture business, not law business, but that distinction eluded the locals.

They told me on January 13, 1972, they would give me a "suspended sentence" for the crime of having a lecture agent if I'd hand them a quarterly summary of my public appearances, press interviews and copies of all my public writings *in advance*—and submit to a public reprimand to boot. I told them I couldn't do that. What a chilling effect *that* would have on my rights to speak freely and frankly! So the locals recommended a year's suspension for me, a reviewing body of the State Bar endorsed that sentence (making sure the press had a release on it) and I had again the considerable expense of hiring one of the best appeals attorneys in the state, Herman Selvin, to defend me before the California Supreme Court.

The court's decision came down in the spring of 1974. It was a victory for me. The court knocked down all of the Bar's charges but one on the grounds that a man didn't lose the right of free speech by becoming a member of the Bar. "The Bar [wrote the court] may not abridge fundamental Constitutional liberties." It added that its own interests in protecting fundamental Constitutional rights prevailed over "the desire of the Bar to minimize solicitation of legal business." Anyway, it noted (agreeing with my original defense), my lecture agent wasn't soliciting law business but lecture business, which was a proper and essential means of insuring that the right to speak would not be "more a hollow shell than a meaningful Constitutional entitlement." The decision set up some important new law both for the layman *and* the lawyer.

As a sop to the Bar's establishment, however, the members of the court suspended me from the practice of law for one month. They dinged me in a six-to-one decision for endorsing the Glenfiddich. They said I had had an opportunity to stop the ad after my return from Africa but hadn't done so. They didn't give very good reasons why I should have. Lawyers have always made endorsements with impunity. When I got the news of my suspension, I noted that Ellis E. Reid, president of the Cook County Bar Association, was endorsing Dewar's Scotch in the pages of *The New Yorker*. He didn't even get his wrist slapped; maybe Dewar's was a better brand than Glenfiddich. It couldn't have been because he was president of his bar association. And a San Francisco lawyer, a member of one of the biggest firms which tried to have me continuously on their back burner, endorsed a line of clothing with impunity.

I took my suspension in May, 1974, lowered the Jolly Roger flying over my office to half-mast and sailed for Japan. When I returned, a pal of mine, San Francisco attorney Fred Furth, threw a party (at my office) for me and *re*crowned me King of Torts. There was something different about this party, however. A number of 22K rock-ribbed establishment lawyers showed up to wish me well. Maybe the freedom of speech issue for *all* lawyers was getting across to all the members of the Bar. I felt good about that.

Still and all, I *had been* suspended for a month, and the news stories about the suspension went all over the world. To that extent, the decision robbed me of something. "Who steals my purse steals trash . . . but he that filches from me my good name robs me of that which not enriches him and makes me poor indeed." So I didn't take the suspension like some contrite sinner. I hadn't done anything wrong. I appealed for a rehearing by the court, directly confronting the issue of advertising and solicitation. The Bar's restrictions against advertising (if advertising it was), I argued, were outmoded. Banning advertising, I said, kept information from people who needed it most. Banks, insurance companies and finance companies wouldn't benefit from advertising. But people in the ghettos and the barrios certainly could.

I also filed a civil action in the U.S. District Court for Northern California against the State Bar of California—for $3 million. My complaint stated, in part:

> MELVIN M. BELLI stands as one of the lawyers at the forefront of the movement to deliver the full resources of today's now exemplary law from the sole and exclusive grasp of establishment institutions and proprietary interests equally into the hands of the injured, the minorities, and the accused. . . . He has spoken for people who needed a clear voice to be heard against establishment concerns, insurance companies, banks, utilities, mortgage and proprietary interests who would minimize responsibility to their victims, and against prosecutions which would circumvent the Constitutional mandate for fair and impartial proceedings under due process of law. In such activities, plaintiff has and does incur the displeasure

of said establishments which have and do seek to censure, throttle and stifle his endeavors, and who treat the law as their own private game preserve.

The State Bar responded to this statement—no surprise —by instituting new proceedings against me, this time for having spoken my mind fearlessly and frankly and spontaneously on "The Merv Griffin Show," more than a year before, on May 14, 1973. I had complained to a national audience about a Washington judge who had reversed an all-time-high jury verdict I had won for a little black girl in Washington, D.C.

In 1972, I had sued Children's Hospital in Washington on behalf of Sharlene Morris, who was then fourteen. Sharlene's mother took the girl to Children's after the girl had several fainting spells and seizures. Without much diagnostic investigation, the hospital treated her with Dilantin, which can sometimes produce a dangerous allergic reaction. Doctors at the hospital advised Mrs. Morris to return the girl immediately in case of bleeding, high temperature or conjunctivitis. A week later, Sharlene complained of a burning in her eyes and was again taken to Children's, where she was diagnosed as having severe conjunctivitis, an inflammation of the eyelids. She was treated with eyedrops and released without instructions to discontinue Dilantin.

The next night, Mrs. Morris again took Sharlene to Children's after the girl developed bumps on her face, vomiting and a 104-degree temperature. The doctors diagnosed her condition as measles, prescribed aspirin and sent her home. On direction, she continued to take the Dilantin. The next day, still running a high temperature, Sharlene was taken to Freedman's Hospital, where doctors described the case again as measles and prescribed alcohol rubs. Late that night, her parents took her to a third hospital, D.C. General, in a semiconscious condition. Her temperature had risen to 108 degrees. Doctors there said she was obviously suffering from Stevens-Johnson syndrome, an acute allergic reaction to any number of causative agents, Dilantin included. Result: a peeling away of the girl's skin, including the protective covering over the cornea of her eyes. (When one of the doctors tried to lift Sharlene, her skin came off in his hands like a suit of underwear!) And without that protective covering, blood vessels and scar tissue spread over the cornea, causing almost total blindness. For the rest of her life, Sharlene Morris would have to look at life as through a muddy windshield.

These were the facts we had to demonstrate to judge and jury at the trial. But in that trial, the judge, John Lewis Smith, Jr., covered me with personal insults. Judge Smith was a Nixon appointee and a man who would later give a suspended sentence to Nixon's moneyman, Maurice Stans, a convicted conspirator in the Watergate affair, not exactly on my ideological wave length. When the defense attorney made a settlement offer of $70,000, Judge Smith insisted I take it. I said they'd have to add a half-million to that. Judge Smith turned on me. "You're trying to go for the jackpot and feather your own nest." He then threatened to appoint "a lawyer of ability and integrity who knows something about torts" as guardian to protect the interests of Sharlene Morris. I told the judge to go ahead and get a guardian for the child—and that I'd pay him myself out of my share of the award—but he dropped the guardian idea.

We finished presenting our case on a Monday in March, 1973, and by that time I was ready to call it quits. The judge was so obviously against us, I'd decided to settle—

not for $70,000, but I was amenable, at least, to another settlement conference. But now the defense lawyers, sensing victory, wouldn't settle for anything at all. Too cocky, they put on a Doctor Thomas Reichelderfer, who testified that medical science could restore Sharlene Morris's vision with corneal transplants. I skewered that doctor on cross-examination; I got him to admit that the first doctor who saw Sharlene Morris at Children's Hospital had actually diagnosed Stevens-Johnson syndrome and that the other doctors there knew it and should have stopped giving Dilantin to Sharlene. I asked him how many times medical science had tried to restore vision to anyone who had suffered from Stevens-Johnson syndrome.

"Four," Dr. Reichelderfer said.

"And how did they turn out, Doctor?"

"Half the cases got worse."

"Two cases," I said. "And the other two?"

"No improvement."

"Doctor," I said, "that is one hundred percent failures!" When I finished my cross-examination, Doctor Reichelderfer stood, his knees buckled and he almost fell off the witness stand.

That turned the case around. The jury, my first all-black jury of six, came back with a verdict of $900,000, the largest malpractice award in the history of Washington, D.C. That's when Judge Smith set aside the verdict and ordered a new trial on the grounds that the jury was "motivated by emotion, sympathy and prejudice." I wasn't there to argue with that decision. At that moment I was flat on my back in the University of California Hospital, San Francisco. I thought I was dying. I'd come down with an unnamed malady of my own: my head whirled, I had double vision and I was alternately delirious and unconscious for three weeks. My chart, which I read on the sly, almost scared the rest of the life out of me. The working diagnosis was: "thoracic carcinoma with metastasis to the brain." (I found out later it was only a bad case of pneumonia.)*

It was only when I got out of the hospital that I learned of Judge Smith's own prejudices. His son was an attorney for the Washington, D.C., Medical Society; because of that, the judge had been asked to disqualify himself earlier in the year from a case involving Children's Hospital. He disqualified himself in that one. (My local counsel should have advised me of this, but he hadn't been of much help. He didn't.) But he didn't disqualify himself in my case—and reversed the $900,000 verdict to boot!

It wasn't long after I learned all this that I appeared on "The Merv Griffin Show," talking about everything under the sun. Almost as an afterthought, I told the Sharlene Morris story, without mentioning anyone by name. The defense counsel for the Washington hospital went to Judge Smith about it, and Judge Smith then took himself off the case and persuaded the entire panel of U.S. District Court judges in Washington, including the redoubtable John J. Sirica, that my statements on TV were an attack on the integrity of the entire court. The judges said my charges

---

* Sometimes doctors have made less than acute diagnoses of my maladies. (I wonder why.) For years, I'd gone to one doctor after another to see if anyone could do anything about my headaches. Then one day I dropped in to see Sam Lucchese at his boot company in San Antonio to get a pair of his fabulous handmade boots, and when he took down my measurements, he wrote down "Length, 11½."

"No," I said, "ten and a half."

"No," he said, "eleven and a half."

"No," I said, "ten and a half. I've always worn ten and a half."

"Lissen, *paisano*," said Sam, putting a friendly arm on my shoulder. "If you wear ten-and-a-half boots, you'll get terrible headaches."

were "without factual foundations and were recklessly made." † I could not continue to carry on the Morris case (without me, the Morrises settled for $150,000) and asked the disciplinary committee of the State Bar of California to "take such action as it deems appropriate in the circumstances." And then the Washington judges, contrary to all custom of waiting until the issue was adjudicated, published a press release announcing their action.

On the Griffin show, I was saying what was wrong with the law in order to improve it. The judges didn't rebut by saying "It's not true." They rebutted by saying, "If it is true, we shouldn't tell the layman, because it may discourage his belief in the law." There was nothing reckless in my charges. Almost everything I had said on TV had already been headlined in the Washington *Post*. If I couldn't criticize the judge for continuing to sit in this case, what was the world coming to? I remembered the words of Supreme Court Justice Felix Frankfurter: "Certainly courts are not, and cannot be, immune from criticism, and lawyers, of course, may indulge in criticism. Indeed, they are under special responsibility to exercise fearlessness in so doing."

"Jesus," I said. "I've been having terrible headaches for almost thirty-five years."

"How long you been wearing ten-and-a-half boots?" asked Sam.

"For almost—thirty-five years," I said.

Sam was partly right. I consulted a chiropractor when I returned to California, Dr. Ted Frigard of Stockton, a man who has since become a great friend. He confirmed Sam Lucchese's diagnosis and ordered me to turn in the old boots.

† I did say, "Some ten years before in a Washington courtroom blacks couldn't sit on the same side of the courtroom as whites." I was in error. Only *after* they came out of the courtroom. They couldn't sit on the same side of the bus.

I told the whole story in a letter I sent to fifteen hundred lawyers across the land. I asked for their comments. Only six were critical of me and all but forty (including some U.S. senators, federal and state judges, governors and ex-governors) submitted affidavits backing me up. Most of the lawyers writing me had said *don't* you dare apologize. The fact is I never did say or infer that Judge Smith was "crooked" or "dishonest." I felt, and still do, this just wasn't the kind of case for him to sit on and consciously or unconsciously bring objective justice to it.

I appealed to the judges in Washington and even apologized for whatever personal offense I had given the trial judge, but the judges did nothing, and the State Bar moved toward another suspension hearing.

So I had another fight on my hands. What to do this time? Wait for first one shoe to drop from the local administrative committee of the State Bar and then wait another year or more for the State Bar to drop another . . . and still another year for the Supreme Court to approve or condemn all this noise from the attic of the Bar? No. I'd try to short-circuit the process. I appealed directly to the California Supreme Court. I cited the court's own opinion of the previous decade in *Brotsky v. State Bar* (57 Cal. 2d. 287):

> In matters of discipline and disbarment, the State Bar is but an arm of this court and this court retains its power to control any such disciplinary proceeding *at any step*. [Italics mine.]

I saw our pretrial appeal to the Supreme Court of California as an important phase of my defense to the State Bar's "case" against me. The State Bar puts other lawyers on the pan if they defraud their clients or get caught in a

Watergate affair. They go after me for speaking freely. So I wanted to stop a trial like this before it ever started; to me the trial itself was a serious infringement upon my own freedom of speech. I was also getting a bit tired of defending myself before State Bar committees invariably composed of lawyers who represented my archenemies: hospitals, utilities, banks, oil and insurance companies.

Could I prove the bias of the Bar? I was so sure I could that I invested five thousand dollars for an analysis of the State Bar disciplinary committees chosen to serve in the last ten years. The independent analysts discovered for themselves how lopsided these committees were. Oh, there was an occasional lawyer like me on a committee, a lawyer who made it his business to go after big corporations on behalf of the little man or take on civil rights cases or a criminal defendant. But for every one like me, there were twenty-eight establishment lawyers from the big corporate law firms.

On the basis of these statistics, I petitioned the Supreme Court that I be tried only by a committee of lawyers that truly represented *all* the practicing lawyers in San Francisco.

As to the central issue of the case itself—my public criticism of judges—I argued that:

> No attorney should be made to sacrifice his well-loved profession as the price of entry into the area of public criticism. None of our institutions can be so fragile or so sacred as to so escape the test of vigorous fair comment, or those institutions themselves will not long endure.
>
> The lessons of Watergate and the echoes of our two-hundred-year history are upon us. The right to criticize the most powerful is the cornerstone of our freedom as a nation, and surely our freedom as law-

yers vigorously representing the public requires
no less.

The California Supreme Court denied my petition without comment, and in August, 1975, I took the stand in my
own defense before a local three-man committee of the
State Bar.

A State Bar disciplinary hearing ought to be a "fra-
ternal" kind of proceeding among respected colleagues. My
young "prosecutor" ignored the protocol. He went after me
with a frenzy and actually recommended disbarment for
life. You would think I was up for murder. I'd only criticized a judge who should have disqualified himself—and
didn't. (Judge Smith later admitted in a disposition that
he *and his son* agreed that juries weren't equipped to try
medical malpractice cases!)

Waiting for a decision was torture. My spirits sagged,
my headaches got worse. Finally, on November 17, 1975,
my own lawyer, Sid Irmas, phoned one of the members of
the three-man committee and said he'd come up with another court decision which might have some bearing on
the Belli case. He was told not to bother: the committee
had already made its decision and handed it in to the office of the State Bar in San Francisco. Irmas called Carl
Heil, an official at the Bar. "Oh yes," said Heil, "the
decision came in on October sixth."

"You mean," said Irmas, "more than a month ago? Six
weeks ago?"

"Uhhh," said Heil, "I've been pretty busy."

"What *was* the decision?" asked Irmas.

"I don't remember," Heil said.

Incredible. I sent one of my young men to the Bar at
lunchtime and a secretary gave him a copy of the decision.
Unanimously, the committee had ruled that while I had
made some "injudicious statements" about Judge Smith,

the Bar's hatchetmen had failed to prove that I had acted with a reckless disregard for the facts or maliciously. As far as this committee was concerned, no judges—not even federal judges in Washington—were above criticism.

For the record, I should say here that more than 90 percent of the trial judges I've encountered are good, able men. But both groups, the good, able judges and the not-so-good, not-so-able judges, constitute the last privileged class in America, the last bastion of unaccountability. Judges still surround themselves with the trappings of dignity, something like the Wizard of Oz, insist on being addressed like kings and popes—"your Highness, your Holiness, your Honor"—and still wear dresses (or, if you will, robes). That's so everyone will bow and scrape before them—and not ask questions. Other officials, from the President of the United States on down, give interviews that help the press interpret and explain matters of concern to the people at large. Supreme Court Justices—like most popes and kings—don't give interviews. No one must ever approach a judge face to face and ask him the meaning of a phrase in his decision. The rationale is probably this: "It's all on paper. If you want to take it to a higher court (and you have the time and money) go ahead."

The press ought to break this stance. The press has penetrated the myths and the mystique of many U.S. institutions: the Presidency, the Congress, the Pentagon, the CIA, the FBI, the world of sports. But judges still seem to be off limits. As Michael Novak once pointed out, only a few judges have made the landmark judicial decision on busing which has so far contributed nothing to the improvement of education for black children and actually heightened the bitterness between blacks and whites in the country. And yet we know very little about these judges. Who are these men? What are their habits of thinking?

What is their range of understanding? Who are the key members of their staffs? Why should citizens have confidence in their judgment? For what favors, if any, were they appointed? As Novak says, "Their decisions are disrupting historic (not merely legal) patterns of social life in city after city. And these judges are not merely passing judgment on Constitutional law. They are now acting as social architects by passing judgment on suitable 'remedies.' They are playing Congress and Executive rolled into one."

How many times have you seen a story in a newspaper or magazine that attempts to present in minute detail just how a man or woman gets appointed to the bench? Or how he conducts the public's affairs on the bench? Or how a Supreme Court decision is arrived at, written and rewritten?

A recent appointee to the federal bench in California came from one of the big law factories in his city. No one ever heard of him, but two giant corporations didn't have a representative on the federal bench at the time and undoubtedly thought they should have this man, their man. So they pulled the required strings, made the proper approaches to the two senators from California, got the President to appoint the man and all of a sudden we had a new federal judge. I am not about to suggest that this judge will always decide in favor of these two corporations. Most of the judges try to put aside their prejudices and preconceptions when they sit on a case (and, in fact, many judges who do recognize that they are, after all, only human, often disqualify themselves on a particular case when they may have some conflict of interest that would prevent them from judging fairly). But I am equally sure that judges would find it easier to put aside their prejudices if they were aware the public knew just exactly what these prejudices were.

I have the highest respect for our nation's courts. If I am asked, visiting any county in the U.S., to pick the most honest, fair, decent person who best represented the total community, I wouldn't pick the town doctor or minister or councilman or even mayor. I'd blindly choose from among the local judges. I'm not a judge hater or judge baiter. In all my forty-plus years of trial practice. I've only found five judges I'd rather not see again on a case of mine. Some judges have decided against me—but I don't have to win a case to make a judicial friend.

CHAPTER THIRTEEN

A Jockey's Silks

A reporter for *Forbes* asked me some time ago what kind of lawyering I did best. I gave him a flashy reply, one I'd like to repudiate right now. I said, "I do anything the client asks of me. If the next guy walks in with an alligator and asks me to wrestle it, I'll wrestle it—and I'll be good at it, too." That was hyperbole. Though I have never been loath to help a rich man who is in a lot of trouble, the fact is that few rich men have sought me out. Anyone who can read the newspapers must know by now that I haven't represented banks, insurance companies, railroads and assorted other octopi. I let the big downtown law firms handle them.

I set a subconscious pattern for myself early in my career. What I really wanted to do in the law was force the system to make good on its promises and bring due process of law to all the elements in our society, not just the rich and powerful. That's why I'm a "radical conservative." Though I shied away from the steady practice of criminal law in San Francisco, I wasn't above taking an occasional criminal case where I saw a chance of helping a man or woman whose rights were being trampled on by official lawlessness. The Bill of Rights was supposed to be a protection against the incursions of government on the individual. Unfortunately, the forces of government did not always understand about the Bill of Rights (not even in San Francisco, the most civilized city in America). Sometimes it would take all my forensic skills to neutralize them.

The San Francisco cops seemed to have the goods on Gertrude Jenkins, an engaging madam who ran a pleasure palace out on Broadway during the 1940's. They had her charged with procuring an abortion for one of her girls, but in order to do so they'd violated about seven of the ten freedoms guaranteed in the Bill of Rights. I could have fought the case on any or all of these counts. But the San Francisco courts weren't buying this kind of defense in the mid-forties and I didn't want to take a client through a lot of appeals if I could avoid it. I countered the law's lawlessness with a glorious flimflam of my own.

I knew that Gertrude Jenkins would have been a terrific witness—against herself—and even if she had survived my questioning, she would have caved in under the Deputy D.A.'s cross-examination. On the other hand, I couldn't let her sit there and refuse to testify. At that time in California, the judge could tell jurors they might infer a person's guilt from his or her failure to take the stand. A judge can't do that anymore. Back then, I jumped the gun for justice. I hit upon a compromise.

After I presented my case, I stood up in court and said, "The defense rests, your Honor. Mrs. Jenkins will not take the stand." I had spent the previous night coaching the woman on her next move. And now in the courtroom, she came across as a real Sarah Bernhardt.

"Wait a minute," she cried, jumping to her feet. "Wait a minute. I want to take the stand. I'm innocent."

"Gert," I said softly (but not so softly the jury couldn't

hear me). "We *know* you're innocent. You don't *have* to testify."

Of course, the judge gave his instructions to the jurors that they could infer what they wished about the woman's refusal to take the stand. But the jury had heard the woman say, "I'm innocent." And the jury had heard me say, "We know you're innocent." And though neither Gertrude nor I was under oath, that's what the jury chose to believe. They found her not guilty. (This is not the procedure I recommend while lecturing to law students when they ask me, "Should the defendant always take the stand in a criminal case?")

Gertrude Jenkins had gotten into trouble with the law in the first place because she'd said too much when the cops arrested her. I wanted to make sure that Molly Regan, a madam who ran a very respectable whorehouse on Green Street not far from Gertrude's place, didn't make the same mistake when she was called before a county grand jury. "Molly," I told her, "you can't say a thing without incriminating yourself. Fortunately, according to the Bill of Rights, you can remain silent."

"Bill Wright?" she said. "Who's Bill Wright? And what kind of pull does he have with the grand jury?" Poor Molly. She was one of the best madams in the City and she knew a lot about people (and the "pull" they could exercise) but she knew very little about the foundations of our freedoms. I tried to explain to her about the Fifth Amendment, the embodiment of an ancient legal principle that no one need accuse himself. "You mean they can't make me talk?" she said.

"Right."

"So I just dummy up?"

"Right."

She couldn't understand that. "Then what's the point of my going before the grand jury?"

"They have a job to do down there. They've got to ask you all the questions." She gave me an uncomprehending look. "Look," I said, "I'll make it simple."

The next day, she appeared before the grand jury with copies of three pamphlets I had given her: the Declaration of Independence, the Constitution and, for show, the Gettysburg Address. Molly dummied up real good. Each time the Deputy District Attorney asked her a question, she pointed to the three pamphlets and held up five fingers. "You're taking the Fifth?" said the startled young prosecutor. She nodded. Never uttered a word. And was never indicted.

San Francisco seemed surfeited then with a number of stuffy young prosecutors who'd either been sleeping during their law school courses on the Constitution or simply didn't give a damn. In 1944, they swooped down on "Father" William E. Riker and charged him with sedition. Father Riker was the founder of something called "Holy City" near Los Gatos in the Santa Cruz Mountains, the head of a kooky religious cult who claimed that he was God. A group of sailors in training visited "Holy City" one day and returned to camp with stories that Father Riker had told them not to go into battle but to lay down their guns.

When the government indicted Riker for sedition, his lawyers were so impressed they announced in open court that they would plead him "guilty," whereupon Father Riker fired them and came looking for me, offering me five thousand dollars now and five thousand dollars later if he were acquitted. I felt sorry for the windy old geezer. He had a mouth like a torn pocket, but I was angry, too. This was one of the things I thought we were fighting for; to allow any man to preach any crackpot ideas he wanted—to anyone.

The newspapers made me a hero in the trial. I sat back and listened to the prosecution's case without making a single objection. The facts didn't add up to sedition and didn't add up to one hundred years in prison, which was what the government was asking for Riker, a shaky sixty-eight. I told the jury so, comparing Riker to all the great crackpots of American history from Ben Franklin to Woodrow Wilson and asking why, if the feds considered this nut so dangerous, they permitted him to continue preaching for one solid year after their investigation began.

I told the jury Riker preached a wacky racist doctrine but I said I'd give fifty thousand dollars to anyone who could understand what it meant. I guess I sounded pretty good, because the *Chronicle*'s Carolyn Anspacher wrote my summation to the jury was "so persuasive that the 68-year old cultist himself was moved to tears."

I myself did not weep, but I have never underestimated the power of tears in the courtroom.*

---

* According to the Supreme Court of Tennessee,

> . . . tears have always been considered legitimate arguments before a jury. It would appear to be one of the natural rights of counsel which no court or constitution could take away. Indeed, if counsel has them at his command it may be seriously questioned whether it is not a professional duty to shed them whenever proper occasion rises.

William F. Howe of New York City, one of the most successful shysters of all time, was also the most accomplished weeper in the history of the New York bar. According to one writer, Howe "could and would cry over any case, no matter how commonplace. His voice would quiver, his jowls would quiver, his great shoulders would shake and presently authentic tears would well up in his bulbous eyes and dribble over. It was a sickening spectacle." But it worked. Howe and his partner, Little Abe Hummel, practically had a monopoly on the criminal-defense business in New York from 1862 until 1907. They were preeminent divorce lawyers and the leading theatrical lawyers of the day.

Needless to say, the jury acquitted Riker on all thirteen counts of sedition, and Riker was so grateful that he named me his "Second Typical God" (whatever that was) in lieu of the second five thousand dollars I thought I had coming. In the presence of the newspapermen gathered about taking pictures the father fixed a benevolent eye upon me, his legal savior, raised his hand in benediction and in tones not unlike those of the late W. C. Fields said, "My son, I shall reward you with a seat in my Kingdom of heaven and that is far more emolument than a paltry five thousand dollars—mere money!"

I declined the offer and said I'd rather have the five thousand dollars. That shocked the father into further communications with his "powers." His "thunderbolts" were not long in coming. Several days later, Father Riker sued me for five thousand dollars on the ground that I had libeled him in my closing argument by calling him a "crackpot"—which was exactly the language that won his acquittal. So it goes.

I didn't fight in the war, because they wouldn't take me. On December 8, 1941, the day after the Japanese attacked Pearl Harbor, I enlisted in the army air corps. I was in the air reserve. But after my physical, the doctors told me I'd flunked. It was my duodenal ulcer.

I would probably have made a terrible officer. I would have wanted to know the reason for every order issued and would have battled my commanding officer every hour of the day. I plunged deeper into the practice of law. A lot of young lawyers were going off to war. Naturally, that meant there would be proportionately more work for me, and I seized the opportunity. I took everything that came down Market Street.

I represented firemen and their widows before the Retirement Board, won nineteen cases in a row and made a further good friend in Bob Callahan, a leader in the firemen's union and a helluva good guy who was as effusive and profane as I. I handled wills and divorces and leases—which was sheer drudgery. But I welcomed the challenging civil cases that not only would tax my legal inventiveness but would give me a chance to help the lone individual being squeezed by society.

Horace Fong, a friend and a restaurateur, was being squeezed—by his neighbors in Oak Knoll, a snooty community up in the hills above Piedmont. The residents tried to have Fong and his blond wife evicted, citing some long-standing restrictive covenant against Chinese. So I sued them, demanding they cease and desist harassing my client, who, I claimed, wasn't Chinese at all. Technically speaking, in California law, he was an American Indian. As such, he was immune.

I justified this outrageous claim by citing a California Supreme Court decision, *People v. Hall,* 4 Cal. 399, which had declared in 1854 that a Chinese murder witness against one George W. Hall was an Indian. Hall's lawyer, appealing the man's conviction, pointed out that an act of 1850 had provided that "no black or mulatto person or Indian shall be allowed to give evidence in favor of or against a white man." But the Chinese witness, he said, was an Indian because when Columbus landed in America, he thought he had reached one of the islands of the China Sea "which washes India." Therefore, he called the natives "Indians," meaning the inhabitants of all lands touched by the China Sea, including China and Japan. The Supreme Court bought the argument: Chinese must be Indians. And who wants to take the word of this heathen against George Hall anyway? Hall was released.

As it turned out, the courts didn't have to make a decision either way about Fong's identity. His wife divorced him, retained the home in Oak Knoll and Fong moved into my home, which was a damn sight more exclusive than Oak Knoll. Fong and I decided to open a new restaurant in Redwood City. We called it "Fong's Iroquois Village." On the cover of the menus, a totem pole rose above a book labeled *Law,* 4 Cal. 399. Around the book was a chicken, an ear of corn, a pumpkin, a fish, a big steak and a bottle of booze. The inscription on the totem said, "Ugh, me Fong."

The restaurant was a big thing in my life for a time. I tried to be the John Sobrato of the Peninsula. (John's Rendezvous was the best restaurant in San Francisco, a favorite hangout for the town's lawyers and judges and a place where servicemen on their way to the South Pacific enjoyed having their last meal in the States. I represented John and I liked his style.)

Ours was not a family-type restaurant, nor was it a place for a man who was merely hungry. Among the dishes, we had strawberry omelettes, cherries jubilee and French prawns a la Fong. We also had a number of other specialties that were variations on Fong's name, such as boiled cabbage O'Fong, McFong hors d'oeuvres, barbecued pork Fongstein and abalone in oyster sauce Fongby.

We never made a dime on the restaurant. In fact, I dropped seventy-five thousand dollars in one year. "Nobody could be that careless with money," said one of the Internal Revenue Service men at first, but after careful investigation, he apologized. "I'm sorry," he said, "somebody could."

Laymen may be tempted to condemn lawyers who indulge in such patent pettifoggery as I had used on behalf of Horace Fong. They shouldn't. Sometimes, a lawyer has to resort to a lot of legal buncombe to achieve the substantial ends of justice. If the buncombe is also laid on with humor, then the morrow will dawn not only fairer but infinitely more amusing. I could have attacked the Fong case head on. But why treat racial prejudice with anything other than the laughter it deserves?

I could never summon up much laughter, however, when I saw an innocent man or woman maimed or crippled by a surgeon's scalpel or a motorist's machine—and then spurned by some thieving insurance company or offered a mere pittance to compensate them for a life of pain ever after. And so, whenever I got the upper hand on an insurance company, I squeezed them—hard. And hang the fine ethical distinctions.

In the case of Irene Kincaid, in the early 1950's, I squeezed so hard the insurance company couldn't get out fast enough. As it turned out, they were a bit too fast for their own good. Mrs. Kincaid had been paralyzed by the maladministration of a spinal anesthetic during childbirth. No trouble proving medical malpractice, and so, in pursuing the suit against Stanford Hospital, I didn't even bother getting a medical expert of my own.

I told the lawyers for the hospital they could give Irene Kincaid every test and examination they thought they needed to verify the facts. Then I took depositions from all of them and found enough discrepancies in their stories to make a good case against each person. I subpoenaed a complete set of the medical records from the hospital, made photostats, added them to the deposition and bound the whole thing into a brochure six inches thick. "Trial by brochure," lawyers call it now.

On the eve of the trial, the case pretty well spoke for itself, and so the defense lawyers offered a settlement of $128,000. They made the offer the very night that Irene Kincaid told me she felt a "tingling" in her right foot. To me, that meant sensation was coming back again; maybe she wouldn't be paralyzed for the rest of her life.

Ethically, what was I to do? Tell the other side that she was on the road to recovery? Not exactly. What I did was tell them that now was the time to get their last and final examination. The defense lawyers imagined that I intended to demonstrate an even more serious injury so I could ask for more money. In this case, my reputation really helped. "No thanks," they said. "We don't want any more examinations. We're satisfied. The point is, are you satisfied with the amount of the settlement?" I certainly was. I took the $128,000, and Irene Kincaid did walk again, though haltingly. For her, $128,000 was not too much—though I'm sure the insurance company would have said it was if they'd known about the "tingling" in her foot—that I offered to let them find out for themselves.

As far as the insurance companies were concerned, whatever sum I asked, for any of my clients, was always "excessive." I succeeded in getting a very modest award in 1955 for Maureen Connolly, a three-time Wimbledon champion at twenty-one whose tennis career was ruined one sunny afternoon in San Diego when a truck ran her down, but the insurance company fought it all the way to the Supreme Court.

Mo Connolly was out horseback riding with two girlfriends on a country road when a cement rig approached them with a frightening roar. The horses started milling and dancing about. The girls held up their hands, signaling the driver to stop and shouting, "Stop, stop, stop!" By his own testimony, the driver could have stopped far short of the girls. But he only slowed down a bit, shifted gears and tried to slip in between the riders—at twenty to twenty-five miles an hour.

It was too much for Maureen's horse, Colonel Merryboy. He shied, then wheeled, throwing Maureen into the truck, which kept right on going for two hundred yards, with pieces of Maureen's leg still clinging to its side. Maureen's leg was broken and, more important, blood vessels supplying oxygen to her foot (*Dorsalis pedes*) were partially torn. To repair them, doctors had her on the operating table for three hours and fifteen minutes—and failed: She would have some slight impaired circulation in her foot forever. Mo Connolly could never play championship tennis again.

San Diego attorney John D. Butler, a former mayor of San Diego, and I asked the jury for $265,000 in general and punitive damages, showed the court movies of Maureen winning at Wimbledon, receiving her trophy from the Queen, being feted on her return to San Diego by a downtown parade. In fact, the San Diegans had given her the horse she was riding. We demonstrated the facts at issue, we proved the damages and produced depositions and testimony from the Australian Davis Cup team captain Harry Hopman, U.S. impresario Jack Kramer and broadcaster Tom Harmon about her projected loss of future fortunes, at a rate of $50,000 to $75,000 a year. "There are few of us," I told the jury, "that are brushed by *the celestial fire*. Certainly this girl was." I told them to remember that fact when they began to calculate the award.

The jury remembered, partially, and awarded Maureen Connolly $95,000, a sum that seems small today compared to the millions already earned by the likes of a Billie Jean King or a Chris Evert, an amount that was relatively tiny, even then in 1955. Incredibly, the insurance-company attorneys appealed on two grounds: (1) that the award was excessive (they said at the trial that $5,000 might be more reasonable) and (2) that the judge had erred in one of his charges to the jury on contributory negligence. (The judge, they said, might have told the jury it could award Miss Connolly nothing if it found the accident was even partly her own fault. More incredibly, the District Court of Appeals in Southern California agreed and reversed the verdict.)

Outraged, we appealed that decision to the California Supreme Court. We argued that Maureen and her two companions had no chance at all to extricate themselves from danger. They were in jeopardy as soon as the truck appeared, for it was then that the horses started to rear; and dismounting in the face of an oncoming cement truck would have been more dangerous than staying on their horses. The truck driver, on his testimony, could have easily stopped, and didn't. We had a lot of trouble with the harsh, all-or-nothing rules that then prevailed on contributory negligence,* but we *did* prove the negligence of the cement company and its driver—and because of it the ruination of the girl's career. And what a career! "Since 1951," I wrote with some exasperation, "she has won every U.S. women's crown, and took her third straight British title at Wimbledon in mid-1954. She was the *only* woman ever to capture the American, British, French and Australian championships—and she did it in a single year. . . . She was the greatest woman tennis player the world has ever known."

The Supreme Court saw it our way. Maureen got the $95,000. "Hardly excessive," said the court. In 1955,

---

* Since the *Nga Li v. Yellow Cab* decision of the California Supreme Court in 1975, a new doctrine of "comparative negligence" has become the rule in California. In the past if a plaintiff was even partly at fault, he got nothing. Now he can recover at least some damages—in those areas where he was not at fault. Negligence of the plaintiff and defendant is *compared* and the plaintiff's award is reduced by the percentage of his negligence. Thus, the California Supreme Court, still the best in the land, has eliminated the inhuman, all-or-nothing standard that prevailed for years.

$95,000, tax-free, might add up to something like a half-million dollars now. But somehow that still seems low.

My divorce from Toni was a fait accompli. Herb Caen chronicled it in the *Chronicle*. "You can say I was over-matched," Toni said. I told Herb. "You can say I am through with women from here on out."

I was involved at the time in expanding my missionary activity. I had gotten my message across to my colleagues at law in *Modern Trials,* now I realized I would have to write a version of *Modern Trials* for the general public. I went through the same up-at-all-hours regime, the same heavy dictation, the same sacrifice in personal terms. On the whole, I'd rather have been home at night with friends. I had installed colored lights on the roof of my digs at 1228 Montgomery. Red meant that I was occupied and my friends better stay away; green meant that I was lonely and wanted company. But during this period, I never put the green light on at all. Well, almost never.

By the end of 1955, I had produced a popular work. *Ready for the Plaintiff,* which told people the truth about the so-called "personal-injury racket." If any private-interest group was enriching itself on a scale that could be called a "racket," it was the large casualty companies of America. They considered it ethical to keep from financial ruin a man who ran another down in his car but unethical for me to try and help the man he hit.

The New York Times gave me a good review in the Sunday book section. "Mr. Belli is brash, aggressive, unpleasant," wrote Jerome H. Spingarn, a Washington lawyer I had never met, "but not entirely wrong." Spingarn found the most pleasing thing about the book was "its author's exultation in his professional life." I was glad that came across. I love the law and I love my place in it.

One of the men who could understand how I felt was Roscoe Pound, dean of the Harvard Law School. We'd met through NACCA, I'd spoken to his students at Harvard (including Ralph Nader) and he liked me so much that when he came to San Francisco for a meeting of the American Bar Association he didn't want to stay in the convention hotel, he wanted to remain with me, so he could meet some real people. I invited about thirty San Francisco cops over for a barbeque and I didn't tell them who he was. He gave a little talk that began, "Law and order begins at the end of a policeman's billy," and when he was finished, the cops gave him an ovation that almost raised the roof.

The ABA discovered that Dean Pound was my guest and tried to get him to leave. But the dean said he was not only happy at my home, he liked it as much as any place he'd ever been. One night, a beautiful strawberry blonde came up to see me, but I was in the back of the house and didn't hear the doorbell, so Dean Pound answered in his pajamas and bathrobe. When I finally emerged, maybe an hour later, I found the girl sitting on the floor next to the dean's bed. He was discoursing on Henry VIII and the laws of Edward II and the Boston Red Sox's chances of winning the pennant and the success of the Marshall Plan in Europe, and she was absolutely fascinated.

After that, whenever I went back to Boston, I'd visit Dean Pound. I had introduced him to my "Pisco Punch" in San Francisco. Now, he took me to his club and introduced me to "Union Punch." Two drinks could knock an ordinary man on his ass. He'd go through six of them. One time, I called on him in Cambridge. His wife took me to his study and the old gentleman—he must have been more than eighty then—was sitting there in a big chair sound asleep with a cigar in the hand that was lying across his chest. He'd been reading, either a book by Sun Yat-sen which was on his right, or a comic strip, which was on his left. A ray of sunlight fell across his snow-white hair, and there was a long ash lying on his vest. It took a while for him to wake up. Like a 1917 Ford on a frosty 1957 morning. You could hear the nuts and bolts, kind of rusty, and the gears grinding. But once the engine got going, it was as smooth as a Rolls-Royce.

Of course I wasn't through with women. On my way to the Mo Connolly trial, I met and fell in love with a sweet stewardess, found out her name was Joy, last name Turney, which I soon changed to Belli. I was forty-eight, she was nineteen, and we were married in 1955, in the Lutheran Church in San Francisco. Soon, I would have another son and I would name him after my father and grandfather, Caesar. For me, it was another new beginning.

I had had a good year in 1955. I had concluded twenty-three cases since June, won all twenty-three of them, for a total of $1.6 million in jury verdicts or settlements, not a big year by my current standards, but a half-million-dollar income for a personal-injury lawyer set some precedents then.

Naturally, I'd rather remember the victories than the defeats. But I did lose one late in 1955. My friend Erle Stanley Gardner might have called it *The Case of the Reluctant Stud*. The stud's name was Otello, a champion, and a potent one. When Bill Stremmel first saw him at work on a breeding farm near Florence, Italy, he bought him on the spot. But the boat trip from Italy was too much for the elderly equine gentleman. By the time Bill had him stabled at his ranch near the Carquinez Bridge near Port Costa, Otello couldn't get it up with a derrick and into the willing receptacles of the fillies they brought to him. So Stremmel got a substitute stud to cover the mares and continued to put the colts down in the breeder's book as Otello's.

Racing is a gossipy business, and word does get around, particularly if the gossip concerns chicanery. Inevitably, the Jockey Club heard of the fraud and hauled Stremmel before them. I thought this was all pretty funny until Stremmel informed me that they wanted to revoke his trainer's license.

"Well," he said, "I didn't feel like I was doing anything crooked. It's just that—you're Italian and you'd appreciate this—I'd just hate like hell to put it down in the breeder's book that this Otello, this Italian stud, can't get a hard-on anymore." So Stremmel conned me with that and won me over. I agreed to plead his case before the Jockey Club and I went back to their headquarters in New York City with a fancy piece of demonstrative evidence: a can of recent color film, duly notarized as to the date, of Otello covering a mare at Stremmel's stables.

So I make the argument and inquire if we can show the film. The officials say that we can, but they ask us to come back on the following day. The reason for the delay is that their wives want to see the film, too. Apparently, these horsewomen all get pretty horny watching, and their husbands do not wish to allow an extra opportunity to go by. So we come back the next day and, before a roomful of people, we put up a screen and a projector and turn it on and we all settle down to watch Otello in action. First, they bring a younger stud to the mare and they tease her as he gets a big hard-on. Then, he rams it into the mare, and then they pull him off and bring on Otello, who has been watching from the sidelines and getting pretty horny himself. Otello covers the mare, and Bill Stremmel and I are feeling pretty good and enjoying the show when all of a sudden this kid with a Brooklyn accent—he was a groom fired by Stremmel some months before—pipes up, "Hey, dat ain't Otello."

So they stop the projector and reverse the film to get a front view of this horse on the screen compared with the description in the breeder's book and, sure enough, it ain't Otello. It is only a horse that looks almost exactly like Otello. This horse has a small star on his forehead. Otello has no star.

I packed up my briefcase, and the stuffed shirts at the Jockey Club ruled Stremmel off the track forever, because he had committed the unpardonable sin. He had corrupted the stud book, which is the sacrosanct genealogy that lies at the heart of thoroughbred racing.

"You didn't tell me about the groom," I said to Stremmel. I realized then I should have cross-examined my own client more thoroughly.

"No," said Stremmel. "I didn't."

"He was blackmailing you, wasn't he, Bill?"

"Yes," Stremmel admitted. "But I told him I couldn't pay him any more money."

Crimes, wills, divorces, racehorses, we've never specialized in any particular branch of the law, civil or criminal, trial or appellate work. I guess we're like the old country doctor, a general practitioner; but there was a time when I was afraid Bill Choulos and I were going to be labeled as specialists—in Mexican jail breaks! Indeed, *Time* and *Newsweek* so characterized us after two very famous jail breaks in that country.

Dyke Simmons, whom I'd never met before, called me prisoner to call outside, anywhere in the world. In fact, terrey. (It's a lot easier than one would imagine for a prisoner to call outside, anywhere in the world. In fact, I've gotten a number of calls from jails all over the United States, even some calls from prisoners on condemned row.) Dyke told me that his family would be getting in touch with me directly but that he had gone across the border from Texas into Mexico and within hours had been arrested for a triple murder. He was vehement about his innocence.

He told me that he had been going to Monterrey in his car on the highway at about the time and place the particularly brutal murders had been committed on the children of a very prominent Monterrey family. The Mexican police threw a dragnet over the whole Monterrey area and picked up any itinerant Americanos who had been there at the time of the murders. Dyke, along with a number of other Americans, was apprehended, thrown into jail and then, in a confrontation, brought before one of the children who was still barely alive. The child raised up and, so Dyke contended, more in delirium than in proper mental orientation, pointed at Dyke as "the man." The confrontation, under Mexican law, was illegal because in Mexico when a suspect is brought before a witness for identification there have to be a number of other suspects alongside from which he will be selected. Dyke was the only person brought before this witness.

Despite this deficiency in Mexico's own law, the police labeled him as the killer and after long and tortuous legal proceedings, most of which were held in the absence of the accused, Dyke was found guilty. He was sentenced to life in prison because Mexico, unlike its more *civilized* neighbor to the north and like all other South American countries, does not have capital punishment.

Dyke convinced me that I should visit him in the Mexican prison. It was an experience. I've visited in a number of South American jails where the family of the prisoner can come within the walls and be locked up at night with the prisoner. The children go to school in the morning from the prison, then go back to the prison.

The homosexual problem in the Mexican prison is

My mother, Leonie Mouron Belli, who scrubbed me constantly and dressed me in Little Lord Fauntleroy velvet suits, and my dad, Caesar Arthur Belli, the handsomest man I ever knew and the most competent.

My office building (arrow) on San Francisco's financial Montgomery Street—as it looked just after the great earthquake and fire of 1906.

On a trip to San Francisco in 1916, my dad and I "drove" an automobile. That was the Cliff House in the background.

In the early days we traveled out of Sonora, my hometown, by stagecoach. That's my mother riding "shotgun."

In 1929, just after college, I sailed around the world on a freighter. Here I am on leave in Hong Kong.

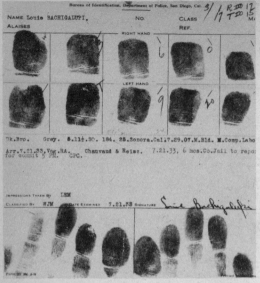

In 1933, with the country in a depression, I rode the rails as a hobo and got booked under the name Louie Bachigalupi by San Diego police.

When a cement truck hit Maureen Connolly and ended her tennis career, I sued and won her $95,000. But the money didn't bring her another Wimbledon title. (UNITED PRESS INTERNATIONAL)

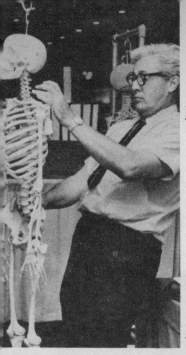

My skeleton Elmer became an integral part of my demonstrative evidence in trial after trial. For this, the press started calling me flamboyant. (TIME—TOBY MASSEY)

My old office on Stockton Street in San Francisco had the cluttered look of a place where a lot of work was done. Perched on my right: my pet parrot, Captain John Silver. (HAROLD LIPSET)

My client, Jack Ruby (center), my co-counsel, Joe Tonahill (left), and I were worried at the trial in Dallas of the man who killed the man who killed President Kennedy. (UNITED PRESS INTERNATIONAL)

Dallas was a nut house where only some of the nuts carried placards. But my expert witness, the renowned psychiatrist, Dr. Manfred Gutmacher, was used to nuts. (WIDE WORLD PHOTOS)

Because my client, Bernard S. Garrett, was weeping, I took over the reading of his statement before a U.S. Senate investigations subcommittee. (WIDE WORLD PHOTOS)

Here I met with two representatives of a California Indian tribe who were opposed to selling their land to the government for over twenty-nine million dollars. I went to federal court for them. (UNITED PRESS INTERNATIONAL)

In 1965 I successfully defended the rights of show girls to show what show girls show. Here I presided over a victory celebration in North Beach. The girls were always grateful for my help. (WIDE WORLD PHOTOS)

In 1969 I came to the defense of Winnie Ruth Judd, famed escaped trunk murderess in the 1930s, but a meek housekeeper when authorities found her decades later and tried to lock her up. (UNITED PRESS INTERNATIONAL)

Here's my friend Errol Flynn, flanked by my great and good friend Franka Faldini and myself. We were on film location off the French Riviera.

After hunting big game on the slopes of Mount Kilimanjaro, the great white hunter needed a bath. Not shown is the countess in the adjoining tub. I enjoyed the safari, but I didn't much care for shooting God's creatures.
(JOAN JONES)

Another beauty contest, this one on the plains of the Transkei, near Capetown, South Africa. Note how similar the smiles here are to those of the California contestants. (JOAN JONES)

Every trial lawyer ought to judge an occasional beauty contest. It's a civic duty, at the very least. Here, in a Miss California contest of the 1960s, the choice was agonizing, worse than picking a juror.

For cross-examining a conventional Scotch drinker in this ad for Glenfiddich appearing in THE NEW YORK TIMES, *I got into a lot of trouble with the California Bar.*

When the baseball Giants reneged on their promises to heat cold Candlestick Park, I sued for the price of my box seats. This headline in the CALL-BULLETIN *summed it up neatly.*

BELLI ASKS DOUGH OR WILLIE MAYS

But then the Giants wouldn't pay the $1,597. So I slapped a lien on Willie Mays, which made him my property—until Horace Stoneham paid me, in dollar bills.

I raise the Jolly Roger flag atop my building after a victory (and lower it to half-mast after a loss). I wonder why the Bar never brought charges against me for this.

Belli At Yale Runs True To Form

By JON OWEN
Register Staff Reporter

Melvin M. Belli, the lawyer who defended Jack Ruby, accused murderer of Lee Harvey Oswald, told a Yale audience Saturday that he felt like "Alice in Wonderland" during the trial of Ruby in Dallas.

"The only time that judge (Joe E. Brown) leaned over backwards," Belli said, "was when he was aiming at the spittoon behind the bench."

Belli spoke at the auditorium at the Yale Law School. The hall was filled to capacity and the students applauded consistently as Belli made his points against Texas.

A Question of Objectives

Belli, who spoke on the subject of "After Dallas, What?", said "I don't say it's wrong to smoke cigars of chew tobacco if you can hit the spittoon."

Referring to Judge Brown, Belli added, "If his aim at the law had been as good as his aim at that spittoon, I wouldn't have been in any trouble."

'Time To Speak Out'

Belli made news in Dallas after the Ruby trial when he charged that the proceedings resulting in conviction of Ruby came after a "kangaroo court" decision. The American Bar Association considered cancelling his membership because of the outburst at the conclusion of the trial.

Belli said of the outburst, "If ever there was a time for a lawyer to speak out, it was then."

Belli took issue with the handling of the Ruby trial, saying that it was a "lynching verdict."

Belli also castigated Dallas because it isn't a "melting pot form of society which has made cities in other parts of the country great," Dallas, Belli added, "is unique unto itself."

As for his "outburst" in Dallas, Belli stated that other lawyers "would have reacted a hell of a lot more than I did" regarding the Ruby verdict.

He insisted that the Ruby trial

Atty. Belli on way to preside at a Yale Law School mock trial. (Dietle Photo)

"wasn't a fair shake" in terms of American jurisprudence.

It took place, he added, "in a rich, powerful city . . . they get vindictive when you go against them." He indicated that "economic reprisals" are not unknown to Dallas.

When asked why he had been openly critical of Dallas even before the jury was selected for the trial, Belli replied that he had wanted "to put the eventual jurors on their mettle, to divorce them from the pervasive community spirit of hatred and bigotry."

He said that he feels the attitude of the city hasn't changed since the trial.

"I have my spies in Dallas too," he said, "and what they are reporting is depressing. First, they report economic reprisals against the few remaining tolerant citizens by Dallas insurance and publishing firms.

"They also have confirmed that Ruby is a depressive psychotic right now and is highly prone to commit suicide any day."

Solid Grounding

Before speaking on the subject of Dallas and the Ruby trial, Belli spoke on the importance of the common law in criminal proceedings.

"Know your legal history," he admonished the law students. "It is necessary to have a good grasping in the common law."

Belli, who is known as the "King of Torts" in his home city of San Francisco, made a volatile, articulate appearance at the Law School. Among the points he made were these:

—The prosecutor in Dallas made one of the "sloppiest" presentations Belli ever saw.

—There is a growing awareness in the United States legal circles of the concept of "trespass of personality."

—The "melting pot" of the country's great cities provides for an interplay between tolerance and intolerance which in turn pro-

(Please Turn To Page 2)

In 1949 my wife Betty Ballantine and I and our four children took a trip to Europe. From the left: Johnny, Jean, Suzie, and Rick. I never wanted a divorce, but Betty insisted, took the kids away, and changed their names to hers. (SAN FRANCISCO EXAMINER)

My second wife, Toni Nichols, and I spent our honeymoon in 1953 up in the High Sierras. Toni was a photographer and a damn good one.

My third wife, Joy Turney, brought our young son, Caesar, then six, to the Ruby trial in Dallas. Now nineteen, Caesar, a lawyer to be, has watched me try cases all over the world. (UNITED PRESS INTERNATIONAL)

Pat Montandon, a San Francisco beauty, and I went through a Shinto ceremony in Japan in 1966, but it was shortly annulled. Pat's a socialite now in the City and has recently written an entertaining non-fiction gothic romance. (WIDE WORLD PHOTOS)

My last wife, Lia, and our daughter, now three. The two of them got all dressed up for this portrait in my office. Lia's a protocol officer for the City, an official greeter.

Some say my office at 722 Montgomery Street looks like a gold-rush whorehouse, but actually it's a museum of my life and travels. San Franciscans love to gawk in the windows. And the Gray Line has the office on one of its tours.

I won several hundred thousand dollars for the families of the Soledad brothers, who were picked off and killed here in this prison yard. The sharpshooter shot the inmates dead right where I'm standing.

minimized. All of the homosexuals are put together in one wing, and in all the prisons I visited, that wing always the neatest, with well-swept floors and lace curtains at the windows, the inmates were the cleanest—shaved, lotioned, washed and bathed.

Every afternoon at four a number of women form a long line in front of the Monterrey prison gates. These are the prostitutes inspected by the government and given license to do business within the prison one day a week. Most prisoners in most prisons had their own "kitchens" and cooked their own food although there was a common mess.

Prisoners say the toughest thing about prisons is—and quite obviously—"doing time." But the communal atmosphere of the Mexican prisons 'makes it much easier to "do time." However, Dyke was sick of prisons when I visited him and set about to tell me of his plans for getting out. He told me he'd never had a sanity hearing and he said that he thought an electroencephalogram, a brain-wave tracing, would show that he had had brain damage somewhere in his past life.

I had become very friendly with the warden, particularly when I admired his chicken farm, which he maintained, with prison help, just outside the prison. Really, he did have some prize hens. I asked the warden if we could get an electroencephalogram of Dyke. From his response I gathered that the warden did not know the difference between an electroencephalogram and a seismic shooting for oil! However, I did explain to him what it was and the warden very helpfully suggested there was a neurologist, of sorts, in neighboring Monterrey who did have such a "machine." The warden said I could take Dyke to this doctor for the tracing.

I was amazed that a lifer would be allowed out of the prison for this diagnostic aid, but even more astounded when on the day of the appointment the warden let Dyke out of jail with one guard and me, in a taxi, to go to the doctor's office!

Dyke enjoyed the ride much more than I because the warden admonished me when I left the prison, "One of you must come back, either you or Dyke—I really don't care which, I just have to have an accurate count!" Dyke was already looking across the countryside, greatly enjoying his temporary liberty, which easily could be stretched to permanent status if he took off from me and the corpulent Mexican guard who sat half-asleep in the corner of the taxicab with a detached "I could care less" look about the whole venture.

We went to the doctor's office and in the back, under dirty, dusty sheets, was the electroencephalogram machine. It looked like a cross between an oil derrick and an Italian expresso contraption. However, the doctor assured me that it would work, but that I'd have to wait in the outer office, which was up at the other end of the building. I sat in the outer office along with the guard for approximately twenty minutes until the horrible thought came to me that Dyke, completely unguarded, could just as easily have hit the doctor over the head and gone out the open window that I'd noticed in the office. I rushed back to the diagnostic room, but my client was still there. I did not leave him after that. We returned him to the jail.

The electroencephalogram turned out "abnormal," but whether this was from the brain damage that Dyke had fancied or the huffing and puffing of the ancient machine, I'll never know. The Mexican appellate courts turned down my writ for release.

However, several months later Dyke was to leave prison without benefit of appellate review, and permanently. Guards and visitors brought their automobiles inside the prison yard and parked them while they were attending their rounds or visiting. One day Dyke got into the trunk of an automobile (he had dressed himself as a woman), and rode out of the prison undetected. He made his way to the border and then across, and showed up in Fort Worth, Texas. One of the young boys from my office who felt strongly that Dyke was innocent met him there, but, he assured me, he had nothing to do with his jail break.

The ending to this jail break was tragic. It wasn't more than six months after Dyke had escaped to the United States—where no effort was made by the Mexican government to extradite him, even if it could—that Dyke walked out of a bar and, while crossing the street, was run down by a speeding motorist and killed.

The other Mexican jail break was even more dramatic. Again, another telephone call from a Mexican *penitenciario*. It was Joel Kaplan. Joel told us enough to interest us in his case, and Bill Choulos and I flew to Mexico City, where we interviewed Joel in the prison. Joel had ample funds, and he was buying everything available in the prison, that is, he had a large, white room with a regular bed, a kitchen, and outside food sent in. Everyone was on his payroll. He lived like one of the mafia dons in the jail. Joel had been sentenced to life imprisonment as a result of a weird homicide in Mexico, in which someone had been killed; but the "someone" was still in doubt, as there were many witnesses who said he was still alive and back in the United States. The CIA definitely was involved, and Joel claimed that he had been framed by his family and the CIA.

We went to New York to see members of the family and found they were extremely wealthy and in charge of a trust fund of millions of dollars for Joel. The trust fund had a peculiar provision that the money would revert to him if he presented himself, in person, to the main office of the National City Bank in New York City. The first thing we did was to change the trust, with the consent of the bank, so that if Joel presented himself to the Bank of America, the branch one block from our office, in San Francisco, he could claim his money.

Choulos took a number of trips to Mexico City and we engaged an old-time friend of mine, who followed me in as dean of the International Academy of Trial Lawyers, the great Mexican jurist, Victor Velasquez. Victor did everything with ordinary and extraordinary writs to the hierarchy of Mexican courts, but to no avail.

Then Choulos and I, according to *Time* Magazine, came upon the brilliant idea of a jail escape by helicopter. This is simply not so. Joel did escape the prison by helicopter (the escape was the subject of a movie, Charles Bronson playing Joel in *Breakout*). The only legal advice we gave Joel was that in Mexico it's not a crime to escape from jail provided no force or violence or deadly weapons are used.

On the given day Joel was at a prearranged place in the exercise yard, and a helicopter flew in low, landed in the yard in the presence of all the startled guards and Joel and his friend clambered aboard and were whisked over the walls to freedom. The helicopter was painted with the insignia of the Mexican attorney general's office, and this was one reason apparently why the already astonished guards did not shoot. In any event, Joel did make his way to San Francisco, where he presented himself at our office one morning. We marched over to the Bank of America, asked to see the manager and I said, "You're holding three million dollars for my client, Joel Kaplan, and this is he. If you'll notice the terms of the agreement, we have but to present him and you are to turn over the three million dollars to him!"

The bank manager perused his copy of the agreement,

shook his head at first in disbelief, but then did pass over the three million dollars to us, but as reluctantly as any banker hates to part with any money—that's not his. Joel wrote all of this in his book, *Ten-Second Jailbreak*. He still comes in to see us regularly, but Bill Choulos and I emphatically deny that we are specialists in Mexican jail breaks.

CHAPTER FOURTEEN

Iron Lungs

In 1968, I published a two-volume work called *The Law Revolt*. It was a prolix treatise, but my point in that book, reduced to its essence, was this: for centuries, the few who knew how to use the law did so for their own profit, while the little people who thought they couldn't afford to play that game continued to be the objects of exploitation by their masters. Contrary to courthouse inscriptions, everyone didn't stand equal before the law. Law was for the rich, who got the protective bills they needed from legislators too prone to listen to the well-heeled. In 1927, for example, the State of California passed something called the California Criminal Syndicalism Act. The captains of the state's biggest industry, the agri-business, used that law for years to keep farm laborers from organizing for a living wage.

Now, I argued, the times were achanging. Many of the little people, the poor, farm workers, women, were gaining power hitherto denied them. And one of the ways they were gaining it (in fact, the only way) was through due process of law, an insistence on the enforcement of laws already on the books, the passage of new laws, the way we the people always intended the law to be, so we didn't need an armed revolution.

On the criminal side, the *Gideon* decision by the U.S. Supreme Court in 1963 (urged by a lawyer who took Gideon's case for nothing, Abe Fortas) opened up the protections of due process to everyone by spelling out the right of even the most indigent accused to the services of an attorney. If a man couldn't afford some one competent enough to forestall his being railroaded into jail by the State's attorneys, then the State had to pay and provide him with a lawyer.

This was a turn which was not only dramatic, but controversial, too. Anthony Lewis's book on the history of that case underlined the almost apocalyptic character of the decision: *Gideon's Trumpet.* On the other hand, some blasted the decision. To hear cops and cartoonists and J. Edgar Hoover tell of it, the *Gideon* decision "coddled criminals." And the *Miranda* and *Escobedo* decisions of the Warren Court, insisting a suspect be advised in advance of his rights, "put handcuffs on the lawmen." The outcry focused public attention, therefore, on the criminal law revolt.

The civil law revolt crept in more quietly. It was the same kind of rebellion, in essence, for it came as a recognition of the rights of the individual. Here, it was not the individual versus the power of the state. It was the individual versus the giant modern corporations: railroads, airlines, public utilities, banks, drug companies, packagers of food and cosmetics marketed for the masses. And the press didn't view this revolt in the same idealistic terms. All the press seemed to see was higher verdicts in favor of those who'd been done in by the giant corporations: more money. Nothing newsworthy about that. Personally, I think there's something as stirring about money as there is about freedom (in fact, money is freedom). But it's generally considered impolite to talk about it. Especially if you have lots of it.

But higher awards (I called them "Adequate Awards") had an effect of giving everyone a crack at life, liberty and the pursuit of happiness. Higher awards, shared contingently by the attorney who helped get the award, were the poor man's ticket to the courtroom, simply because now an attorney could afford to work "for nothing" on the chance he'd get one-third of an award that was now worth fighting for.

New case law helped the civil law revolt along. But the glare of publicity didn't focus too strongly on court decisions. Headline writers couldn't summon too much enthusiasm on a story dealing with the modernization of outmoded legal rules: A man in North Carolina got injured when his Corvair cracked up going around a curve. In the old days, he'd have had to sue General Motors in Michigan; now he could do so in North Carolina. "Big deal," said the editors. "Put it on page fifty-seven."

And when the courts started reversing the old (but not ancient) principle of caveat emptor, let the buyer beware, neither press nor public (nor many lawyers) foresaw the import. I myself didn't see all the implications of an early decision in this line—and it was my own case, *Escola v. Coca-Cola*, way back in 1944.

The *Escola* opinion was like one of those far-reaching integration decisions of the Warren Court, more a legislative act than a judicial one, inasmuch as it tried to enunciate some new legal guidelines that would bring greater justice to all the people. It was such a departure from the law we'd all been taught in school, however, that we could hardly believe our eyes.

As in so many landmark cases, the central figure in this case, Gladys Escola, was a humble individual, a waitress in a Madera restaurant, who started putting bottles

of Coca-Cola into the restaurant refrigerator one day and
had one of them explode in her hand, mangling it almost
irreparably. In the lawsuit, I claimed that I would have a
hard time proving *negligence* on the part of the Coca-
Cola Bottling Company of Fresno (and even if I could,
it would be far too costly to do so). I maintained that I
didn't have to. Instead, I relied on a common-sense doctrine lawyers call *res ipsa loquitur* (literally, the thing
speaks for itself), a doctrine that hadn't been overly used
in the law since medieval times, when they cut the sword-
maker's hand off with his own sword if the blade wasn't
any good. In essence, that doctrine meant that I didn't
have to prove any special negligence on the part of the
Coca-Cola Bottling Company, I could simply assume
there was something wrong somewhere if Coke bottles
started exploding in people's hands for no reason at all.
It wasn't fair to Mrs. Escola, I argued, simply to say this
was just a stroke of bad luck for her and that she couldn't
seek some reparation from the bottling company. Yet,
according to the way the law had been going ever since
the onrush of the industrial revolution, maybe she
couldn't collect a dime from anyone.

Why not? Because the law said that there had to be
some kind of a contract (implied at least) between Mrs.
Escola and the bottling company before she could ask
for damages. And there was no contract. This doctrine
(called privity) had the effect of making things easy for
industry. If people got poisoned by some of industry's
products or mangled using industry's machines, that was
just too bad. You couldn't stop progress, could you?

I argued that the time had come to change all that.
Manufacturers—even Coca-Cola Bottlers—ought to stand
behind their products. They had a general duty. If those
products didn't do what their makers said they would

or if they injured us during normal use, then the manufacturer should pay.

The California Supreme Court agreed with me, and Justice Roger Traynor wrote a special seminal opinion that went even further than I had hoped. He made a rational case for the principle of absolute liability—whether the manufacturer was particularly at fault or not, and his argument went far beyond anything strictly legal. In effect, he said that little people like Mrs. Escola shouldn't have to pay for an unlucky accident like hers. The logical one to pay for it was the fellow with the deepest pockets, who set the action up in the first place.

Traynor's opinion was a decision for the little people, entirely in accord with the winds of change that were blowing through the country—and the world. It was a time when people were becoming increasingly conscious that we were all brothers and sisters; that no one need be alone; that, acting in concert and in justice, we could all make life more worth living.

It wasn't until the mid-fifties, in a suit against Cutter Laboratories, that I tried to apply and broaden the principles enunciated in the *Escola* opinion.

How could I sue Cutter Laboratories? On the face of it, the Cutter scientists were heroes, Cutter was manufacturing a revolutionary new vaccine that would immunize an entire nation from the deadly effects of infantile paralysis, the disease that had crippled President Franklin D. Roosevelt. Suing Cutter was like suing Florence Nightingale.

As a lawyer, I had to do it anyway. To me, it didn't matter that almost 409,000 Americans had received the Cutter vaccine and hadn't contracted polio. The fact was that in a two-week period in the spring of 1955, 79 persons had been paralyzed because of something wrong in the Cutter vaccine. It was a wrong I had to right. I didn't care how much I delayed the vaunted program of FDR's sacrosanct National Foundation for Infantile Paralysis or how much of a threat I was to the future of medicine (as the president of another drug company, Eli Lilly and Company, was later to charge). In my kind of law, I worried most about individuals who had no defenses against the corporate juggernauts driving for profits and power.

Something, obviously, had gone wrong at the Cutter Laboratories in the inscrutable East Bay, and now some innocent little children were suffering the consequences. Whose fault was it? Who should pay? Little ponytailed Anne Gottsdanker, who was five and a half and would never run again? Or James Randall Phipps, thirteen months old when he had gotten his shots and now unable even to crawl? Or the heartsick doctors all over the country who had administered the ampules of vaccine to their patients with no knowledge that this miracle vaccine was somehow contaminated by a hidden enemy? Or the man who developed this vaccine in the first place, Dr. Jonas Salk? Or the people at the National Foundation for Infantile Paralysis and the National Institute of Health who had helped him do it?

No. I'd have to go after Cutter. They'd rushed the vaccine to doctors even before the government gave its final approval on April 12, 1955. Less than two weeks later, polio cases began to break out. Was it because of the vaccine? That's the way it seemed. On April 27, the Surgeon General of the U.S. telegraphed Cutter to take its vaccine off the market. Cutter did so. The other manufacturers put on the brakes, the National Institute of Health completed a two-week re-review of the whole program and then told all the other companies—except Cutter—that they could go ahead with their vaccines.

(Cutter never marketed a Salk vaccine again.) There was no doubt about it. An NIH report found that seventy-nine persons got polio from the Cutter vaccine.

Naturally enough, the parents of those children who contracted a permanent crippling disease from the Cutter vaccine consulted their lawyers. Their common sense made them ask, couldn't they sue someone? The government and the National Foundation and the medical profession and the press were all hailing this new wonder drug, urging everyone to undergo inoculation—and the stuff ends up giving their kids polio.

And another irony. Doctors got the vaccine first and gave it to *their* children. One told me he was listening to the news on his car radio. Came the flash that the vaccine was suspect. Chills and aches in the inoculated leg or arm. Trembling, he pulled over to the side of the road. His child had had a sore arm and fever that very morning—fourteen days after inoculation. The exact incubation time. All he could do was wait. There was no antidote and the child's whole blood couldn't be drained and exchanged. For a week he suffered. Then his child recovered. The doctor and his youngster were among the lucky ones.

Most lawyers thought they had a case—if some smart fellow could prove Cutter Laboratories was negligent. Some of the lawyers referred their wondering clients to me. Others, knowing I'd jump right in and do the early thorough investigation that was needed, sat back and waited to see how I'd proceed.

I am sure those lawyers who referred their clients to Belli didn't think these lawsuits would be easy. It is generally believed that tragedies must occur if science is to advance. For the sake of many, public opinion refused to condemn experimentation that might harm a few. And no one imagined that Cutter Laboratories would just come right out and confess what went wrong with the preparation of the vaccine at their labs. I never did discover the whole truth. Cutter Laboratories and the whole goddamn pharmaceutical industry covered up the facts effectively enough to prevent my proving to a jury's satisfaction that Cutter had been guilty of any wrongdoing (what is technically called *negligence*). But I was able to win the first two suits (on behalf of Anne Gottsdanker and Randy Phipps) by proving that Cutter had sold a vaccine that was harmful in its end result and had therefore breached something that lawyers call *"warranty."* It was the application, at last, of Justice Traynor's concurring opinion in my early *Escola v. Coca-Cola* decision, and it was better than proving negligence, because the decision helped affirm new public policy that led to consumer crusades across the land. If there is one legal decision upon which Ralph Nader built, this is it!

"Warranty? How you going to sue on that?" asked Lou Ashe. We were holding a strategy session at Jack's Restaurant in San Francisco. Jack's, not far away from my present office, used to be a brothel, and some of the finest waiters in America preside over its private upstairs dining rooms. These rooms provide just the right mixture of aromas and atmosphere conducive to serious conversation. Bernard Witkin, also from Boalt Hall, friend and a great legal scholar with hundreds of books to his credit, was there, too. Bernie agreed with Ashe. "The law of warranty applies to a sale," said Witkin, "not a service. You have it in foods. But not yet in drugs."

Witkin was right—at that time. I knew the legal precedents. The old law of warranty held that there had to be a contract between seller and buyer before the seller was liable; the concept of privity, mentioned earlier. Here it applied to the druggist who sold the drug but not to the manufacturer. We didn't think that was right. At least, that's the way we decided to argue. Maybe—it was just a hunch—the courts were ready to apply the concurring opinion in *Escola v. Coca-Cola*. The time was now ripe, I believed.

But—as Ashe and Witkin pointed out—we couldn't proceed in such an important lawsuit on my hunches alone. (There were seventy-seven other victims of the bad Cutter vaccine depending on our two pilot cases to give them direction.) So we decided we'd go ahead with a double-barreled attack on Cutter, concentrating in the trial on Cutter's *negligence* and laying what common-sense groundwork we could to win on breach of *warranty* in the appeal.

I think we proved negligence all right—though not so well as we might have today, when the courts insist that adversaries disclose much more to each other in advance than they did twenty years ago. Even so, we did some good detective work. Cutter Laboratories wouldn't tell us anything. In fact, they did their best to hide what they had. So we went to Dr. Jonas Salk, who was helpful—up to a point.

Salk said it wasn't the recipe, it was the cooks. Well, we could have figured that. Five other companies weren't having any problems. Only Cutter. But then Salk gave us an instant education, told us in meticulous detail how he and the colleagues in his Pittsburgh laboratory produced their polio vaccine. They grew live polio virus in flasks containing kidney tissue from rhesus monkeys, harvested the live virus, filtered it, then inactivated it by progressively adding formaldehyde to the virus solution under a controlled temperature of 37 degrees Centigrade—until there were apparently no *live* virus elements remaining. There were, of course, some virus *elements* still present; otherwise the vaccine would have had no antigenic properties. It would be useless. Like all vaccines, the Salk vaccine gave a person a little bit of harmless, controlled polio that immunized him against an attack of the real thing.

Salk's basic problem in making the vaccine: knowing when to stop the inactivation process so that it would cook long enough to produce a safe vaccine but not so long that it would render the vaccine impotent. Salk solved this problem by making continuing tests of the virus solution during the inactivation process. Five times during the process, he would extract some of the solution from the batch and perform a tissue-culture (or titration) test. He and his colleagues did so by injecting some of the viral solution into a culture of monkey kidney tissue and then noting what percentage of the kidney cells were progressively killed. They would proceed to plot the results on graph paper. If there was any departure from a *constant* rate of kill, Salk would know that the process had gone awry. If the tissue-culture tests revealed a constant rate of kill, however, there would be a straight line on the graph and Salk could *predict* that the same kill rate would continue even after it was no longer possible to detect the presence of live virus by the titration tests. The postulated result gave Salk the hoped-for margin of safety he felt necessary working with such a potentially hazardous vaccine. To establish this safety, Salk said, a *single* negative test wasn't enough. There might still be some deadly polio virus lurking in the solution. To be absolutely safe, he said, he needed a *sequence* of negative tests. This was his safety key.

"If Cutter produced some bad vaccine," said Salk, "my guess is that they weren't following my straight-line theory."

"But how do we confirm your guess?" we asked.

Salk shrugged. "Cutter has to have records, protocols."

"A kind of lab diary?" said Ashe.

"Yes."

"We'll try to subpoena those," I said.

"In the meantime, maybe you have another line of inquiry open to you," Salk said. "In the April crisis, when the government held all the polio vaccine off the market for a time, it tested samples of every manfacturer's lot. The government let the others go ahead—and held back Cutter's. Why? Obviously because the tests showed Cutter's vaccine was bad—or that some of it was bad. Maybe you can get the results of those tests."

We got them, much much later, by court order and after the trial had already begun. Before the trial, the government provided little help. Too often, a so-called regulatory agency is more concerned with protecting an industry than with acting as a public advocate. Here, the National Institute of Health's Laboratory of Biologics Control threw a cloak of secrecy over its entire stewardship. One of my partners, Dick Gerry, went to Bethesda, Maryland, and returned empty-handed. Ashe smiled and pulled an important-looking piece of paper out of his pocket. "Maybe we'll just have to help ourselves," he said.

"What's that?"

"One share of Cutter stock," Ashe said. "It is mine. As a stockholder, I am going to the meeting tonight to offer a resolution that the company not only turn over all the records to us but explain them as well."

And he did, too. Oddly enough, the stockholders voted him down. If it made money, the stockholders didn't care *how*.

It wasn't until the trial began—months later—that we finally got the Cutter Lab records we were looking for. We did so by calling Dr. Walter Ward, Cutter's medical director, to the witness stand and letting the judge, Thomas J. Ledwich, see the shape of the Cutter defense (which, as far as I could see from preliminary encounters with the Cutter principals, consisted of three parts denial and one part not remembering).

Finally, it became obvious to Judge Ledwich that if there were records available, why try to remember what they said? Why not bring them to court? The judge turned to Cutter's counsel, Wally Sedgwick, an insurance stalwart. "Have the records here at nine-thirty in the morning," he ordered.

At last, the records. Now we were able to tell just how Cutter had cooked its vaccine—and whether Cutter had been following the recipe. The records showed Cutter hadn't. We saw the protocols for each batch and noted that the lab technicians had not followed Dr. Salk's method. Randy Phipps and Anne Gottsdanker had been inoculated from Cutter Lot Number 19764, and it was clear from the protocols, written in Dr. Ward's own hand, that Cutter hadn't performed the five tissue-culture tests recommended by Dr. Salk. Furthermore, a history of the vaccine production at Cutter showed that as Cutter proceeded to manufacture the vaccine, it was getting poorer and poorer results. It produced twenty-eight lots of vaccine. Ten of these were bad. Five of the last seven were bad. *Something was wrong.* In producing Dr. Salk's vaccine, Cutter was ignoring Dr. Salk's methods.

When I got Dr. Ward back on the stand, I asked him about Cutter's inconsistent results. (In at least one instance, Cutter had produced good vaccine which would make a person immune from each of the three types of polio, then, after mixing the three vaccines into one polyvalent pool, found that it tested positive: some dangerous live virus was still remaining.) With such inconsistent results, Cutter should have put on the brakes. Instead they rushed to the marketplace with the vaccine. "Do you mean to tell the jury," I asked Dr. Ward, "that you put out the vaccine not knowing what the word *consistent* meant?"

"Yes," said Dr. Ward, "and as far as I know, everyone else did, too." (This would be the heart of the Cutter defense: *everyone* was ignoring Salk's recipe. But everyone wasn't.)

"Didn't that prove to you one of two things?" I asked. "One, that your tests were not accurate, or two, the way you were manfacturing was wrong?"

"Well," Dr. Ward said, "I can't answer your question. Something odd, or something was going on which scientifically you couldn't explain."

"You knew, then, in some of your tests—one-third of them, in fact—you were getting live virus, and that 'something odd was going on,' to use your words. Either these tests were not good or your manufacturing was not following the Salk process?"

"I just can't answer that question," replied Cutter's medical director.

Dr. Ward could answer most of the questions, though. To some questions, he gave both yes and no answers. What the hell else could he do? Lot Number 19764 tested out negative, and Cutter sent ampules of it all over the country. But Anne Gottsdanker and Randy Phipps took injections from that lot and came down with polio. (Thank God, thousands of others did not get polio. The experts said they did not contract the disease because they already had some kind of immunity to polio.) There was no doubt about that: Anne and Randy's symptoms appeared exactly twelve days after inoculation, and their paralysis took hold first in the precise anatomical areas where they received their shots. Even Dr. Ward conceded that. I asked him, "It is your opinion presently that there was live virus in the lot with which Anne Gotts-danker was inoculated and with which James Phipps was inoculated?"

"That would be my best opinion, yes," Ward responded.

Could you fault Cutter for marketing vaccine containing live virus? I could. The jury might have—except for a constellation of scientific stars, virologists, immunologists and serologists, who testified that Dr. Salk was not necessarily right and that, if he was, then, in any event, Cutter was not violating any of the minimum standards set by the U.S. Government. The government witnesses who rushed to Cutter's defense admitted that their minimum standards didn't pretend to prescribe a particular manufacturing process, and Dr. Howard J. Shaughnessy, an adviser to the U.S. Public Health Service, admitted on cross-examination that if he had known that one-third of Cutter's lots were turning out bad, he wouldn't have recommended licensing the vaccine. (He gave no excuse why he didn't know.)

Cutter didn't tell us who their defense witnesses would be. In those days, the defense didn't have to reveal this information before trial. But after we'd finished putting on our case, I noticed a lot of flashbulbs popping in the corridor and learned that Wally Sedgwick was out there introducing one of his star witnesses to the press. It was Dr. Wendell Stanley, a Nobel Prize winner. It took Sedgwick half a day to run through all of Dr. Stanley's degrees and honors and associations and another half a day for Dr. Stanley to snow the jury with his tales about viruses, which, he said, are "almost like crystals." You don't know, he told the jury, whether the crystals are living or dead, they can procreate, they have "a personality." Jesus, the jury was spellbound.

That night, I phoned my NACCA colleague in Chicago, Leo Karlin, and asked him about Stanley. Then Karlin got on the phone to Washington and talked to another NACCA buddy, Dr. Paul Cantor, who discovered that Stanley had testified before a crash committee of the Congress on the vaccine. Early the next morning, Cantor read me a transcript of the hearings. When a congressman had asked Dr. Stanley about the polio vaccine, Stanley had said, "I know very little about polio. My work has been with the tobacco virus. If you want to know anything about polio vaccine, I would refer you to Dr. Jonas Salk." On cross-examination, I confronted Dr. Stanley with this statement: Here he was in court shilling for Cutter and bad-mouthing Dr. Salk. What about his congressional testimony? The great Dr. Stanley could only sputter on that one.

But the cumulative effect of all these expert witnesses for the defense put the jury into something of a quandary. Sedgwick even had someone from the NIH testify that he and his team had investigated the Cutter operation and state flatly "there was no negligence." When Fred Cutter took the stand, he painted a pretty little picture. The Cutter Laboratories was just a little country store that he and his brother and mother had founded. He was behind the counter, and Mrs. Cutter was rolling the little pills and putting the sugar coating on them so they wouldn't be bitter for the baby and another Cutter was going out into the woods and gathering the medicinal berries. For a while there, we thought we were looking at the family of Daniel Boone, making elderberry wine for salvation and for society.

On cross-examination, I tried to cut through that bullshit. "Now, let me see," I said, going to the blackboard and drawing a genealogical chart. "There's Papa Cutter and Mama Cutter and there's one son, Fred Cutter. But there's another Cutter. Henry Cutter. Who's he?"

Fred Cutter said, "Oh, that's my blind brother."

And so I wrote down the name of Henry Cutter, and under his name I put "blind brother." I asked, "By any chance, was he in charge of testing?" The jury liked that. They laughed with me. And then they saw another Fred Cutter, because, at that point, he completely changed character on the stand and became the sophisticated, sharp-tongued, accurate-speaking entrepreneur that he really was.

But my cross-examination of Cutter was only a diversion. Before I had gotten deeply involved in the case, I was afraid I couldn't prove that Cutter was guilty of negligence (or, rather, that no Oakland jury could bring itself to convict their hometown industry). After I learned what Cutter did (and did not do), I was damn sure Cutter was negligent and went all out to prove that charge to the jury. But it was a mistake. In trying to prove negligence, I gave Cutter an opportunity to show how careful they were in many other ways. And that took the edge off our victory. For victory it was: the jury came in with a verdict of $131,500 for the Gottsdanker girl and $15,800 for the Phipps boy, whose paralysis was far less severe—but not on negligence. They found against Cutter on breach of *warranty*. So the new law.

The jury had decided Cutter breached its warranty, and in its appeal Cutter had to fight that decision. I was glad. Now, in the appeal brief, I could concentrate on warranty and drive its new use home. If the appeals court upheld this principle, we would try the other Cutter cases on warranty alone, and better yet, we would make a fantastic step forward in the field of warranty law. "This is not going to be a simple brief," I told Ashe and Gerry. "This is going to be an outline of new warranty law. It is going to change the face of the legal map. We'll have thousands of them printed, ship them to law libraries and law offices and courts all over the world." They agreed. There was no doubt about it. We had made law. For both in the judge's instructions and the jury's verdict, we had jumped the traditional barrier of privity—there didn't have to be a "contract" between the person getting the vaccine and the drug company. And no one noticed that we had done so.

Well, almost no one. The big drug companies took note and vigorously joined in the lawsuit at the appeals stage. The Pharmaceutical Manufacturers Association, the American College of Physicians and the American Pharmaceutical Association all filed "friend of the court" briefs defending Cutter. For this, I was grateful, because out of their own self-interest these friends of the court had to argue my strongest point.

The brief of the American Pharmaceutical Association claimed, in Cutter's defense, that the pharmaceutical industry had been subjected by our lawsuit to "the danger of becoming the victim of its own excellence." What the industry was saying—rather insouciantly, I thought—was that "if you are the one person in a million who gets a bad result from our drug, it means there's something wrong with you, not us, and therefore we owe you nothing."

I felt the opposition was jumping up and down on the weakest branch of the tree. The chances were slim that any appeals court judge had a child who had contracted polio from a Cutter shot or knew someone who did. But the big boys helping the defense were saying, "This can happen with any drug." *Any* drug? That was diferent. That could only help our appeal. The very thing that had cost us a negligence verdict—the very weight of the big boys on Cutter's side—was turning now to our favor. The big boys didn't know when to quit.

Why should Parke-Davis, which had marketed only effective Salk vaccine, scream now on Cutter's behalf? Because, they were arguing, they didn't want to bear the future consequences of the Cutter verdict—the notion that a drug company could be liable to pay damages even though they were "without fault." In fact, while our case was before the appeals court, the Pharmaceutical Manufacturers Association called several press conferences and issued news releases warning the general public what dire things would happen if we won the appeal. E. N. Beesley, president of Eli Lilly and Company, told one group of reporters, "The suggestion that the pharmaceutical industry should be subjected to the doctrine of liability without fault is a novel and shocking concept. In my opinion, its imposition would be a threat to the future of medicine and to the welfare of the people." And then he made a threat: acceptance of that novel principle "would delay and even prevent the introduction of many life-saving medicines." He asked, "Who could afford to pioneer in pharmaceutical research? Who would dare to try anything new if it could mean undeserved ruin of their company?"

For the record, the appeals court upheld our side on warranty. The court backed our argument that the marketing of polio vaccine was a sale, not a service; we weren't suing the doctors for administering the vaccine. They didn't mix the stuff, they simply took a sterile hypodermic needle, drew the entire contents from a sealed ampule and injected it into their patients. The doctors, in fact, trusted Cutter implicitly—just as the public did. In effect, the appeals court endorsed the novel idea of liability without fault and, as a result, *Time* Magazine's law section said this was "easily the most spectacular development in modern tort law—the most potent new weapon aimed at making business safeguard consumers."

I had started out to prove *warranty*. The court went *beyond* my contentions and held on *"absolute liability"* or "liability without fault."

The decision didn't hurt business *or* consumers. Since then, the pharmaceutical industry has gone ahead with their pioneering medicine—to the health of the public and, I must add quietly, the swelling of their own purses.

Cutter's attorneys had claimed that unless our breach of warranty verdict was overturned, neither the Cutter Laboratories nor any other pharmaceutical manufacturer could obtain liability insurance—and they'd be forced out of business. Not true, I countered. Practically everyone in these times could and did buy absolute liability insurance: manufacturers, wholesalers and retailers; drugstores; restaurants; hotels; grocery stores; meat markets; candystores; fish grottos; cigar stores; soda fountains; sandwich vendors; even hot-dog stands and nuclear power plants. Cutter itself had liability insurance, twice as much as it then needed to settle every "Cutter incident" filed. If Cutter's report to the appeals court was honest, then its report to its own stockholders (Lou Ashe included) was dishonest.

In Cutter's 1956 Annual Report, the company assured stockholders that the polio-vaccine suits would not reach beyond the first two layers of insurance. And in its 1958 Annual Report while our judgment was still on appeal, Cutter told stockholders that its contingent liabilities would not result in any significant financial liability in relation to the net assets of the company and its subsidiaries.

So the appeals court affirmed our judgment. Cutter then appealed to the California Supreme Court, but by then we knew where we were. Our answer before the Supreme Court was short, but it was all warranty. We thundered about it, we roared about it and we practically ignored the negligence aspect. The Supreme Court of California refused to review the case. The verdicts stood. On that basis, we (and our colleagues in the law) were ready to take on some of the other Cutter cases—on warranty or absolute liability alone.

I got a letter from one lawyer with a Cutter case pending in San Diego, David S. Casey, now the president of the California Bar Association—one of the few plaintiff's lawyers to achieve that position. "To my mind," wrote Casey, "this is the greatest single blow for justice that has ever been struck by any lawyer and to you must go the satisfaction of having almost singlehandedly produced some relief for these poor unfortunates who ten years ago would have received no compensation."

We got a phone call from Los Angeles. There was a boy there named Brian May who lived in an iron lung. He had been given Cutter vaccine, then a paralysis set in that affected everything except the mind of Brian May —which was decidedly superior. Would we try the case? We would. On warranty alone. For almost three years, we had labored to make new law. Now, we would ride the course of the law we'd made. Warranty. You stand behind your product. If 999,999 people trust and buy your product, you take their money. If one person trusts and buys your product, you take his money, too. If your product benefits those 999,999, that is as it should be. If your product hurts that one, then by God you had better make it good to him the best way you can— because he trusted you to stand behind your goods.

Since this was the way the law was going (the law was not standing still then, and it isn't standing still today), Cutter turned to something rather desperate. Brian May was so bright that Cutter's attorneys could have claimed, citing other crippled geniuses of the past, that Brian's useful life and contribution to mankind were actually not impaired by his physical ailment. For some weird reason they didn't take this approach. (Perhaps they were deterred by the spectacle of a movie I put on in the courtroom—*A Day in the Life of Brian May*—a straightforward cinematic representation of what life was like for an eleven-year-old boy in an iron lung.) What they did was a far uglier thing. They had a doctor get up on the witness stand and say that Brian didn't have polio at all.

That made me angry. When I realized what the doctor was claiming I could hardly believe my ears. By the time I rose to my feet to begin my cross-examination, I was nine feet tall and I was Clarence Darrow and Louis Pasteur and Albert Einstein all wrapped in one. Dick Gerry said later that my performance that day was "the greatest cross-examination I ever saw." When I finished with that doctor, finished slamming, riddling and destroying his pandering presentation, I knew I'd won for Brian May. The judge, a man never noted for his sadism, was grinning. I think he thought the doctor deserved everything I gave him.

And I guess the jury agreed. The jurors came back from their deliberations and awarded the mother of the injured boy the amount of $75,000. And for Brian May, they found damages in the amount of $600,000. It was, up to that time, the highest personal-injury award in history. Today, that verdict would easily have gone $6 million or more.

Did it break Cutter? Hell, no. All the suits against Cutter ultimately ended up costing the drug manufacturer $1.1 million above and beyond the $2 million the company had in insurance coverage. But by 1963, Shields and Company, a member firm of the New York Stock Exchange, recommended the purchase of Cutter stock "for substantial long-term capital gains." Despite its bad experience with the Salk vaccine, Shields and Company said that Cutter had intensified its research efforts with great success. Cutter discovered a chemical compound that doctors could use in the treatment of mental illness, an antispasmodic for ulcers and a superior local anesthetic particularly useful to urologists and dentists. In a joint effort with Parke-Davis, Cutter was working on a product to dissolve clots in the bloodstream. And, on its own, Cutter had developed (and was ready to market) a live measles vaccine. Company profits, Shields and Company reported, had risen from $26 million in 1961 to a record $29 million in 1962.

And wouldn't you know it? Lou Ashe still had his original share of Cutter stock.

I tried to apply the doctrine I'd established in *Cutter* to cigarettes and cancer. At one time, in the 1960's, I had seventeen cases pending against the biggest cigarette manufacturers in the country—for I believed (as did my clients who were dying of various respiratory ailments) that not only was cigarette smoking harmful to one's health but that the manufacturers had an absolute liability in tort and ought to stand behind their product. Some of my friends in the plaintiff's bar believed as I did; we thought that it was only a matter of time before one of us could prove legally what we thought we already knew scientifically. A victory here could change medical history. With a clear precedent to sue on behalf of others who had gotten cancer from smoking cigarettes, the cigarette companies would have had to start pouring some of their excess profits into cancer research. By now, maybe we'd know the cause of cancer.

Unfortunately for our clients (and for us), we won none of the cases. In the few that we tried in court, we couldn't convince the jurors that the cancer victims didn't bring the cancer on themselves. No one forced them to smoke. If they got cancer why should the manufacturer pay? Federal Judge Herbert W. Christenberry of New Orleans put it this way when we discussed the matter in chambers: "Mel, you get what you buy. When you buy a pack of Luckies, you get smoke. I know you say you can get cancer, but I say you get smoke. If that has a side effect, that's tough luck. If I let you get by with this, then pretty soon you're going to be suing Elsie the Borden cow for giving too much cholesterol or Jack Daniels for giving you cirrhosis of the liver."

That was a major test case, *Lartigue v. Reynolds Tobacco Company*, and I had as my co-counsel one of the best trial lawyers in America and one of my closest friends, a former Louisiana legislator everyone called "The Kingfish." The late Senator H. Alva Brumfield was red-bearded, portly, with an eloquence overlaid by the accents of the bayou that won him some judgments that are a legend in the South.

Lartigue v. Reynolds came to a premature (and disastrous) conclusion when Brumfield's investigator put his bright, eager (but untried) sister in charge of looking into the potential jurors' background. She went right to the veniremen and asked them everything but their underwear size. The information *was* helpful; but we'd almost finished picking the jury when one of the jurors seemed compelled to tell the judge that someone had phoned him and asked him what brand of cigarettes he smoked.

I jumped right up and said, "Judge, those cigarette companies again. Now they're tampering with our jury." The judge took us into chambers, brought in lawyers from the U.S. Attorney's office, the FBI and, of course, the opposing attorneys for Reynolds. I let them have it. I said that anyone tampering with the integrity of a

Southern jury should be sentenced to the chain gang. After my diatribe, an FBI man marched our investigator into chambers, and she proceeded to tell the whole sordid story. The judge declared a mistrial—and I was lucky *I* didn't have to march in a chain gang.

The case was tried later and went for a defense verdict—which means we lost this one. But I have others of this kind pending all over the United States. Eventually, to the great good of mankind, I'll win one. That's the kind of practice I have.

The next case I tried with the Kingfish had a happier outcome. It was in Anchorage, Alaska. A young man named Jones had had a horrible accident working on the railroad. The railroad people should have settled the case right away. Instead, they got cute. They hired two private investigators named Kraut and Schneider who went to the extraordinary length of traveling all the way to Oklahoma and taking surreptitious films of a man they thought was my client, Tom Jones, unloading a truck, riding horseback, swimming and diving in a public pool and square dancing on a Saturday night. Only it wasn't Tom's activity they were filming. It was his twin brother, Bill. When Tom told us that story, the Kingfish and I knew how we could use it to advantage.

We just sat back and let the other side put on their movies and then stipulated that a man who could do those things (and ask for compensation) was a phony and a fake and entitled to nothing more than a horse whipping. On the other hand, we said, if our client was telling the truth, then he should get an award, and a good one, because the railroad that could afford to send a film crew to Oklahoma obviously had a lot of money to spend.

Then we called Bill Jones—our client's twin brother—as a witness, and he convinced the federal judge (there was no jury) that he was the star of those movies, not

his brother! The judge was furious—and then happy to
see how I made Kraut and Schneider squirm on the stand.
The judge gave us $160,000 on that one—an all-time-
high verdict in Alaska.

We celebrated by going fishing with Bailey Bell, the
Anchorage lawyer who brought us up there for the case.
We loaded up a private plane with cases of beer and Rus-
sian vodka for our hosts in Kotzebue, who were Eskimos
and couldn't get booze then, legally. We got the whole
town drunk. They closed up everything; guys were falling
into the fire they were so drunk. Then we got into this
little, single-engine plane with a door that was fastened
by bailing wire and went fishing. We flew over a mountain and hit a snowstorm (this was early fall, as I recall)
and landed as soon as we could, right on the pebbly beach
of a pristine stream. "You're not going to fish in there,"
I said to the pilot. "The stream's full of rocks and moss."
The pilot just laughed. The "rocks" and "moss" were
Dolly Varden trout and the stream was full of them. We
had no bait, no flies. We just used bits of red flannel on
a barbed hook and the trout fought one another to get
caught. Inside of a half hour we had five burlap potato
sacks full of Dolly Vardens. We brought them back to
the Eskimos—coming back to life after their binge. They
just grunted at the fish and threw them to the dogs, who
ate them. The Eskimo gal that the pilot was courting explained that ten-pound Dolly Vardens were all too
common to excite her townspeople. "You got any more
vodka?" she asked.

CHAPTER FIFTEEN

Red Velvet

I am not sure when they started making my office a stop on the Grayline Tours of San Francisco, but it seemed like a natural thing for them to do. The office was a bistro about one hundred years before I bought it in 1959, right after the Cutter case. Exquisite Lotta Crabtree, a chanteuse celebrated in more than one tale of San Francisco's Gold Rush days, sang there. The building next door, 728 Montgomery, which I also bought, had an even richer past. That's where Bret Harte wrote "The Luck of Roaring Camp" in the 1850's. It was the birthplace of the first Masonic Lodge in California and a home, in turn, for dealers in gold bullion, a Spanish newspaper, a mining company, an antique shop and a puppet theater. But neither building made the Grayline Tours until I arrived.

I called 728 "Caesar's Annex" (after my father and grandfather, Caesar Arthur Belli, and for my son, Caesar) and 722 "The Belli Building" and had them both restored to what I imagined they were (or should have been) during the City's pioneer days. We found to our surprise that the buildings were floating on redwood rafts—no other foundations, just a network of redwood planks, six to eight inches thick, twelve to eighteen inches wide, and crisscrossed to a depth of eight feet. When we sank the elevator shaft, we found tidal water rising and falling in it. Though we were now some eight blocks from the Bay, we still had Bay tides right inside our building. We left the floating foundation as we found it. We also let stand the pillars supporting the inside of the building—they were made of turned ships' masts—and some of the heavy ceiling beams and the outside cast-iron pillars that had come from New Orleans. I had the floors and the walls sandblasted back to the honest wood and fire-red brick that lay beneath aged layers of paint and plaster. I also left room for a brick courtyard open to the sky, put in a decorative pool and filled the yard with staghorn ferns and leafy rhododendrons, chrysanthemums, azaleas, camellias, poinsettias and salvia. In front, I installed a giant wrought-iron gate hammered in New Orleans, then painted black the cast-iron frames running around the tall blue-tinted windows. Below the windows I affixed black flower boxes filled with pink-blooming ivy geraniums and planted lots of Virginia creeper that soon ran up the building's facade where a small shingle reads "MELVIN M. BELLI LAWYER."

I took the front office, looking level out on Montgomery Street, so I could see passersby, so they could look at me. Inside, I installed a huge fireplace, mahogany bookshelves floor to ceiling, a window seat, a solid mahogany bar, almost as wide as the room, which had come around the Horn and served the thirsty citizens of Sonora (including my father) at Ellsbee's Saloon until I brought it to San Francisco. I had the high white ceilings trimmed with gold and an occasional gold cherub and my coat of arms and hung an old four-bladed wooden fan that groans as it whirls in-between four crystal chandeliers.

I furnished the room in red velvet drapes and mostly

Victorian pieces. One small desk is a Wells Fargo original. An old rolltop came from the Bank of America. An ancient safe "Made by the American Safe Company" was a bequest from one of San Francisco's most effulgent madams. I filled the room with velvet upholstered chairs and banquettes and covered the library ladders reaching to the ceiling with more red velvet.

It was then that I began bringing home souvenirs. I was an eclectic with a taste for everything. Everything, every kind of clock and bottle and book caught my fancy, local menus and recipes, native tools, pinball games, flutes and pipes and ceremonial hats. Nothing human was beyond my interest. The office became a museum of man—and of myself. Those who peek in today might see:

A very defunct armadillo, gift of Joe Tonahill, from Jasper, Texas. The statue of a Swiss madonna, adorned with a copper bracelet from the Congo and topped with an ostrich plume from South Africa. Three old U.S. passports, their accordian inserts extended and covered with the entry stamps of dozens of countries. A picture of Queen Victoria (on the label of a bottle of Bombay Gin). Dozens of apothecary jars from my grandmother's drugstore in Sonora, many of them filled with mysterious liquids, one of them with Grandma Mouron's remedy for malaria and one plainly labeled "The Great Gonorrhea and Gleet Remedy, Prepared Only by Penn Drug Co., Inc. of San Francisco, Price $1.50." A cuckoo clock from the Black Forest. A campaign sign circa 1905: "George H. Cabbanis for Superior Judge," hung at an angle so I can tell tell visitors the judge wasn't as crooked as his picture.

Demon masks from Katmandu, and a buffalo hide from Nigeria. A certificate appointing me as attorney general of E Clampus Vitus, an historic fraternity of the Gold Rush days, signed by Emperor Norton I. A large wooden box secured with a padlock, inscribed "Jury Box No. 1," from Anaconda, Montana.* An antique barber chair. A skeleton named Elmer whom I have been known to take to court. A plaque bearing my coat of arms, done in fun one day with the help of my then less-than-sober partners: the words REX TORTIUS (King of Torts) over a shield and

* Like all the items in my office, this one has a history. Montana was the so-called "treasure state," but no one there had ever seen a personal-injury award (despite the horrible catastrophes in the mines) of more than $30,000. Montana's awards were horrendously low. I took it as a personal challenge to raise the ante there. I did it with the Ridgeway case.

Bill Ridgeway had been tending his little ice-cream store in Anaconda one day and kind of watching out the window at the construction activity next door. Cahill-Mooney Contractors were excavating for the enlargement of a Standard service station. One of their diggers hit the natural gas line, and before anyone knew what had happened, the gas filled Ridgeway's store. When the automatic refrigerator sparked to "on" it blew up the store and Ridgeway, too. Luckily, Ridgeway didn't lose his life. Just one of his legs.

I went into that trial loaded with paraphernalia: skeleton, blackboard, anatomical charts, a diagram of the accident scene, an x-ray box and Bill Ridgeway's prosthetic limb. I spent almost three weeks on trial in this case and then late one afternoon, after we were finished for the day, I paused on my way out of the court when I saw that one of the lawyers appearing for Cahill-Mooney Contractors (call him Tom Foley) had stayed behind for another matter. He was seeking the court's approval on a settlement in another case seemingly unrelated to mine. A little girl had lost a leg in a bus accident and Tom Foley, representing both the girl's father and the insurance company, had arranged a $30,000 settlement on behalf of the little girl.

It seemed more than a coincidence to me that Tom Foley was bringing a little girl's case before the court in the middle of the Ridgeway trial. The Ridgeway jurors had gone home for the night. Before they returned to court on the morrow, the last day of trial, they would have read the morning paper. The paper was almost sure to mention the child's case and the $30,000 settlement. Was this an attempt to remind the Ridgeway jurors of the going rate for lost legs in Montana? I was determined to stop it. I asked Judge William Taylor to appoint me as *amicus curiae* (friend of the court) in the case of this girl so that I could investigate the scroll, a crutch in one quadrant of the shield, an ambulance in another, a dollar sign in a third and a corkscrew in the fourth. (In the tort business, you need a little drink now and then.) The scroll reads "The Holy Grail Insurance Company," my pet name for the insurance industry in America, which in its self-aggrandizements affects such sanctimonious claptrap. I see the moguls not

---

liability in the case and, if the findings so warranted, bring suit for a much greater amount than $30,000. I asked that he hold the cause of the little girl until the Ridgeway verdict, "so this verdict will be untrammeled by any prejudice or any sympathy which may appear as a result of this prospective news story in the Anaconda *Standard* tomorrow morning."

Tom Foley interrogated the father of the little girl right there. "Do you now desire Mr. Belli or any other lawyer to represent you in this matter?"

"No sir," he said, "I do not."

At this point I became a little upset. "I have offered to appear as *amicus curiae* on behalf of the court; and not on behalf of this man. He not only does not want a lawyer but he is satisfied to settle this case for thirty thousand dollars. He disdains any help. It's the little child who needs it."

"You claim," said Judge Taylor to Foley, "that this settlement that you are effecting at the present time isn't made, like counsel here intimated, to jeopardize their case?"

"That is correct," said Foley.

"Well . . . if that isn't your purpose, nothing is to be lost by passing over it at this time."

I cooled down, gave the judge a thankful look, grabbed my briefcase and stalked off. "The gall of that guy!" I said to my co-counsel, Montana lawyer Horace Dwyer. "I could just see the headline in the Anaconda *Standard*, girl gets thirty thousand dollars for loss of leg."

Our jurors evaluated Bill Ridgeway's leg at a little more than that: They gave him $183,000, not an adequate award, I thought, to compensate him for his loss, but a hell of a lot better than the $30,000, and it set a new standard, in the *Standard*, at least.

I think Judge Taylor was impressed. After the case was all over he gave me the old battered jury ballot box that had been used in that courtroom for years. "Here," he said, "you've taken everything else, you might as well take this too."

as Knights of King Arthur but as bandits. In fact, I have a picture in my window facing the street of some musta-chioed Mexicans, with muskets, era of Pancho Villa, captioned "Adjusters of The Holy Grail Insurance Co."

More artifacts: a sword used by my father in Knights of Templar parades. A metal helmet, "Truck 8, S. F. Fire Dept." A ticking clock that adorned the wall of my grandmother's drugstore in Sonora. A stethoscope and a bedpan. An old miner's pail. A brakeman's lamp. A wood-carved human fist from the Philippines, middle finger extended. Mongol stirrups. Bottles of Jim Beam and Chivas Regal. A case of Calso water. Ceremonial hats from Samarkand, Jerusalem and the Andes. An old Rugby jersey, number 7. An X-ray shadow box, in good working condition: turn on the light and you see a human stomach playing host to a pair of surgical scissors. Certificates of membership in the Federal Bar Association, the American Trial Lawyers Association, the American Academy of Trial Lawyers. (I keep a parchment of the American Bar Association hanging upsidedown—in the john.) A solid gold lifetime membership in Local 41, San Francisco Bartenders Union. A recipe for Pisco Punch.*

A collection of keys from several hundred of the best hotels in the world. Most of the keys have a tag that pleads "Drop in nearest mailbox." Inscribed pictures from Mae

---

* Put some pineapple in the bottom of a crock and let ferment for two or three days. Then pour straight pisco Peruvian prune brandy over it and let ferment for a couple more days. Crush the pineapple and add fresh orange, pineapple and lemon juice, some angostura and lots of ice, and, if necessary, sugar, but try to keep sugar out completely. Stir with an ossick, and serve in tin cups. (This recipe never seems to turn out for anyone other than me and Caesar, possibly because no one else bothers to stir with an ossick, which is the petrified pizzle of a walrus. I found two of them on a beach in Alaska, gave one to Errol Flynn and hung the other in my office.)

West, Marlene Dietrich, Harry S. Truman, Flip Wilson, Lenny Bruce, Johnny Carson, Mike Douglas, Merv Griffin, Herbert Hoover. A plaque presented by some cons working for prison reforms. Another, from Governor George C. Wallace: "Melvin M. Belli, Honorary Colonel, Alabama State Militia." And an heroic portrait of me above the fireplace painted by Frank Ashley, a Marin County artist, who made me look more like Dorian Gray than Melvin Belli.

I put the reception room at the other end of the courtyard and had it done in red drapes and flocked red wallpaper, with another huge oak bar serving as the reception desk. It wasn't long before someone said that room looked like the hallway at a high-class whorehouse. (The late Professor [and Dean] Snodgrass of Hastings Law School looked at the layout, on opening night, and dryly commented, "Mel, I'll take my champagne down here in the reception room. I'm a little too old to go upstairs to visit the girls.") There were times when I looked over the motley collection of humanity waiting to see me at any hour of the day and thought that description almost apt: cops and con men and crooks, mining engineers, male models, heirs expectant and executors of wills, maniacs and murderers, pimps and prospectors looking for a grubstake, psychotics and psychics and grandmothers with clacking teeth who were sure they were being done out of their fortunes, and young ladies seeking theirs.

Late one day in a week of grinding hard work, exhausted, I stepped into the reception room to find it full of the lame, the halt and the blind all waiting to see Mr. Belli. I had had it. I slipped into the john, lathered up a bucket of soap suds, smeared them all over my face and came out on all fours, growling. "Hooo! Heee! Haaa! Hey!" My receptionist, a quick brown fox named Gretchen, yelled, "Mad dog! Mad dog!"

Hardly anyone even looked up. One woman finally noticed and nodded—could it be her approval? I could only guess her thoughts or those of the others. Maybe: If Mr. Belli had occasional attacks of Saint Vitus's dance or *dementia advocatus,* well, that, apparently, was just one of the costs they'd have to bear. I walked slowly back to my office, sobered by the nonreactions, and dug out of a lower drawer an essay that a young fan of mine, Judy Hatcherd, had written about me when she was in the seventh grade. She had quoted Cesare Lombroso. "Good sense," he wrote, "travels on the well-worn paths; genius never. And that is why the crowd, not altogether without reason, is so ready to treat great men as lunatics."

My taste in things exotic ran to people, too. But I think the exotics in my life have made it richer for their presence.

I'll never forget Errol Flynn was living in Jamaica when he agreed to write his foreword to my *Life and Law in Japan.* "Dear Sporting Blood," he wrote, "even though a lawyer, you are still a man. I will do the foreword and anything else you might have in mind." He said he had just spent three of the hardest months in his life getting down his own autobiography, *My Wicked Wicked Ways.* "I have just cast off my last wife," he added, "and have a new mistress who is certainly no worse than any of the predecessors but, as you would say, that is irrelevant, immaterial and frivolous, and I am delighted. *Merde a toil!* Errol."

The girl Flynn was delighted with was Beverly Aadland, a long-legged blond beauty who was only sixteen when Flynn passed through San Francisco with her in November, 1959. They stayed with me and Joy and little Caesar, the only issue of my marriage to Joy. It was clear then, even to Caesar who was only two and a half, that Flynn, now bloated and puffy, was a sick man. Joy pleaded with Flynn to take things easier. He told her, "Look, I've done everything twice. Why should I bother? If I had an attack, there wouldn't be anyone to give a damn."

I wasn't home when he left for Vancouver, sad because he had to sell his yacht, the *Zaca.* He told Joy, "Tell the guy I love him. Just tell him that for me." I would never see him again. Flynn died in Vancouver. Beverly Aadland came back to us, stayed at our apartment and had me put in her claim to part of Flynn's estate—which the courts turned down despite my charge that Flynn had introduced her to "immoral debauchery and sex orgies and taught her a lewd, wanton and wayward way of life." Was that any way for me to speak of a friend who was like a brother to me? Hell, no. That was just lawyer talk. Flynn would have appreciated it.

I wouldn't forget Mickey Cohen either. To me, Cohen wasn't a "pug ugly." He was a gentleman of great courtliness and charm who was doing the best he could with the lot he'd been given in life. The press (no doubt acting on information leaked by an FBI which could prove nothing on Cohen in a court of law) had convicted him of high crimes. The press suggested Cohen had rubbed out Bugsy Siegel as part of a gang war stretching all the way from Las Vegas to Los Angeles.

But Mickey passed one test of mine. My little boy, Caesar, has been a great judge of character almost from infancy, and Caesar took to Mickey Cohen as to the loving grandfather he never met. So did Caesar's dog. For a time, Mickey Cohen was Caesar's babysitter. Caesar may have been about six when Joy and I had a second home in the Hollywood Hills above the Sunset Strip. One night, during a party there with Randy Hearst and some Los Angeles judges in attendance, Caesar and Mickey appeared at the top of the stairs. Caesar was in his pajamas, and Mickey had a pink chenille bathrobe on over his clothes. Caesar had a banana in Mickey's back, a make-believe pistol. He was going "uh-uh-uh," and Mickey said, "Don't shoot, don't shoot. I'll tell the boys. I'll be good." My guests gulped at that scene. Some of them even hurried off into the night—though they hadn't yet drunk all they'd planned.

Was Cohen a crook? On many counts, I'd put Cohen up against the high priests and hypocrites in the ABA or some of the fixers in certain Washington law firms who never go to court, who stay out of print and out of the public eye but operate behind the closed doors of their office suites, in congressional corridors and out on the course of Burning Tree, to the great detriment and great injury of the American public. I would have put Cohen up against J. Edgar Hoover himself. And certainly Richard Nixon.

Eventually, however, in 1962, they got Mickey, sent him to Alcatraz for tax evasion. He had thought that if he received some of his money in the form of "gifts," he wouldn't have to pay income tax on it. Lou and I told him that he'd have to declare the gifts as income, but he wouldn't listen to us and he got in trouble. They only sent him up for a short while. It was obvious when he got out of Alcatraz that it had been no vacation. I don't know whether doing time is a deterrent, but it is a punishment and especially for a guy like Mickey Cohen: because he's famous as a tough guy, the other prisoners take a special pleasure in hurting him.

A few years later, a crazy con at the U.S. penitentiary in Atlanta (where Mickey was vacationing) hit Cohen on the back of the head with a piece of pipe. The blow crippled Cohen for life, and we won a damage suit against the government on Cohen's behalf. Then the Internal Revenue Service attached the entire sum of $110,000, including *my* 20 percent fee. That wasn't Mickey's $22,000, that was mine. But the IRS took it, and I made no move to stop them. Those were the days when you didn't insist too strongly against a federal agency with unlimited powers of retaliation. Mickey, a true gentleman, was more concerned about my loss than his.

Lenny Bruce was as much of an outcast among polite society as Mickey Cohen. More so, because Bruce was better known, the most notorious of the so-called sick comics, who couldn't stand the hypocrisy in America and focused the full light of his brilliant mind on satirizing our pretensions.

When I first encountered Bruce, he'd just been arrested in Philadelphia on a drug bust. (Not that the cops really had anything on him. All the dope they'd seized in his hotel room was legally prescribed, but Bruce was beginning to go too far in his nightclub acts. For instance, a bit he did was called "To is a preposition, come is a verb"— which wasn't intended to arouse prurient interests, and didn't.) With this routine, Bruce was criticizing the hypocrisies of contemporary society. And, naturally enough, society didn't like it. In Philadelphia, the establishment had decided to get rid of him. As Albert Goldman, Bruce's brilliant biographer, tells the story, "Not only was the act becoming a little too outrageous for many middle-class patrons, *he* was becoming a little too outrageous for many of the presumably sophisticated people with whom he associated. . . . He was getting pretty intolerable." One night, someone who was thinking of backing a movie idea of Lenny's invited him to a party in North Philly and insisted he put on a show for the people there. Lenny took offense at the guy's manner and when the party gathered around him in their fashionable suits and cocktail dresses, he said. "Okay, people, here's my act." With that, he whipped out his schlong and pissed on the carpet. Goldman wrote: "Someone in that crowd, some nice Florida-tanned businessman or martini-hoisting senior partner or aspiring political big-shot, blew the whistle on Lenny Bruce. He wanted Lenny driven out of town, forever; and he knew that the scandal of a drug bust—whatever the outcome—would do the trick. He put pressure on the heat and the cops were sent in to make the kill."

And then, to make matters worse, Bruce publicly exposed the corruption of the cops and the magistrates in Philadelphia. The justice of the peace, David Keiser, had asked for a payoff of ten thousand dollars to dismiss the charges. When Lenny wouldn't pay off, Keiser went ahead and bound Lenny over for trial. Lenny told his audiences about Keiser (who later resigned in disgrace and committed suicide) and the cops, and that did it. The narc network all over the country picked up the news that Lenny had declared war on them. They'd have to fight back. Before, they would look the other way when they suspected that Lenny was on something. Now they would bust his ass whenever they could. And they did.

I had other things to do and couldn't take Lenny's case in Philly. But I would have other chances in the coming years, when Lenny was arrested in Chicago, San Francisco and Los Angeles. I tried to come to his aid, but Lenny couldn't be helped. One night he told a San Francisco nightclub audience that he wanted to apologize for not being so funny that night. "I'm not a comedian," he said. "I'm Lenny Bruce."

For Bruce the comedian, that was the beginning of the end. After that, his act became a cause, and though his cause was right (in fact, precisely *because* his cause was right), the law-and-order establishment set out to get him.

Once he was arrested in San Francisco for doing "To is a preposition, come is a verb," then compounded matters by making each successive act more outrageous, reducing the San Francisco police crusade against him to an absurdity. He came right out on the stage of the Jazz Workshop and said, "Motherfucker." The people were shocked. They tittered. And he said it again. "Motherfucker." And they tittered again. "Now, ladies and gentlemen," he said, "to show you how silly all of this is, the U.S. Supreme Court has just decided, so my lawyer, Mel Belli, tells me, that my act's obscene if it creates prurient desire in you. So I'm going to say 'motherfucker' and you're going to see two of San Francisco's finest starred and blue-coated policemen come down and arrest me. Rather than arrest me, they ought to be taken to a psychiatrist if my saying 'motherfucker' raises a prurient desire in them."

And sure enough, two red-faced policemen came and took him off the stage. The owner of the Jazz Workshop would bail him out each time—Bruce was a big act and would fill the house for any nightclub owner in the business who had the guts to book him—and Lenny would come back and go through a recitation of what had happened to him on the way to jail, in the jail, before the judge. Some of that was funny, some of it was tragic, some of it was a bore to anyone who wasn't really that interested in the criminal-justice system.

But Lenny was interested. Though he had me as his lawyer, he liked to do his own legal research in my office, and I saw nothing wrong with that. For a period of three or four months, he came down to the basement, surrounded by all those law books, and read Supreme Court decisions. Sometimes, he'd ask me to explain a point or take the opposite side and make arguments against his own briefs, which were quite passable. He didn't make a pest of himself, but he would ask the legal secretaries to type his stuff for free, and because he had this ingratiating, almost little-boy quality, they would do it. He'd get into the girls' working hours as well as their pants. Regularly. He had a fine mind and a marvelous glibness. He'd read dictionaries as I read novels. Once I went backstage at the Jazz Workshop and found him all excited over a big thesaurus, a whole new world of words.

Lenny Bruce offended the deadly dull, and finally the deadly dull in San Francisco and Chicago and L.A. got him. For that reason, I'd go out of my way to defend him. I had the same feelings about others who were fighting other establishments. I went out of my way to defend osteopaths and chiropractors, many of whom did less harm and much more good than many M.D.'s that I knew.

And I took up the case of Muhammad Ali at a time when he was supposedly one of society's outcasts.

Ali phoned me one day at the Hilton Hotel in New York, where I was staying, and in minutes he was knocking at my door. "Mel," he said, slipping in quick as a panther, "shut it, shut the door." I shot a look down the hallway and saw seven beautiful black and white foxes by whom it would be a pleasure to be torn to shreds. I looked over at Ali, who rolled his eyes and raised his arms. I shut the door, and Ali stretched out flat on my bed to talk. This was the time when his conviction for refusing to join the army was on appeal before the U.S. Supreme Court. He wanted to know what else he could do or what I could do for him.

I hold him I thought he should take his case directly to the White House, promise he'd take the patriotic trail, tour the country talking cold turkey to dope addicts in the ghettos and inspiration to children everywhere. He agreed with the plan. He was losing the best years of his professional life unfairly and, I thought illegally, because no boxing commission in the land would let him fight. I went to Washington and talked to presidential aide Leonard Garment about Ali's offer. Garment thought the move could do nothing but help Nixon and said so. But he had to check with someone else first. I guessed it was John Mitchell. A few days later, I phoned Garment to see if he had an answer. He did. The answer was no. I told him that with this Nixon had lost his last great opportunity to become a human being. "I know," said Garment, a likeable guy and a bright one. "But what can you do? Mitchell has the last word."

The next time I ran across John Mitchell was in 1974, when I sued him for divorce on behalf of Martha. For his part in Watergate, Mitchell was playing the covering-up game with Tricky Dick. Martha had had enough. I flew to Phoenix's Camelback Inn to talk to Martha. She was a tough lady, a sweet Southern girl in crinoline one moment and Gold-Tooth Gertie of the Klondike the next. She said she wanted me because she wanted a lawyer who wasn't afraid of Nixon and couldn't be bought off. With one of my New York colleagues, Richard Creditor, to help me handle Martha, I took the case and finally settled it with the exception of one little thing. In a divorce case, it is always "one little thing." It's the damned good-for-nothing parakeet or the spoiled poodle or the cut-glass Viennese sugar bowl given as a wedding gift by Aunt Tillie—but to whom? With Martha and John Mitchell, it was *his* black alpaca suits. I had everything squared away, except those goddamn suits. John wanted them back, but though I'm sure Martha was never going to wear them even to a masquerade, she wouldn't give them up. Hanging there in the closet, they looked like John Mitchell, without John Mitchell inside. They were shiny, baggy at the knees, black conservative, confidence-instilling East Coast establishment, salesman suits. We were at an impasse, because I told her to give John his suits. Never, but never agree with "the other side" in a domestic relations battle no matter how reasonable and fair it is. She began to consult other lawyers and finally got my good friend Henry Rothblatt—whom I couldn't see wearing John Mitchell's suits either.

It's too bad Martha didn't do her story on the Nixon gang. It would have scared hell out of everybody in America. She told me that John Mitchell would come home every night while he was Attorney General, they would have their drinks and then he would meticulously relate everything that had happened in the government that day from Nixon and the National Security Council on down. The experience was a heady one for Martha. "Who do you think was running this country for those months? I was." But then John Mitchell stood by while government agents belted her, drugged her and tied her up. I had to doubt about that. Martha? I liked her. I think she was a great gal, but done wrong more by Mr. Nixon than by Mr. Mitchell.

Not long ago, I got a phone call from someone who might still be heavyweight champion of the world if it weren't for Ali. It was George Foreman. I recognized his voice because I'd already faced him in a legal action brought by the mother of his child. Now he wanted me on his side. He had had some difficulty finding a San Francisco lawyer who would battle one of the City's most prestigious law firms. He said, "Are you afraid of taking them on?"

I said, "George, I'm not even afraid of taking *you* on." (But I was especially pleased to sue this particular firm: They had represented a litigant against me personally and had taken the case all the way to the Supreme Court—and lost.)

Foreman liked that. He sent his manager over to tell me how this law firm had purportedly helped bilk Foreman of $350,000, money he had received as part of his purse in the Foreman-Muhammad Ali fight in Zaire in 1974. Foreman had gone to this law firm with a business proposition that had been presented to him. He wanted to know if the deal was any good; he wanted to know if it was safe. The firm handed the matter over to one of its own attorneys for investigation. This man allegedly hustled over to the promoters of the deal and said he would recommend the matter to Foreman if the promoters would give him $25,000 "under the table." We contend in our suit that they did and he did. And the law firm asked Foreman to "bring over" the $350,000. They invested it for Foreman. Inside of a month the business went "belly up."

As a courtesy to my brothers in the bar, I asked them if they cared to settle: the liability seemed so clear. They said they weren't interested in even discussing the matter. Before the sun had set I filed suit against them on behalf of George Foreman for the $350,000—plus another $5 million in punitive damages.

I do not expect much acclaim from my colleagues at law for filing this suit. And if I win it big, I expect to hear some pretty harsh comments from some who believe that lawyers shouldn't sue lawyers.

But I do not work for acclaim. Acclaim doesn't bring me love, peace, pleasure or fill my pockets with gold. In forty-three years of practice, I have had more than my share of acclaim. But I would willingly trade all of it for the privilege of practicing another forty-three.

CHAPTER SIXTEEN

Mildewed Wool

Though I represented many of the so-called "haves," I devoted most of my time and attention to the "have-nots"—who came seeking me more and more as my reputation grew. A profile in *The Saturday Evening Post* identified me with one of Flynn's movie personae, Robin Hood. That was a mixed blessing. As a result of the *Post* stories, I received several bagsful of mail from men and women who'd been denied justice so long they had given up hope until they read the *Post* article. Their ills were a catalog of the disasters that society itself—particularly government bureaucracies—could create for people who had never grown up enough to do for themselves. One letter from a black man in prison was typical:

> The real reason I'm writing to you is that all of my petty thievery life, my dreams were to have an attorney of your standards. Another thing: here I have been did everything except castrated. I'm afraid to talk about that too much but if you would just mail me a card with your name on it, it might save me a few knots off my head. At this time, I have the

flu, but if I don't smile right or scratch my head, I don't get to eat.

Most of them didn't need lawyers, they needed head doctors—like the shaggy young man who stood on the sidewalk one day in front of the office shouting, "Melvin, where's Melvin? Hey, Melvin, gimme some of your money!" Or the woman—Mrs. Johnson—who writes to me at least once a week, special delivery, with no return address, preparing me for her imminent arrival at the office.

> I will be in your office sometime between 10 and 11 on Monday. You and I will go straight to the Hilton, you can have the police deliver the clothes I am going to wear about 4 o'clock. After I am ready, hopefully by 7 o'clock, we will leave at once for a hideout. Can a helicopter land on top of the hotel, so we can leave in that?

Mrs. Johnson never arrives. But her letters continue to come. Of all the cases that come to me and I have to turn down, most of these latter are due to stale claims, having let the "statute of limitations" run.

I tried to help some of those whose problems were mainly legal, attempted in other instances to find lawyers who would share some of the less hopeless cases *pro bono publico*. But I was overwhelmed. Being in the tort business was part of the problem. There are as many different kinds of torts as there are ways for people to get into trouble. They all seemed to come knocking at my door or ringing on any of the four telephones on my desk. Injuries to a person's back, eyes, head, every bone in the body, singly or in conjunction with multiple injuries, nerves, veins, bone, muscle. Injuries from likely and unlikely sources: the fender of an automobile, a defective wheel, a bad tire, a faulty derrick, a poorly made prosthesis, wrong or contaminated blood, bad care by a doctor, a lawyer, an architect, an engineer. Catastrophic cases—paraplegia or quadriplegia, blindness or mental damage. Funny cases, too, which were all part of a day's work for a tort lawyer.

One client had felt the need to blow his nose while walking down Mission Street. He said he didn't have a handkerchief (looking at him, I could believe that), but I gave him one star when he said he didn't want to blow his nose on the sidewalk. He went to the curb and, holding one nostril, arched his neck over the gutter and blew into the passing traffic. An automobile coming along whacked him alongside the head and broke his jaw. That was a tort. Committed on him. I went to court and pleaded "last clear chance." That means that the one who had the last opportunity to prevent the tort should have done so. The motorist had the last clear opportunity to prevent the accident and didn't, even though the plaintiff was negligent. So I got a jury verdict for the plaintiff.

Another client, a petite opera singer, bought a ticket to the movies one day in San Francisco, groped her way down the aisle and sat down on what felt to her "like a bag of marshmallows." She put her hand on the seat and found, to her horror and shock, that someone had actually defecated on her seat. We never did determine how the former occupant of this seat could have performed this feat (during the show?). But we had unmistakable evidence: the fur coat was ruined. Over and above that, there was the "pain, humiliation, ridicule and embarrassment"—words that no tort lawyer could live without.

I assigned the case to a fresh, brilliant young woman in my office, Betsy Fitzgerald Rahn (now a municipal judge). *She* was shocked and humiliated when I presented the case to her, but I pointed out that a tort is a tort and she'd better get used to trying the bizarre in our offices. I also told her to go to a dictionary and learn how to say "shit" ten different ways without repeating herself. To this day she has a beautiful way of saying "shit," even though she doesn't get much chance to use it. I wrote a letter to the theater saying that I was amazed that they would keep their theater in the manner of a stable. Perhaps, I suggested, they had just finished showing *Eagle Squadron* and that was the cause of the deposit in the seat: they hadn't cleaned out the eagle's nest. I said other flamboyant things in my letter, but they wouldn't settle. Betsy went to trial and won the Case of the Eagle Squadron Tort.

Lou Ashe said it was my own damned fault that I was overwhelmed. I didn't have to take every case that came along. And if I weren't so self-promoting . . . He urged me to go easy. I didn't *have* to raise the Jolly Roger atop the building and shoot off that little cannon every time I won a big case, he said. It was just a question, he said, of style. But I do not believe it was my style that angered the legal establishment, it was my substance. Some of my capers were only an excuse for their anger. It was my cases (and their implications) that made the business community—and the lawyers who served that community —nervous.

Reviewing the big cases I had during this middle period of my life, I now realize that I was stomping on some pretty big toes. My Cutter case could have repercussions throughout the world of American business. Other lawyers in NACCA (which had now changed its name to ATLA, the Association of Trial Lawyers of America) were driving through the wedge I had opened. A young attorney named Ralph Nader had stepped into national prominence as an advocate for the public at large which, he claimed, quite properly, had a right to expect that a manufacturer ought to stand behind the goods he offers for sale.

In 1956, I used the doctrine of liability without fault to win a suit against United Aircraft, maker of helicopters, on behalf of a navy pilot's widow who lost her husband when his helicopter crashed on its maiden flight during military maneuvers. I could sense that the verdict was causing every contractor doing business with the Pentagon to tremble with fear that he would be slapped with lawsuits every time one of his planes or ships went down or some ordnance went awry.

And with good reason. I was going after the big guys—and would continue doing so with gusto. I went after railroads and airlines and the telephone company and a newspaper tycoon and a man who owned the Giants. And when I became involved in one of the largest will contests in the history of Georgia, I was not surprised to find myself on the side of a woman who had to fight almost the entire establishment of Savannah for ten years before she got what was coming to her.

It was a little thing that started me off on a nationwide crusade against the telephone company. Ma Bell tried to take away a number I'd had for years. YUkon 1-1849, and replace it with 981-1849. "I am not a San Quentin convict," I wrote in my complaint. "YUkon is a colorful name. So is KLondike and SUtter and the more lyrical VAlencia. They are not going to make numbers out of my people."

Jimmy Breslin, then a columnist for the New York *Herald Tribune,* picked up the ball and ran with it.

The Telephone Company [he wrote] is a public utility, and it should act like one. . . . Digit dialing is only one of the many things the Telephone Company does which must be stopped. This is a public utility which has been getting away with murder for so long that it now figures it is in the right. Well, this is going to stop.

Breslin got an overwhelming response from readers all over the country. I became general counsel of the Anti-Digit Dialing League of America and Richard Gehman, the writer, became director of an active Metropolitan New York chapter. "Harassment," said Gehman, "is to be the major function of our group." Hiram Johnson III, the grandson of our illustrious California governor and U.S. senator, joined me in a bit of West Coast fun. We sued Ma Bell and held up digit dialing in California for six months. They were ready to convert to diesel oil and we kept them on gasoline. It must have cost the phone company millions. That gave me a lot of satisfaction, but I have continued to pay for it: one of the telephone company's principal lawyers keeps harassing *me* by continuing to relate tales about me to the Bar—always eager to listen. My solace is to keep reminding myself that his epitaph can only be: "Here lies a 22K stuff-shirted bastard."

I took on one of the country's great press lords, John S. Knight, for waging a campaign of vilification against Bill Brautigan, the Dade County District Attorney, in the pages of the most powerful newspaper in Florida, the Miami *Times-Herald*. On the morning that Knight was scheduled to take the stand, he was waiting in the judge's chambers, a very important person who was getting special treatment from the judge. I wanted to make sure the jury knew that, so when I called Knight as a witness, I deliberately turned my back to the judge and looked expectantly toward the rear of the courtroom. In the meantime, Knight had slipped in and got on the witness stand, as I knew he would. I played dumb, still looking toward the back of the room. "Bailiff," I said, "where is John Knight?" The bailiff waved toward the witness stand and I turned around very slowly and said, "Oh, *there* you are. How did you get there?" Knight blushed, and the judge hid his face from the jury. But of course the jury knew how Knight had gotten there. And it knew, too, that common people don't wait in the judge's chambers.

"What is your address?" I asked Knight.

"Well," he said, "I have *several* of them."

That gave me another opening, to help me impress upon the jury that they were now in the position of judging one of their betters, a heady feeling for any jury. "Well, just give us one of the more modest," I said.

And with that, Knight was finished. Paul Louis, my great friend and colleague from Miami, and I had the excruciating pleasure and agony of overhearing the jury deliberate that one (we could hear them through the walls of the judge's chamber and all of us, defense attorneys, too, listened together). The jury foreman was too much with us. Paul Louis had told me to keep him on the jury because he was "a Klansman buddy of my uncle's." When the other jurors said they wanted to give our client one million dollars, their redneck announced. "Look, I'm for the plaintiff more than you are, but we give him one million dollars, the judge will set it aside. Let's be realistic and give him a hundred thousand and save plaintiff an appeal."

I groaned, "Jesus Christ, just bring in the one million dollars. Let me handle the appeal."

But no. When the jury filed back, the foreman was winking and smiling at me, as if he'd done me a big favor. He was like the cocker spaniel bringing in the morning chronicle, panting and wagging his tail. The verdict was $100,000.

The next day, I ran into John Knight at Hialeah Racetrack. Knight's a square shooter and I became very fond of him. That day he could not have been more charming. "I want you to meet my wife," he said. He took me to his box, where the fashionable Mrs. Knight had a cocktail in one hand and a racing form in the other. "Honey," he said, "this is the man who took a hundred thousand dollars from me yesterday." She gave him a look of scorn that included me, too.

"Yesterday," she said to Knight, "you should have stood in bed."

And I had absolutely no compunction at all over suing Horace Stoneham, who was then a hero in San Francisco for bringing the New York Giants and big-league baseball to the Golden Gate. Horace Stoneham didn't know how cold the wind blew in San Francisco when he brought his team to Candlestick Park in 1958. Candlestick Cove was right on the Bay at the bottom of a natural wind tunnel bearing breezes, it seemed, directly from Alaska. When Stoneham realized how cold it could get at Candlestick, he had a radiant-heating system installed (or thought he did) in the box-seat sections and advertised the fact with a feature in the club's own yearbook.

I was delighted to see major-league baseball in San Francisco. I bought a season box but after a few games, I came to the conclusion that if there was radiant heating, the pipes were filled with refrigerant and brine. I sued Horace and the Giants for fraud and breach of warranty and went to jury trial in San Francisco Municipal Court.

I proved my case in a rococo, funning style that absolutely enraged the stuffy establishment lawyers Stoneham had hired. I had expert witnesses, Giant fans, come into court wearing long underwear and Arctic survival gear to testify this was their normal attire for a Giants' game at Candlestick. I took the stand myself in my Alaskan parka and swore that not even this fur could keep me warm in one of Horace's boxes. Finally, I brought in the owner of the plumbing firm that had installed the radiant-heating system. He said the system worked, but the Giants were just too cheap to turn it on.

In my summation (I was still wearing the parka), I argued warranty. "*Fraud* is a sinister word," I said. "Let's be true, generous San Franciscans and knock out the count of fraud." I told the jury all I really wanted was my money back. That and a victory which would teach a large national audience the real import of legal *warranty*. The jury was out for *two minutes* and came back with an award of $1,597, the full price of my box.

That night, the *News-Call Bulletin* carried a banner lead: "CHILLY BELLI BEATS GIANTS, 1597-0." Horace Stoneham never forgave me for that. He said I put a jinx on his whole season. In fact, I caused a little more grief for him when he dragged his feet on paying me the $1,597. I got a writ of execution on Willie Mays (arguing successfully that player-owner contracts made the likes of a Mays, Stoneham's chattel). The sheriff's office actually served the execution on Mays and after the deputy explained to the great center-fielder that he was now the property of Melvin M. Belli, Lawyer, Mays giggled and said, "Well, I dunno, but if Mr. Belli owns me, I hope he's got a good ball club." That's when Horace paid up, but to avoid having a photostatic blowup of his cashier's check grace my office (as it surely would have), he sent over the money with my good pal Jake Ehrlich—in dollar bills.

I gave the cash to the City for a clump of Lombardy poplars that now grow at the top of Montgomery Street just below Telegraph Hill. It's called "Caesar's Park."

And then I took on the Diamond will contest. Barney

Diamond was a bridge builder in Georgia and the South and, apparently, such a damn good one that he was worth more than $20 million when he died. But he hadn't done so well by his wife, Delores, not if she was to believe the terms of the will written and witnessed a year before Barney died, which gave her an income of only $400 a month.

Barney and Delores, his second wife, had broken up several years before his death, then gotten back together before the signing of this curious will but not before Barney had promised her he'd stop drinking and deal her in on a third of his estate. In California, consortium was not good "consideration" (as lawyers delicately call the goods that people exchange in their multifarious dealings, financial and otherwise). A wife was *supposed* to live with her husband; she wasn't to be paid extra for it. In Georgia, not so. If we could prove the oral promise in a court of law—and then show *why* Barney Diamond didn't follow through on that promise—we might break the will.

Showing why he didn't follow through, however, wasn't so easy. Some men who'd been closest to Diamond— particularly four officers of Diamond's several companies who were also trustees of the will's prime beneficiary, the Diamond Foundation—stoutly maintained that Diamond was in fine fettle when he signed the will. And Diamond's doctor said he'd just died of old age—at sixty-eight.

"But there was something wrong with him," his widow said. "Something radically wrong." I picked up on that and went into a huddle with Delores's brother, Donald E. Austin, an able Savannah lawyer himself who had telephoned me from Georgia I told him we might break the will if we could exhume the body of Barney Diamond. He sounded stunned. "Dig up the body? Mel, what good would that do?"

"We might find some brain damage that would account for his not remembering and keeping his promise to your sister."

"You could prove it *now*?" asked Austin, "Two months after his death?"

"We could," I said, "if there was anything organically wrong. Pathologists make these findings all the time. I was with Dr. Emile Brietenecker during an autopsy once in Vienna and—"

"Jeez, Mel," Austin said, interrupting. "We don't do things like that down here in Georgia. The people here wouldn't stand for it. We'd be bound to get some rednecks on the jury—"

"Leave the jury to me," I said. I told him I'd take the case if I could get Doctors Milt Helpern and Andy Cyrus down to Savannah and have them take a look at Barney's brain.

They were two of the best. Cyrus was a neuropathologist from the Wisconsin School of Medicine (formerly Marquette) and Helpern was from Bellevue in New York. They both expressed their doubts about my hunch. "It's a long shot," said Helpern. Cyrus said, "If we don't find brain damage, it'll hurt your case." I told them it was a chance I had to take. I had a hunch. (And that's what separates the "great" trial lawyers from the just "good" ones.)

When we exhumed Barney Diamond out of the damp red Georgia earth, his blue serge suit had taken the color of its wearer, gray beyond the cyanosis of death. The smell of wet wool commingled with the effluvium of the tomb, of mildew from head to toe and a fungus that seemed to thrive most particularly in the corpse's nares. An overpowering blue-gray miasma rose from the casket. The two trustees from the bank who had come to watch the autopsy tried to excuse themselves. "We'll stipulate," they said, "to the identification of the body, Mr. Belli."

"No, gentlemen," I said somberly. "That wouldn't be fair." Among others, I was suing them as executors of the estate of Bernard F. Diamond and I insisted they stick around for this important inning. If anyone was going to rob Delores of what was hers, I would make them suffer. They did suffer, fainting only occasionally when Bill Choulos made offers of orange juice and rare roast beef sandwiches through the three hours that followed. They had to watch as the pathologists took a rotary saw to Barney's skull, pulled the skin of the forehead down over the face and sectioned parts of the brain with a razor-sharp scalpel into slices thinner than a sheet of carbon paper. Down they went.

When we finally got to trial in Savannah, Drs. Cyrus and Helpern told the court why this will couldn't be Barney Diamond's: For at least several years before his death, Barney Diamond was non compos mentis. Cyrus said he found ten cysts in Barney Diamond's brain and added, Sherlock Holmes-like, from an inspection of the brain alone, that Barney Diamond probably walked with a gimpy left leg, couldn't read and would have had some speech impediments. All three deductions turned out to be true. We found friends of Barney's who came to court to confirm them. And Dr. Helpern testified that Barney's brain was deteriorated from the ingestion of too much alcohol, a fact Delores Diamond only admitted much later and with extreme reluctance.

I sent my investigator, Gene Marshall,* a former narcotics agent in charge of Florida and the Caribbean,

---

* Much of a great trial lawyer's success rests on the ability of a great investigator to do the unusual, come up with the impossible, retrieve the irreparably lost. He's the key to the "who done it." Marshall ranges the United States for me— sometimes abroad—and his well-padded (but meticulously

around Savannah to find our best witnesses. One of them was an affluent member of Savannah society named Jack Middleton, who owned a shipping line or two. Marshall told him what he wanted. He just grunted and picked up the phone and called me. "Mel," he said, "I've got your henchman here. You better come yourself."

I went. The Middletons had his and her kitchens, a poker table dominating his. We fenced for a time in *his* kitchen over sour-mash bourbon and branch water. Finally, Jack Middleton said he didn't like lawyers and he didn't like courts, but if I agreed not to lollygag around in court, he'd come in and tell the truth. I said fine, I'd like to prepare him. He said he'd been preparing for seventy years.

In court, he handed his Panama hat to the bailiff (as if to his own valet), nodded to the judge, Harrison Dunbar, reminding him of their lunch date on the morow, and raised his right hand. "I'll tell you the truth about Barney Diamond," he announced to the jury of twelve, all of whom knew who Jack Middleton was. "When I heard about the will, I was having dinner at the Oglethorpe Club and I saw Tom Adams [the attorney who drew up the disputed will] and I went over and told him, 'Tom Adams, you're a goddamned liar. That's not Barney's will. He wouldn't have approved a will like that.'"

I didn't ask Jack Middleton a single other question. And neither did the other side.

I had no trouble with the jurors, a cross-section of Savannah, and they came in with a verdict that Delores A.

documented) expense sheets are well worth the little extra. But equal to him in importance is another non-lawyer, Leslie, my secretary. If there were a fire in the Belli Building I'd tell Choulos to save these two even at the cost of letting all my law books burn!

Diamond was entitled to one-third of Barney Diamond's huge estate.

But that wasn't the end of the affair. The trustees of the local bank, the officers of Diamond's several companies, and a team of lawyers went through all the appeals they could. And then when the Supreme Court of Georgia affirmed the trial verdict in our favor, they tried to get the tainted will probated anyway, and we had another trial on our hands in the Superior Court of Chatham County, Georgia. In this one, we charged the four officers of the Diamond companies with various kinds of illegal connivance, asserting they'd drawn up the will to their own benefit and got Barney Diamond to sign it because in those last months before he died, he'd sign anything they put in front of him. The four reacted as I expected they would and even brought in witnesses to affirm their good character. Character witnesses? I poohpoohed that move, "Why, if General Sherman were charged with arson in this community," I said. "I could bring in his mother, a reverend and five or ten others to testify that he never even played with matches."

The trial went on for weeks, well attended by the Oglethorpe Savannahians and the nouveaus, with the establishment cheering for the bank attorneys upholding the will and the nouveaus rooting for Delores Diamond. We brought Dr. Cyrus and Dr. Helpern back and we cross-examined a whole host of doctors now testifying for the other side, including the man who had been Barney Diamond's regular doctor, Dr. Thomas McGoldrick, who insisted that Barney Diamond had never been an alcoholic (as Dr. Helpern had surmised). I wondered why.

On cross-examination, I challenged Dr. McGoldrick. "You're not an objective witness here, are you?" I said.

He sputtered. "I trust I am, sir—"

"You put in a bill for twenty-five thousand dollars?" He gulped. At the first trial, he said he hadn't charged anything for advising the attorneys who were trying to uphold the tainted will. Since then, I'd learned he sent a bill for $25,285. I pressed on and wondered if he didn't think that fee was exorbitant.

"If I thought it was exorbitant, sir, I would not send it." He paused a moment and I let him try to tell me what it was (if it was not exorbitant). "It's exceptional," he said.

I went to the blackboard and together we worked things out. We agreed he was charging something like one hundred dollars an hour. I returned to the aggregate figure. "And you think you're nonpartisan as you sit there with a bill outstanding for twenty-five thousand dollars?"

The doctor said he understood the meaning of perjury.

I asked him about the meaning of notations he'd made in his records about Barney Diamond. One of them read, "9/8/69. Has quit drinking for two weeks. Going through torture." Another: "2/1/68. He's afraid that if he's taken off alcohol, he would drop dead." The doctor explained them both away in a rambling, though ingenious, way. I asked him how he could explain a notation (made by another doctor) that Diamond had the DT's.

"He didn't have the DT's," said Dr. McGoldrick. And the opposition attorney objected to the introduction of this business about the DT's because it was in the doctor's "personal records."

I passed on that and turned to the doctor. "Doctor, let me put it to you this way. The hour is late and we know your time is—I was going to say valuable but I—"

The judge interjected here and asked the jury to disregard that remark.

I made an elaborate bow. "I don't want to keep you on overtime, Doctor."

Now Dr. McGoldrick got into it, too. *He* turned to the jury and he asked them to disregard that, too.

All this amused the jurors, but they couldn't agree on a verdict. We ended up with a legal stalemate on the written will, but we still had a jury verdict, affirmed by the Supreme Court of Georgia, awarding Delores Diamond one-third of the estate. I urged Don Austin, who was handling all the delaying motions that the other side persisted in filing, to try and settle the case, even if he had to take less. "Let's settle this once and for all." I wrote. "By the time we finish with all the trials and appeals, there won't be anything left for your sister. They say now Diamond only left $8.5 million. Someone on the other side may be pirating the estate."

However correct that surmise, I learned some time later (the case was still unsettled) that the opposition lawyers had submitted a bill for $383,275, plus $8,826 in expenses, which would all have to be paid out of the Diamond estate. I wrote Austin:

If they charge this much for *losing* a case, what in Christ's name would be their bill for winning one?

Did this guy drive a cab before he went to law school? I note on page 22 that he has over $1,500 for "stand by time" during the jury deliberation! What the hell was this for, does he want us to pay for his biting his fingernails or was he actually working getting a pipeline into the jury room?

I'd like a little stand by time myself, such as "dreaming of next day's procedures—$50 an hour." How much did he charge for "wetting of pants when jury came in?"

I've got some clients over in San Quentin for arson and safe blowing. They only got away with $150,000, half of what this gang is asking for and the work is 100 times more dangerous than theirs. Ask them if they will take some apprentices and I can send them any number of men from San Quentin who would like to go straight—if "going straight" is sending bills like this.

P.S. My bill for this letter is $37.50, plus $11.00 overtime.

A year later, Delores Diamond finally saw some of her money. The trustees for the estate consented to give her a third of the figure they had computed as the full value of Barney Diamond's estate. It was les than she deserved, but far more than the munificent $400 a month they'd tried to bestow upon her—before we exhumed Barney Diamond.

CHAPTER SEVENTEEN

Cowboy Hats

In 1963, I had reached a pinnacle in the law. Then, all of a sudden, I was plunged into a whirlpool of hatred from which I have never completely emerged. My crime was daring to defend Jack Ruby, killer of the man still officially designated as the assassin of President John F. Kennedy. In the public's mind. I might just as well have been defending Lee Harvey Oswald.

At first, I wasn't really sure I wanted to take the Ruby case. I wondered if I—or anyone—could get a fair trial for Jack Ruby in Dallas. Dallas was a city of hate, a city where Adlai Stevenson was spat upon and hit on the head with a picket sign and where the American flag was hung upside-down by General Edwin Walker, a man relieved of his command in Germany for indoctrinating his troops in the right-wing extremism of the John Birch Society. It was a city where the "Minutewomen" would get on the telephones and call all over with such messages as "Mental health is communistic" and "Fluoridation is a Communist plot." And this was not just a lunatic fringe, this was the prevailing mood of the Dallas obligarchy who ran the town and told it what to think. But I didn't necessarily have to try the case in Dallas. If I could get the trial shifted to San Antonio, perhaps . . .

My doubt about representing Ruby disappeared when I read a wire story out of Tulsa on the morning of December 13, 1963. In Oklahoma to attend a meeting of the Tulsa Bar, a man I'd never met before attacked me for agreeing to take the case in Dallas. The man's name was Edward W. Kuhn of Louisville, Kentucky, president-elect of the American Bar Association. "Melvin Belli of San Francisco is just in it for the publicity," said Kuhn. "He's a negligence lawyer."

In Kuhn's book, of course, "negligence lawyer" was a dirty word—as "insurance-company lawyer" is in mine.

Kuhn went further in his Tulsa interview. "I don't like the idea of making a Roman circus out of Ruby's trial," he said. He was blaming *me* for tentative plans *they* were making in Dallas to televise the Ruby trial. But those were not my plans. The TV networks were behind that. And the presiding judge in the case, Joseph Brantley Brown, was going right along with the networks—until the Citizens Council, a semiofficial, semipublicized, self-perpetuating group of businessmen who ran Dallas, put the screws on that plan. Allowing TV in the Ruby trial wouldn't help the image of Dallas. The oligarchy was ashamed enough of Lee Harvey Oswald and Jack Ruby; they didn't want to remind the nation of their shame any more than they had to.

Allowing Judge Brown to sit on the case wouldn't help the Dallas image either (lawyers in Dallas snidely called him "Necessity" Brown because "necessity knows no law"). But when the Citizens Council found out they couldn't get him off the case, they had one of their council members, Sam Bloom, serve as the judge's "public relations man" to help keep him out of trouble. There was little question who was boss. When Bloom told

Brown he couldn't have the TV coverage he wanted, the judge wailed, "Ahh, Sam, cain't I have just one TV camera?" Bloom shook his head.

I took the Ruby case for a variety of reasons. But even now, more than a decade later, I cannot say which are the chief reasons. Money? Not a factor. Earl Ruby, Jack's brother, promised me a $50,000 fee, piddling enough on a big case like this, but I ended up getting less than half that—and spent $30,000 of my own on the case. There were other more compelling reasons.

Jack Ruby was a sick man, and I thought I could do something for him. It was a legal challenge: I get bored easily, but I am not bored when I am doing something that no one has ever done before. And here was the first time in the history of man and the law that anyone was going on trial for murdering another man on television— on live television with a national audience. Okay. Millions saw Jack Ruby (or at least a man whom the press identified shortly thereafter as Jack Ruby) shoot Lee Oswald. But Ruby deserved a fair trial anyway. On television, no one could see Ruby's state of mind.

From the first, I suspected that either Ruby shot Oswald to keep him quiet about the involvement of others or he was overcome by some crazy impulse on a weekend when all of us were slightly mad. Since there was no real evidence that Ruby was part of an assassination conspiracy, I had to lean toward the second explanation. And if Ruby was crazy, then maybe I could help the nation and its lawyers think more creatively in the future about the problem of mental illness and crime.

In Texas, they still used the outmoded M'Naughten Rule (the so-called knowledge of right and wrong test to determine legal insanity), and any lawyers who wanted to use it were caught up from the start in the anomalies of M'Naughten—getting doctors to come into court and say, unconvincingly, that this or that defendant couldn't tell right from wrong. When they did this, doctors were operating outside their competence. Doctors don't deal in "right" and "wrong," which are ethical and legal concepts, but with sickness and health. Sometimes, a man who is mentally ill can differentiate between what is right and wrong even as his illness leads him to the wrong conduct. What are the courts going to do about these people? In Texas, judges and juries have generally said send 'em to the chair. The Ruby case was no different. Excuse me, it was different. Because it was a BIG case and Texans seem to go a little crazy themselves when they're confronted with anything big.

It was not only because I was a good lawyer with a practical and an academic background in forensic medicine that I got the case. I defended Ruby because I was a colorful lawyer, too.

The Ruby family didn't have much money for Jack's defense. Soon, Earl Ruby, Jack's brother, realized there was only one source of funds to hire a lawyer: the media. A damn good Hollywood writer named Bill Woodfield and an entrepreneur named Lawrence Schiller persuaded Earl to syndicate Jack Ruby's story worldwide. They told him that the story *would* be easier to sell and make more money if he had a colorful lawyer. They suggested Mel Belli. Jack Smith of the Los Angeles *Times* had written a long feature on Belli during a recent murder trial in Southern California, "L.A. WATCHING NEW COURT IDOL EMERGE." Belli, they said, was the man to take the case, *if* you could get him. Earl didn't know. He'd already considered Charles Bellows of Chicago, Charles Tessmer of Dallas, Jake Ehrlich of San Francisco and Percy Foreman of Houston, four of the best criminal lawyers in the country. He thought they all wanted a lot of money. What would Belli want?

In a private meeting in the kitchen of my home in Los Angeles, I told Earl my fee would be between $50,000 and $75,000. Earl said that Woodfield and Schiller thought they could probably get him $25,000 for the Jack Ruby story. Only $25,000? I wanted to try the case. "Okay," I said. "Don't worry about the rest."

All I ever got from Earl Ruby was $11,000. After the trial, Earl gave me another check—which promptly bounced.

I thought I might get back my expenses with a book on the case and entered into a collaboration agreement with Alvin Moscow, the Hollywood writer who had helped Richard Nixon write *Six Crises*. We were given a contract and a $20,000 advance from David McKay. But after a few days at the trial, Moscow left in a huff because, he said, I was giving everything away to the newsmen and women who had flocked to Dallas. By the time David McKay published the book, he said, there'd be nothing new to tell. But hell, this was a public trial, and I had to try to educate people, particularly the people of Dallas, about the peculiar nature of this case. There was a popular feeling that since Ruby had shot Oswald, and on television, why even have a trial? Furthermore, District Attorney Henry Menasco Wade, Jr., had already promised the world that he'd see to it that Ruby would get the electric chair. I wanted to overcome that kind of prejudicial statement and I couldn't do so by keeping quiet. I had to talk to the press. Wade complained that I had called four press conferences before he could call one. He was wrong. He called one before I ever got into the case, talking about death for Ruby, and thus influencing public opinion. That infuriated me.

If talking to the press hurt my book, so be it. I was

first and foremost a trial lawyer, and my first obligation was to my client. As it turned out, I found another good writer whom I liked to help me, Maurice Carroll. He was covering the trial for the New York *Herald Tribune*. *Dallas Justice* was the fruit of our joint effort. David McKay published it in October of 1964, and it presented my views about this most celebrated and most misunderstood case. My royalties came to zilch. The book barely made back the advance. (Six years later, the Lyndon B. Johnson Library in Austin sent me a copy of the book and asked that I "suitably inscribe" it. I did. I wrote, "To LBJ, the biggest thief to come to the White House up to Richard Nixon." And to think I'd filed suit in September, 1964, to stop Barry Goldwater from running for President of the U.S. against Johnson—on the grounds Barry Goldwater wasn't a native-born U.S. citizen, having been born in Arizona ten years before it became a state.)

In retrospect, then, I was chosen to defend Jack Ruby because I was, in addition to everything else, colorful. Boy, was I colorful! To read now the newspaper and magazine accounts that appeared then makes me blush in a way I haven't since I was seven.

John S. Knight, president and editor of the Knight Newspapers, sent his own signed editorial to each of the papers in the Knight chain and told how I took him "to the cleaners" in the Miami libel suit. He noted an AP story describing my moist-eyed reaction to Jack Ruby's own story and said, "That's pure, unadulterated Belli for you. Even Texas has never seen a performance that can match Belli at his best. . . . The urbane Belli, with his cowboy boots and Savile Row suits, is the greatest actor since John Barrymore. I should know. It cost us $100,000 for a seat in the witness chair."

The repeated references to what I wore puzzled me the

most. Was I the only lawyer in the world who tried to dress up to the dignity of the court? Bill Flynn of the Washington *Post* wrote about my Savile Row suits, my handmade shirts with diamond studs (I never had a pair) and flowing Byronesque ties, my starched cuffs, my black boots, high-heeled, highly polished. *Time* focused on my Chesterfield overcoat with fur collar. The Toronto *Telegram* described my red velvet carpetbag full of legal papers (resembling something usually found strapped to the top of a stagecoach). *The Saturday Evening Post* gave the inside story on my suits, which themselves were dark and conservative: My tailor had "added certain nonconformist modifications. The jacket and matching vest are lined with bright red silk, and the pockets of the sharply creased trousers are cut parallel to the waist, frontier style."

What all this had to do with my lawyering, I'll never know. But that was the press for you. Maybe it was easier for a reporter to describe what I wore than go back into the appeals court decisions on the Cutter case (for example) and tell readers how I had made new law in the warranty field. Or maybe the reporter had learned from experience that his editors didn't want to overburden their readers with that heavy stuff, they simply wanted to entertain or excite or appall them. *The Saturday Evening Post* piece, "A Flashy Lawyer for Oswald's Killer," by Richard Warren Lewis, did precisely that. Oh, Lewis wrote about some of my courtroom and appeals court victories. But he wrote a helluva lot more about my flamboyant lifestyle, my Silver Cloud Rolls-Royce, my three luxurious homes, my law offices around the world,* my

---

* I now have my name on the door of legal offices in Los Angeles, Washington, D.C., New York City, Munich and Tokyo, as well as San Francisco. It's simply good business to maintain my presence in those places.

historic office in San Francisco and the grand banquets therein where, once, a shapely harpist "unencumbered by any clothing" provided dinner music. (That was a damn lie: the girl wore slippers and earrings.)

Still, though Lewis had emphasized the flash and the trash, he helped me get across a declaration of my most serious intentions in the case. His article ended with my view of the issues: "We have to overhaul our concept of insanity in the courtroom. What we're trying is whether Ruby was deprived of his senses—that's what no one saw. It will require the testimony of the finest psychiatric experts in the world to determine what went on inside this man."

As it turned out, few really cared about that. This was a state trial, one of those courtroom events that impinge on the deepest subconscious feelings of an entire nation. It was to be like the trials of presidential assassins Leon Czolgosz and Charles Guiteau—the murderers of Presidents McKinley and Garfield—where the verdict was already preordained by public opinion. It was like the trials to come of Sirhan Sirhan and Arthur Bremer, who each, though clearly afflicted with grave mental illnesses, got the maximum penalties under the law. It was like other notorious miscarriages of justice in American history: Sacco-Vanzetti, Scopes, the Scottsboro boys or maybe the Rosenbergs.

What was Ruby's mental state when he killed Oswald? I never thought that Ruby himself knew. I finally came to the conclusion that Ruby shot Oswald during some kind of blackout—he never could recall the moment when he pulled the trigger—but rather than admit that to himself, Ruby concocted a story. "We know I did it for Jackie and the kids," Ruby told me during an early conference in his jail cell. He said he wanted to save the

President's widow the trauma of appearing in the Oswald trial. But I couldn't accept that. I knew that his first lawyer, Tom Howard, had, perhaps unconsciously, planted that idea in his mind or watered and fertilized it. But it didn't add up. Mrs. Kennedy and the kids would never have had to come to Dallas for the trial of Oswald. From everything else that I knew about Ruby's movements in November, 1963, I knew that an incredible series of chance happenings had put him in a position where acting on an unthinking impulse, in a blackout, he could shoot Oswald.

But what kind of blackout? After my first visit with Ruby, several weeks after the shooting, I couldn't say. Something was mentally wrong with Ruby. I was sure of that. But what?

Ruby was not what I had expected at all. He had been brought up in a tough ghetto section of a tough city, Chicago. He had operated a striptease joint in the Southwest's gaudiest big city, Dallas. In my imagination, he should have been fat, oily, with polished nails, wearing a sharp, shiny suit, with rings on his pudgy fingers.

I found him in white jail coveralls. He had a face like a ferret, he was clean shaven and neat, and his thinning black hair was combed straight back. There was something odd about his eyes. They shone like a beagle's.

"I'm Belli," I said.

"Yes, I know," Ruby replied. He shook my hand mechanically. Then he turned to Tom Howard—who was in the case until the day the trial began—and poured out a litany of complaints, about the way the case was going, about the little slights he was receiving in the county jail, about how they weren't giving him his diet pills. He was very matter-of-fact. He gave no sign that he was even aware of his celebrity status or the possibility of impending disaster. He seemed like a guy on the outside who just happened to be on the inside.

Jack Ruby was a great talker. He talked to anyone and everyone who came by his cell. One day, wondering to myself how the District Attorney and his men seemed to know so much about our case, I asked Ruby what he'd been telling his favorite guard, the one who talked religion and read the Bible to him. "I told him everything, Mel, what happened when I shot the gun, and about Jackie and the children and about the story we're telling for the trial."

I groaned. "Jack, you *don't* remember all of that." It was just Ruby filling in the blanks in his memory again—the doctors would call it "confabulation." (Really to comprehend the Ruby case one must understand the convoluted process of confabulation, a kind of defense mechanism used by psychotics to conceal the fact that their minds are cracking up. They really can't remember. So they fill in.)

I honestly thought Ruby was insane. But try to convince a Texas jury of that in a big case. Jurors generally find it difficult to acquit a man on grounds of insanity if they themselves, in his position, might have been strongly tempted to commit his crime. In effect, they're rejecting their own antisocial impulses (we've all got them) by punishing the man who had yielded to them. And if ever there were a case where jurors were inclined to feel this way, the Ruby case was one. Especially Dallas jurors.

That's why I wanted to get the case shifted out of Dallas. Under Articles 560 and 562 of the Code of Criminal Procedure of Texas, the judge presiding at a criminal trial can order the trial moved out of his county if he is satisfied that prejudice against the defendant would prevent him from obtaining a fair and impartial jury. And so, in a change of venue hearing in Dallas on February 10, 1964, I tried to show that Dallas was a cesspool of prejudice. Out of that pool, I argued, we couldn't get a jury that was unbiased. How was it biased? It was my primary contention that the city of Dallas itself would be on trial as much as Jack Ruby was. Dallas had been shamed by the assassination of President Kennedy, doubly shamed by letting the President's assassin be killed in the Dallas police station itself. And so, a Dallas jury had to convict Ruby in order to acquit Dallas.

But how could I prove such prejudice? Few of the city's leaders—or anyone else, for that matter—would admit such a thing under oath. I put Sam Bloom, the judge's public relations man, on the stand. He only had to move over a bit, since he was occupying a place on the bench next to the trial judge! "I don't think Dallas has any sins that need be washed away," said Sam Bloom. There were only a few who would try to gainsay Mr. Bloom. One was Stanley Marcus, president of the justly famous Neiman-Marcus department store. "I have grave reservations," he told the court, "whether the defense *or* the prosecution can get a fair trial in Dallas." District Attorney Henry Wade asked if he didn't think anti-Ruby feeling was prevalent everywhere else, too. "In Dallas," replied Marcus, "the feeling is more personal."

I got a few others on the stand who agreed with Marcus. But Judge Brown said we ought to try to pick a jury. If we couldn't get one that was unbiased, then he'd move the trial elsewhere. But that was a lie. Later, I found out from one of Brown's fellow judges that he never had any intention of moving the trial to another city. He had a passion for publicity, and this would be the biggest case of his career. Moving the trial might mean handing the case to another judge.

We got a bad jury. Judge Brown summoned several

hundred potential jurors to appear. We examined 172 of them before Judge Brown forced upon us an entirely WASP jury eager to do its Dallas duty. Some were so eager to serve that, though they admitted they'd seen the shooting of Oswald on television, they pretended they had no "fixed opinion" who did it. I couldn't believe that. These jurors wanted a ringside seat for the big show. Mrs. Louis Malone, the aunt of the Dallas police department's public relations officer, seemed pretty eager. Joe Tonahill, a Texas attorney who assisted me during the Ruby trial, asked her if she might be curious why a shooting had occurred, and she gave this amazing answer: "Yes, I am—*if* it happened."

Now everyone in the U.S. knew it happened. That wasn't an issue here.* But if anyone said he had serious doubts that Ruby shot Oswald, he was trying very hard— too hard—to qualify himself as a juror. We didn't want Mrs. Malone. We tried to reject her, but the judge denied us: we'd run out of our rights to challenge jurors without proving due cause, what the courts call "peremptory challenges." So the policeman's aunt became our twelfth juror. And the drama began.

The principal actors were Joe Brown, the judge; Henry Wade and Bill Alexander for the prosecution; Joe Tonahill and I for the defense. Jack Ruby? For a time, it seemed as though he was the least important person in the courtroom.

At least, Joe Brown *looked* like a judge, with a wrinkled face, heavy gray hair and an ever-present pipe. But he was weak and he let the District Attorney make his decisions for him because he knew he was too ignorant

---

* Caesar, who attended the trial, asked me, "Father, why are you pleading Mr. Ruby not guilty when everyone saw him do it?" I replied, "We didn't see what was going on in his mind. That's the only thing we are going to try."

of the law to make many decisions on his own. He had not even graduated from high school. He did pass the Texas Bar after attending a third-rate (and short-lived) law school in Dallas. He practiced law for one year before he became a justice of the peace and moved from that position two decades later to the criminal court. Once when we were arguing a legal point that I thought called for the citation of some cases and an application of res gestae, his Honor called me up to the bench and whispered to me, "Mel, I wish you'd lay off that pig Latin." And when I cited a series of cases to show that Ruby could be released on bail under Texas precedents, he filled me in on Texas ways by whispering, friendlylike, "Mel, them's nigger cases. Don't cite 'em." Well, at any rate, Judge Brown was friendly.

That was more than you could say for the District Attorney, Henry Wade, or his assistant, Bill Alexander. To Wade, any means at all seemed justified by the end. Wade was a shark. He'd bragged that he'd asked for the death penalty twenty-four times and got it twenty-three. Before the trial had even begun, he told the press, "Belli is a very interesting, international lawyer. He has written a book on Roosha." It was an ex-FBI man's attempt, Hoover-style, to color me pink, and he did so, I suspect, in anticipation of his last words to the jury, "Let communism know we believe in the right of law here." Wade played the country boy. He never offered a legal citation. He bellowed at witnesses he didn't like. He was invariably slumped in his chair, chewing an unlit cigar. Wade was a competitor who liked to win—at any cost. "If you go hunting," said one Dallas lawyer, "Henry gets the biggest deer, and if you go fishing, he gets the most fish. If you play bridge or dominoes with him, he'll beat you."

I didn't dislike Henry, but Bill Alexander, Wade's number one assistant, was something else again. He was a tall, taunt, aggressive man with a pockmarked face, jug ears, narrow eyes and thin lips that never smiled except in contempt. Dallas lawyers were afraid to tangle with him, for he carried a concealed gun with him at all times, even in the courtroom. But not in this courtroom. I think, for once, he was scared of his opposition, for if he had worn a gun in this case, I would not have made a scene, I would have stopped the trial then and there. Bill Alexander's rod was all the evidence I needed to demonstrate the climate of violence that prevailed in Dallas. Even without the gun, Alexander's climate was violent. One day in court, he referred to Ruby as "a Jew boy." I challenged that slur, the judge tried to smooth it over, and after the furor had died down, the assistant District Attorney offered to be less blunt in his phraseology. He, too, was ex-FBI, and, like Wade, burning with a zeal to convict. Once, he reluctantly gave me some police reports. He told reporters he did so only "because the goddamn liberal northern Supreme Court makes them available to the defense."

Joe Tonahill of Jasper, Texas, was a wonderfully exuberant 250-pound bear of a man, a lifelong friend and a fellow member of the American Trial Lawyers Association, a member of the board of my Belli Foundation and rich enough to waive his fee in the Ruby case. As a Texan, he seemed genuinely ashamed of the railroading we were to receive at the hands of the authorities. He could hardly hide his disgust for a proceeding where the prosecuting attorneys could invariably tell the judge what to do—and get away with it.*

I think I surprised everyone by not doing Act One of

* Later in the trial, Joe rose to make an objection: "Incompetent, irrelevant, immaterial and—un-Texan." Judge Brown replied, "It's not incompetent, irrelevant or immaterial. But I'll sustain the objection." It was "un-Texan."

The Music Man. I was the soul of decorum in the court. Dorothy Kilgallen, in Dallas for most of the trial and a frequent lunch companion of mine, along with Bob Considine of the Hearst papers, said that I was "Chesterfieldian" in my approach to the court. Invariably, I would rise out of respect when Judge Brown entered the courtroom, while Henry Wade and Bill Alexander sprawled in their chairs. Invariably, I would begin with the time-honorable salutation, "May it please the court?" When Wade and Alexander wanted the judge's attention, they would shout out everything short of, "Hey, Joe!" On one occasion, Wade said that, too.

The brunt of our defense—in fact, our only defense—was that Jack Ruby was incompetent when he killed Lee Harvey Oswald. The corollary of that was simple enough: as a civilized nation, we didn't execute crazies even though they do kill. It was an opportunity, at least, to show the rest of the world how fair and humane our justice system could be. Trouble was, our system wasn't fair or humane.

Hubert M. Smith, chancellor of the Law Science Academy of America at the University of Texas had written to me two weeks before the trial started. "Mel, I feel that the Ruby case might well develop into one of the historic medicolegal cases in the criminal field and I am certainly hopeful that there will be further affirmative findings by the scientific experts." From the experts, I was hoping for a medical diagnosis of a *functional* psychosis, which could lead to a simple insanity plea, one that any juror would have to acknowledge and say, "Well, okay, he's crazy."

What the doctors came up with, it turned out, was a diagnosis infinitely more subtle, infinitely harder to back up in court, a diagnosis that jolted me so much that I telephoned one of them and almost begged him to tell me I had misunderstood what he had found. But as all the doctors came in with their reports, my fears began to shrink. Their findings all fell with honest precision into a consistent scientific pattern, the most perfect defense backed by diagnostic reports I had ever seen.

But the ignorance of the judge, jury and prosecuting attorneys (who would help the judge and the jury feel justified in ignoring the psychiatric and psychological evidence) precluded a courtroom victory—the only thing, alas, which the press and public would accept as "proof" of our case's validity.

We proved that Ruby was incompetent. We used only three witnesses in our direct presentation. Each traced his own trip into the inner space of Jack Ruby. Dr. Roy Schafer, one of the nation's most eminent clinical psychologists and a professor at Yale, laid the foundation with his psychological tests, which he said showed a clear indication of brain damage. Dr. Martin Towler, a Texas psychiatrist with a strong expertise in neurology and electroencephalography, pinpointed the precise variety of that brain damage. And Dr. Manfred Guttmacher of Baltimore, one of the country's most respected authorities on mental illness and crime, put it all together by showing how Ruby's mental disabilities had exploded into irrational action.

Maybe they were too good. The morning after Dr. Guttmacher testified, I dropped into a barber shop near the courthouse. The barber had just placed the towel around my neck when I heard someone say, "—and they got those Jew psychiatrists out from Maryland."

"Yeah," said another voice, "those slick Jew psychiatrists with their slick Jew lawyers."

This was simply Nazi stuff. I swept away the towel and the barber stepped aside as I leaped and gave the Nazi salute. "*Achtung!*" I yelled. "*Achtung! Heil Hitler!*" And

I goosestepped out of the shop while these locals stood there with their mouths open.

There was a kind of bullying nazism that prevailed in the courtroom, too. The prosecuting attorneys tried to keep my star witness, Dr. Schafer, from testifying at all. I had to fight for almost two hours, in and out of the presence of the jury, before *they* would allow the eminent clinical psychologist to tell the court what he had discovered about Jack Ruby.

From Dr. Schafer's psychological tests alone (he took no case history from Ruby and saw no other doctor's reports before he made up his own mind), he concluded that Ruby had organic brain damage and that the most likely specific nature of that brain damage was psychomotor epilepsy. As I was trying to get Dr. Schafer's description of psychomotor epilepsy (which was *not* grand mal epilepsy, the so-called falling-down sickness characterized by loss of consciousness and violent convulsions), Bill Alexander objected that I hadn't asked Dr. Schafer whether Ruby knew the difference between right and wrong.

The judge agreed with Alexander. He wasn't interested in anything now but the answer (from the wrong kind of expert witness) to what he termed "the legal question," the right-wrong M'Naughten inquiry. The prosecuting attorneys looked so smug in their ignorance I wanted to scream. I gritted my teeth and tried to explain that Dr. Schafer could no more express an opinion concerning sanity than a lab technician could diagnose appendicitis.

Judge Brown didn't understand and told me that I could have an exception if I wanted one—in other words, that I could play the rest of the ball game under protest and let the Texas Supreme Court decide who was right. I shouted, "I don't want an exception. I want [the court to know] what this man has done laboriously over a hundred hours, your Honor."

The judge knew I wasn't going to sit back meekly. So he put the jury in a holding room while I tried to explain—again—what I was trying to do. Apparently in Texas they'd never seen a psychologist give this kind of careful testimony as a predicate for other experts, particularly a psychiatrist.

By now, however, the heads over at the prosecution table were huddled together—Wade had twenty-seven assistant prosecutors working on this case with him and ten investigators—and it was apparent from the buzzing that they knew they'd gone too far. Alexander rose and interposed with a suggestion that might allow the judge an escape from his serious judicial error. He wondered whether I was assuring the court that the other doctors in the case would use Dr. Schafer's report as a basis for their opinion.

I was angry and ready now to let these turkeys choke on their own giblets. "I'm not telling anything. I'm going to play it by Texas law—" where, I figured, it was now becoming apparent, trickery and ambush seemed to mean more than a search for the truth. "I'm not telling nobody nothing."

Now the prosecution was backpedaling furiously. Judge Brown wanted Schafer off the stand. The prosecution now wanted to keep him there.

Finally, the light began to dawn on Joe Brown. He wondered about the relation between Dr. Schafer's reports and the conclusions of the doctors to come. I explained—again. "We had no psychiatrists there at the time, we had no psychologists at the time of the shooting, so we have to reconstruct. . . . Modern medicine is teamwork, many tests and many men. In every major hospital in the United States where they have any of these problems, they have someone like Dr. Shafer to assist the psychiatrists to make a determination."

The judge was wavering now—and looking over at the prosecution table for some guidance. They'd gotten him into this. Now maybe they'd tell him how to get out.

"Ah, Judge," said Wade, "let's let him go on. I think we could have finished by now. So let's go on and let him testify."

"All right," Judge Brown said.

Astounded, I tried, as best I could, to pick up the threads of Dr. Shafer's testimony. Dr. Schafer tried to describe psychomotor epilepsy. "The attack may involve expressions of rage, but it doesn't always. Some patients with psychomotor epilepsy act very bizarrely during their attack, and frequently they are thought to be schizophrenic until neurological exams are conducted on them, and they may be capable of more or less organized action during their attacks." The state, said Dr. Schafer, could vary "from a second or two . . . at least up to a day or two."

The beautiful thing about Dr. Schafer's hunches was that they found confirmation in the brain-wave tests administered later by the court-appointed psychiatrist, Dr. Martin Towler. To build the bridge between Dr. Schafer and Dr. Towler, I asked Dr. Schafer one more question. "And you ultimately, then, at the end of your report, requested electroencephalographic studies, did you not?"

"Yes," Dr. Schafer replied.

Wade was so enraged by what Dr. Schafer had said on the stand (and by what he knew was coming) that he subjected Dr. Schafer to a cross-examination that was a symphony of whines, shouts and supercilious snarls about this funny disease called "motorcycle epilepsy." Wade got nowhere with his questions. That only made him angrier. In a final effort to discredit Dr. Schafer, he demanded the doctor recite from memory one of the stories he would read to patients as part of their memory test. "We'll see how good *his* memory is," he said in a smirking aside to the jury.

Dr. Schafer flushed and then, pointing out that a testing psychologist needn't himself memorize the stories, proceeded to rattle the story off with precision—and a small, triumphant smile.

We gathered that night in the Cork Club of the Hilton Hotel—the only night that we had all our doctors together: my wife, Joy, and me, Dr. Schafer and his wife, Dr. Guttmacher, who had been waiting for some days to testify, and Dr. Towler, who came to dinner angry. Over Texas sirloins and a good Pommard, Dr. Towler told us why he was angry. Judge Brown had dropped Towler as his court-appointed consultant; because his defense findings didn't help the prosecution, the judge ruled he was "a defense doctor." Could Judge Brown have tipped off his own prejudice in this case to any greater degree? Well, yes, he could. Dr. Towler said that Judge Brown had sent a state trooper from Dallas to Austin a few days before to pick up copies of his brain-wave tests—and then handed them over to the prosecution.

The next day in court, we unfurled those brain tracings, six hundred feet of spidery black lines on white chart paper that folded out like an accordion. Dr. Towler, who had done more than four thousand EEG's a year for twenty years, pointed to the significant fluctuations that proved what Dr. Schafer had suspected. To make sure, Dr. Towler had sent the EEG's to the world's leading expert on the electroencephalogram, the man who had helped devise the test in 1932, Dr. Frederic Gibbs of the University of Chicago. Dr. Gibbs had confirmed Dr.

Towler's reading, and now Dr. Towler announced in court that Ruby had "a seizure disorder, most likely psychomotor epilepsy." Furthermore, Dr. Towler pointed out in his lazy Texas drawl, at the time of a seizure, a man could behave like an automaton. "He may have smattering bits of memory. Most patients will be amnesic for the entire episode."

And if he only remembers part of what happened? I asked. Dr. Towler said he could "confabulate"—"fill in memory gaps with something which may not have transpired. . . . It could be an unconscious thing in a confused individual." He'd be open, the doctor said, to suggestions from the people around him—to help him fill in the gaps. This was precisely the picture I had of Ruby after he had shot Oswald. He didn't know what he'd done. But when the cops started telling him, those were all the clues he needed.

Wade's cross-examination of Towler was good. He hit on the weakest point in our case: though we had ample medical testimony that Ruby had brain-wave tracings indicating that he suffered from periodic seizures, we obviously couldn't prove that he was having one when he killed Oswald. In a case like this, we didn't have to prove this contention beyond a reasonable doubt, only according to a preponderance of the evidence. We had some witnesses in the Dallas police station who testified that at first Ruby didn't seem to know what he'd done: Captain Will Fritz asked Ruby, "Jack, why did you do it?" And Ruby replied, "Do what?" And we'd destroyed the testimony of others who said that Ruby had called Oswald a son-of-a-bitch just before he'd shot him. It was a *cop* who had cried at Ruby, "You son-of-a-bitch, Jack. Don't do it." For the right jury, that could have been good enough. For this jury, it wasn't anything.

Wade asked Dr. Towler whether he had an opinion

on Ruby's condition at the time of the shooting. He did not.

Right away, without preliminaries, my third medical witness, Dr. Manfred S. Guttmacher, said *he* had an opinion on Ruby's condition on that historic Sunday morning in the Dallas police station. "I don't think he was capable of knowing right from wrong or understood the nature and consequences of his actions," Dr. Guttmacher testified.

Who was Guttmacher? He was one of the most eminent men in the field. Johns Hopkins- and Harvard-trained, postgrad work in London and Prague, he had been the director for thirty-three years of a psychiatric clinic attached to the criminal courts of Baltimore. Each year, he was involved in some five hundred criminal cases having psychiatric overtones, many of them homicide cases, and most of the time he testified on behalf of the prosecution —against defendants who were faking insanity. He was an impressive man, tall, heavyset, with a prominent nose, deep dark eyes, a high forehead framed by a fringe of white hair. His voice was cultured, resonant, and he didn't try to snow the jury with big words.

He was also a man of principle. He believed that on the day Oswald was shot, "Ruby was struggling hard to maintain his equilibrium, and his sanity, really. And then this situation arose where there was a great deal of excitement and the lights, and the man suddenly coming out, and I think that he just decompensated. I think he just—the lid came off, and this violent act took place. And then I think after he reorganized his defenses again, he became a relatively normal person, on the surface at least." But he wouldn't go so far as to say that Jack Ruby was having a seizure at that moment. No one, he said, could *prove* that. "What we have," Dr. Guttmacher wrote to me on the eve of the trial, "is that Jack has a definitely abnormal and damaged brain . . . definitely abnormal brain waves. Whether we call them discharges of psychomotor epilepsy or a psychomotor variant is, I believe, of no real importance. . . . There is abundant evidence in the medical literature that people with brain waves like Jack's, showing a disturbance in the temporal lobe, in most instances, behave abnormally and are given to psychopathiclike behavior, particularly to irrational outbursts of aggression, often when under stress, which can or cannot be actual seizure attacks."

And that, basically, is what Dr. Guttmacher said on the stand. Or at least tried to. Wade got right into the middle of the testimony. "Judge," he whined, "we object to this ramblin' on."

I flared at that. "I resent this cornball talk, 'ramblin' on,' Judge. This man is a learned scientist, and to say he's rambling on is insulting to him—"

"Well, I object to it," Wade persisted, "and I think he's ramblin' on something that has nothing—"

"That's because you don't understand," I said. "And for a person who doesn't understand to say someone is rambling, I think is the height of ignorance." There were more than a few moments of silence while everyone mulled that one. Finally, Judge Brown told us all to "git along." He meant, I guess, to let Dr. Guttmacher say anything he had a mind to. Judge Brown wouldn't accuse him of rambling. No sir.

After Dr. Guttmacher had had his say—he was on the stand for most of the afternoon—Bill Alexander plunged into an effective cross-examination, which shouldn't have hurt us a bit. He addressed his questions to Dr. Guttmacher in a half-incredulous, half-contemptuous tone. He asked when this seizure state began. "In my opinion," said Dr. Guttmacher, "when he walked down the ramp there and saw all the people, the bright lights."*

"Did he know what he was doing?"

"He was very much like a sleepwalker."

"When did he come out of this . . . state?"

"It could be a matter of less than a minute."

"As little as two seconds?"

"As little as ten seconds."

"Your diagnosis?"

"I call it epilepsy," Dr. Guttmacher testified, "but I hadn't maintained that this man was *in* a state of psychomotor epilepsy. I think he *has* psychomotor epilepsy. I don't think there's any question about that, but this state can occur, this kind of disassociation—I was going to read what Dr. Menninger calls episodic dysfunction—can occur in people who are not epileptics, who have very weak ego structures."

Bill Alexander then asked, "If you say he wasn't in a psychomotor epileptic seizure at the time he committed the act, what is your diagnosis? What was he suffering from?"

"I think he had a rupture of the ego, and a period of episodic dyscontrol, and I think it's impossible to tell whether this was in a psychomotor attack or if—it does occur, for instance, in battle. It occurs in people who don't have psychomotor epilepsy. It can occur under great stress in people who have a damaged—particularly a person with a damaged functioning brain that this man has. . . . We have no data to tell whether at that moment it

* Doctors can induce an epileptic state in a patient by stimulating the patient with rapidly flashing bright lights. If he's an epileptic, the blinking lights will generally bring on a seizure.

was a spasm of psychomotor epilepsy or whether it was episodic dyscontrol."

"Your diagnosis?"

"A mental cripple, carrying an unbearable load, who cracked."

"A *bad* personality?"

"A *sick* personality."

Dr. Guttmacher had helped us. Unwilling to specify that Ruby had had a psychomotor seizure just as he shot Oswald, he insisted nevertheless on some sort of mental upheaval at that point instead and had linked it to the strong evidence of brain damage that we had already seen. The jury, which had listened to Dr. Schafer with huffy neutrality and had followed Dr. Towler's EEG's with open boredom, looked interested and alive. I thought we had tipped the weight of the evidence over the line toward the likelihood of insanity. I would have liked to have gotten on the stand Dr. Gibbs, the psychologist who had devised the EEG back in 1932, but he didn't want to come to the trial. So be it. It was enough. I announced to the court, "The defense rests."

If the jury could have considered the evidence then and there, we might—just possibly—have won. But the prosecution had its time now for rebuttal. And we had time for a surrebuttal. And they had time for a counter-counterrebuttal. Too much rebuttal. By the time we'd ended all that (we even got Dr. Gibbs to change his mind at the last moment, fly to Dallas and defend the EEG), the jury was thoroughly confused. And exhausted.

Judge Brown compounded the confusion and the exhaustion. He wanted the verdict to go against Ruby. (He finally ended up confirming our suspicions rather openly when he confessed to Tonahill, an old friend, that "a suspended sentence would hurt me," paused, then added, "I know it would hurt Henry [Wade], too.") Now, he would keep the final day of the trial wheezing along until 1:06 A.M. That's right. We ran more than an hour past midnight, bone-tired, bleary-eyed, our minds reeling.

The scene was more like a championship prizefight than the windup of a jury trial. Judge Brown had a live TV camera in the rear of the courtroom for the verdict and mikes set up for radio coverage of his jury charge and the summations, which, he insisted, would have to go on that night, "even if it took until nine o'clock in the morning."

An unnatural shimmering light filled the high-ceilinged old courtroom and the smell of the ringside, cigar smoke and bodies and sordid expectation all commingled together. For the first time, the ban on standees was relaxed. All the benches were filled, the walls were lined and a crowd bellied out around the bailiff's desk near the door to the judge's right. The crowd itself was a tony one—not the usual courtroom audience at all; some of the cream of Dallas's society came from the opera dressed for parties afterward. These people didn't stand in line with the peasants, they strolled right up past the evangelists outside who were still parading with their placards that read, PSYCHIATRISTS ARE TOOLS OF THE DEVIL," past the portrait of Judge Roy Bean, the famous hanging judge of the frontier, who would have regarded this kangaroo court with nothing but approval, and whispered their names to a guard at the door or got a nod from one of the courthouse officials. Down in the lobby stood a marble drinking fountain. Hastily painted over for the "outside press" to see was the legend, dimly still visible, "for whites only."

Instead of having dinner, I hurried down the street for a steambath, then got back to the court at 8 P.M. for Judge Brown's charge to the jury. When we first saw that charge earlier in the day, Joe Tonahill had complained that it called for "a directed verdict of guilty of cold-blooded murder." Phil Burleson, the young lawyer who was protecting our appeals record, drew up a list of 134 separate objections and exceptions. But the judge went right ahead and read the charge pretty much the way Henry Wade had written it for him. He read it in a friend-ly fashion, but that didn't make it any easier on Jack Ruby.

Then it was time for our summations. I don't know why I ever went ahead with anything at that hour of the night, a Friday night after a long week. We should have balked. They couldn't have held the party without us.

There were seven of us scheduled to speak: Phil Burle-son, Joe Tonahill and I for the defense, and four mem-bers of the prosecution team, Bill Alexander, Frank Watts, Jim Bowie and Henry Wade. There was a lot of wasted oratory in Joe Brown's court that night. The seven of us yammered on for more than four hours. I knew the jurors had made up their minds long ago. They weren't interested in the medical evidence. Two women jurors had slept during the important testimony of Dr. Towler, and Judge Brown actually read comic books. Eleven of the twelve had seen Ruby shoot Oswald on TV. Ruby should pay for that—never mind why he did it. It was that simple.

In his summation, Bill Alexander gave the jurors the justification they needed. "American justice is on trial," he said. "American justice had Oswald in its possession. Oswald was entitled to the protection of the law. Oswald was a living, breathing American citizen." And then Al-exander wheeled around and pointed theatrically at Jack Ruby sitting next to me and bellowed "—just like *you*, Jack Ruby, who were judge, jury and executioner."

Poor little Jack, who had shriveled down to almost

nothing during the months of his trial and incarceration. He gave a start of surprise. Amid the legal wrangling of the trial, no one had paid much attention to Jack Ruby. I didn't even put him on the stand, because I didn't think he'd help the case. He did not know why he shot Oswald and he would rather go to the electric chair than admit he couldn't remember shooting Oswald. He would have made up a story and put on a brave show in court.

I got up to speak just before midnight. Everything seemed unreal. "Is this really a jury trial?" I asked myself. "Am I ready to ask an American jury to spare a man's life at this hour?" I walked the five miles from counsel table to jury rail. It took me several hours. I felt like Alice in Wonderland falling through the looking glass. My feet weren't touching the floor.

Apparently, I handled my pleas with some eloquence. I don't remember. But Reporter Harold Scarlett wrote in the Houston *Post*:

It turned out to be a voice whistling at the waves. Still, some who heard it may remember it to their graves. . . . .

Many lawyers have argued before many jurors. Some fine ones argued eloquently that night, before and after Belli. But at the moment he sat down, Belli seemed to be truly one of the anointed ones.

In less than an hour, he had ranged over a lifetime of learning. Like a mountain goat, he leaped unerringly from Pasteur to the hunchback of Notre Dame, to Anatole France and "Penguin Island," to Humpty Dumpty, to President Kennedy.

And Jack Ruby.

"The village clown, the village idiot . . . the little guy who trots coffee to the police station . . . Everything is fine until something happens, but then . . ."

Belli was gifted by nature with a velvety, hypnotic voice that could charm cobras out of their baskets.

Arguing before the jury, he played that voice like a symphony. It was by turns a Stradivarius, a bugle, an oboe, a snare drum racing at breakneck speed through key pages of the trial testimony. . . .

Belli himself said later he was too tired, he talked too long, it was not Belli at his best.

But Clarence Darrow would have liked it.

Clarence Darrow wouldn't have liked Henry Wade's summation. Wade acted like a country bumpkin who ridiculed everything in the trial he couldn't understand and asked the jurors what they wanted history books to say about them. It was a measure of Wade and of the jury that they went out and voted a verdict which history—and the Texas appeals court—would soon reverse and condemn.

They didn't vote that night. It was 1:06 A.M. when Wade finished, and Judge Brown told them to try to get a night's sleep. The bailiffs led the jurors out, Ruby's guards escorted him down the corridor to the jail elevator. The newspapermen and women bolted for the telephones in the pressroom. The society folk who had lined the courtroom walls drifted out in little knots.

I walked uptown. Dallas is an early-to-bed city. The beer joints close at midnight, and by 12:30 you can play cards in the middle of the main street without fear of being run over. Sybille Bedford, the renowned English journalist in Dallas for *Life* Magazine, and I had a chicken sandwich at a glaring, all-night lunch counter that reeked of rancid deep-fry oil, and then I walked to my hotel and lay awake until dawn.

It took the jurors one hour and fifty minutes the next

morning to come up with a verdict. The two women jurors who had fallen asleep in the jury box during Dr. Towler's explanation of the EEG tests asked to have the transcript of that testimony read to them so they could fill in the gaps. But one of the men on the jury told them they wouldn't need the psychiatric testimony. Good Lord! That was our whole case.

I had rather expected the jury to come back with a verdict—a guilty verdict—in the afternoon sometime. It was Saturday morning. I had slept until ten, dressed casually (putting on a black Italian sport shirt without a tie), expecting to return to my hotel room after I had had a chat with Jack Ruby in his cell. I started up the street toward the courthouse and the jail with Sam Gallu, the movie producer who had been shooting film for a documentary on the trial. The streets were full of tootling high school bands, girls on prancing horses, drum majorettes twirling their batons, officials running around with clipboards. The Dallas Saint Patrick's Day parade—three days early—was about to start.

There was a crowd milling about the courthouse. "Hey," someone said, "they were looking for you. The jury has a verdict."

So soon? I thought, and my heart leaped. No civilized community, I told myself, could vote death that quickly. It would be hard for them, in that short a time, even to find him guilty. Maybe we had a victory after all.

I was wrong. The verdict was guilty, the penalty death. As Judge Brown read the decision, one of the jurors flicked a piece of lint off the knee of his well-creased trousers. So much for Jack Ruby. "We expected it all along," I whispered to Ruby, "but we tried this case for an appeals court. We'll make it there." They were leading Ruby away, and the TV cameras focused on the jurors as they started to file out.

I rose and erupted, "May I thank the jury for a victory for bigotry and injustice?" The jurors were embarrassed. That, at least, pleased me. "Don't worry, Jack. We'll appeal this to a court outside Dallas where there is justice and due process of law." I kept on raving. "I hope the people of Dallas are proud of this jury."

By now the room was bedlam. The ever-watchful sheriff had packed the place with lawmen; for the first time since the trial started, the courtroom broke into disorder. Men with cameras, floodlights and microphones surged in from the door. Newsmen were standing on the benches and tables and the deputies started swinging on them. Groups of newsmen and women clustered around the principals. Eileen Ruby, Jack's sister, was sobbing. Henry Wade was grinning. I continued to rail at how American justice had been raped, shouting in tears. "This is a disgrace to American law," I told a TV reporter with a live mike in his hands. I added: "Ruby was railroaded, this is a kangaroo court."

I was still standing amid a cluster of reporters in the corridor outside, calmed down by now, when Judge Brown broke away from the newspeople who were interviewing him and pushed his way through to me. He extended his hand. There were tears in my eyes, some of them for this fundamentally humane and descent man who had been a prisoner of his community's prejudices. "I can't shake hands with you, Judge," I said. "You've got blood on your hands."

Pain flickered across his face. "I'm sorry you feel that way about it, Mel," he said. "Come back and see us again." He walked away.

Later on, I would get a friendly letter from Joe Brown.

Dear Mel [he wrote], Appreciate your note about

my ankle. It's doing fine. You, like me, are misunderstood. It seems that everything went wrong. However, it gives them something to talk about. I'm good for the next four years or so. I'm not too weiried [sic]. Thanks again and lots of luck to you.

Joe Brown

And I heard even later that Brown made it a point of telling his friends that Mel Belli was the "most brilliant" lawyer who'd ever appeared before him in a court of law.

Not everyone in Dallas thought so kindly of me. One skinny fellow with a long crimson neck stood there in the corridor and repeated over and over, "Hey, Belli, maybe yer the one who needs a psychiatrist. Hey, Belli, maybe yer the one who needs a psychiatrist."

I gave him a pitying look and proceeded down to the street, newsmen at my heels. I locked myself in my hotel room and started to pack. I'd had it with Dallas, for good. And I wanted to get away from—everything, for a while. I booked a train to Mexico City and then, as I waited for the train's departure, I answered the ringing phone in my room. I told a reporter for ABC Radio: "I've reassessed my feelings about Dallas. I think that it's sicker than I originally felt when I came here—those horrible bigoted, little, narrow nasty people that sat in judgment of this 'Jew boy.' I hope to get back to New York, and stand on Times Square and see some free Jews, and niggers, if you will, and some Puerto Ricans, and some dagos, and Chinese, some free Americans walk by and take 'em by the hand and say, 'Thank God, I'm back in America and out of Dallas.' "

I told him that with this jury I should have tried the case like a Dallas "nigger killing." "A second-year law student," I said, "could have done better than I did in this case. I tried to bring law, medicine, impartial consideration to this case, to Dallas, and what did I get down there? I got a lot of hog calling. And you fellows heard it, too."

I told a reporter for Dallas radio station KBOX: "Any relaxing? My relaxing is going to be done in the law library to write this appeal as fast as I can. I am ashamed of my profession, and I apologized to Jack for the law."

The reporter from KBOX asked me if maybe I shouldn't have put Jack Ruby on the stand. I said, "You couldn't have put Our Saviour on the stand to have done anything good in Dallas."

I told a reporter for radio station KLIF in Dallas: "I am going to damn Dallas with every breath. I say that Jack Ruby got an unfair trial. There wasn't a law book cracked in the whole trial. When I cited law, the judge practically held me in contempt for misconduct. This is a sick, sick, sick city, and I think we should do something about it nationally."

This reporter from KLIF asked whether I was afraid that Jack Ruby would be killed. "What I am scared of," I said, "is that they might take the watch off him and then someone will slip one of his men in there with a shiv and that will be the end of Jack Ruby and the appeal, and that will then nicely seal all of these things forever as far as Dallas is concerned."

And then I told him: "I think if the oligarchy, if the Citizens Council would just leave you people alone and someone would get rid of the Dallas *Morning News,* you wouldn't have any more trouble. Tonahill and I have gotten a group of people who are going to talk to the Dallas *Morning News* to see how much they want for us to buy it."

"And what," asked the reporter, "would you do with it if you did buy it?"

"I would put some honest, tolerant Texas editors in

charge of it and see if we couldn't change this city back to an American city."

"I'm about out of questions, Mr. Belli."

"You call again," I told him. "I have just started. I may start slow, but boy, I end up fast."

It didn't take long for the president of the American Bar Association to react. Walter E. Craig was in San Francisco on the day of the verdict, March 14, 1964. He called a press conference (right in my home city!) and declared that in my outbursts on radio and television I was guilty of "unethical conduct." That made me feel awful. Craig pretended to be speaking for "the lawyers of America." But he wasn't speaking for them (in fact, in my outbursts, it was *I* who was doing that) or even for the ABA—for Craig had had no time to consult the ABA's grievance committee, and therefore he could have had no official authorization from the committee. Unless that committee had a standing order authorizing the president to "get Belli" any time the president thinks Belli is stepping out of line.

In fact, Craig was speaking only for himself. He was an insurance-company lawyer from Phoenix. I had clashed with him and his firm in the past. This was just a matter of Craig trying to even some old scores—and get a few extra licks when I was down.

Bob Considine, the Hearst reporter, tried to put Craig's silliness in perspective for me. He found me still in Dallas and told me, "Mel, don't worry. Being thrown out of the ABA is like being drummed out of the Book-of-the-Month Club."

I didn't mind going back into Dallas. I had nothing against the people there, only against the oligarchy. When I'd left town, the cab driver wouldn't even let me pay my fare. "Ride's on me," he said. "You're our guest in

Dallas. We're not all like that goddamn D.A.'s office." And in the airport coffee shop, a little blond waitress said, "God bless you. Don't think too badly about our city."

Now, five months later, I was back to see Phil Burleson. Phil said, "Jack told me you're the only person in the world he trusts completely."

"I'd like to see that guy again," I said.

"Why don't you?" Phil replied. Consciously, I had come to Dallas to work, gratis, on the appeal. Subconsciously, I wanted to see Jack. Late that night, we drove over to the Dallas county jail.

"Hello, Mel." Ruby gave me a little, twisting, secret handshake that meant nothing.

"Hello, pal." I was shocked. Jack's skin was flabby, his hair was wispy and there were sores on his scalp. One of the guards later told me he'd been pulling hair from his head and from his arms, too.

"These civil rights riots," he whispered to me, his eyes wide, his voice husky and confidential. "They're a cover-up for a pogrom against the Jews, my people. I brought this on them." Those were just about the only coherent words he had to say. And they were crazy words.

The trial had been too much for him. Showing the nature of his peculiar insanity in public as we did provided the last disintegrating blows to a personality that had been held together with bubblegum and bailing wire for years before Ruby ever saw Oswald. Everyone at the trial should have seen that, even Edward Linn, a writer for *The Saturday Evening Post,* who, though he covered the trial, never seemed to understand what I was trying to do at Dallas. However, he was almost right on the mark when, noting that the full protection of due process drove Ruby mad, he concluded, "It would have been kinder to have stoned him to death."

But of course Ruby didn't get the full protection of due process of law. That was why Phil Burleson was writing an appeal and why I was doing a friend of the court brief—to demonstrate to the Texas Supreme Court on the trial record itself that Ruby didn't get a fair trial. The court ended up agreeing with me and reversing to remand the case for a new trial—in another city. (There were so many errors in the prosecution's case that the court reversed without even getting to the most interesting question of whether prospective jurors who have seen a murder on TV are "competent.") By then, Ruby couldn't appreciate much of that. He died of cancer of the brain two months later.

So we didn't lose the case. The State lost it. Henry Wade and Bill Alexander were the ultimate losers. Neither one got the federal judgeship he should have had.

That wasn't exactly the end of Jack Ruby. The assassination buffs who believed that Oswald and Ruby were part of a conspiracy to assassinate President Kennedy picked over Ruby's bones—and are still doing so. They even offer reinterpretations of Ruby's testimony in Dallas after the trial before Chief Justice Earl Warren and the Warren Commission's chief counsel, J. Lee Rankin. You can look it up yourself in Volume 5 of the Warren Commission's full report. There you can see ample evidence of the disintegration of Ruby's personality, his rambling, incoherent monologue and Warren's occasional, embarrassed interjections. You may puzzle, as I did, over Ruby's pleas that Warren take him back to Washington to testify because he was too frightened to say what he had to say in Dallas. He had told me once, "If I go on [the stand], I'm liable to get a lot of people in trouble." But I do not think this had anything to do with an assassination plot. For one thing, Jack Ruby had a weird, almost pathological love for President Kennedy. Jack

Ruby's worries were nothing but pathological: he was obsessed by the imagined shame and destruction he, personally, was bringing on the Jews of the world.

I was (and am) puzzled about the inability or unwillingness of most members of the Warren Commission to stand up in public and defend their report (though I understand that one of the Commission's ablest members, Joseph Ball, is now doing so). I am convinced that it is partly because of the Commission's "what we have written, we have written" attitude that a majority of Americans do not now believe the Commission's conclusions that there was no conspiracy to assassinate JFK. Men like Mark Lane could then give their own highly tendentious reconstruction of the facts (facts given them by the Warren Commission itself in its twenty-six volumes) and no one could or would gainsay them. I wish Lyndon Johnson had left some skeleton staff to speak for the Warren Commission; issues raised by the assassination buffs are with us still in the election year of 1976. Honest Americans without any ax to grind want answers—and they're getting damn few from the government.

In 1964 and 1965, I tried to do what I could. I sparred with Mark Lane in New Haven and New York City where a disorderly crowd of New York liberals hissed and booed me and applauded Lane. *The Village Voice* reported that "a middle-aged Lochinvar came out of the West and walked into an ambush." I guess I did.

Lane was bright and he had an almost encyclopedic knowledge of the facts in the JFK assassination. But his own friends among the assassination buffs have charged that Lane has played games with the facts.

Lane took some of Jack Ruby's ramblings and attached conspiratorial significance to them, and on that score at least I tried to assure Lane in private and in public that

Jack did not know or act with Oswald and knew nothing about a plot or a plan as Lane still charges.

Lane wasn't alone in his suspicions. The FBI itself investigated Ruby for longer than it ever cared to admit. The Bureau found that Ruby was a compulsive communicator, and so, while Ruby was in the Dallas county jail, it was arranged that he'd have access to a phone and a sackful of change. Then the agents sat back to see whom he would call. It turned out that Ruby phoned *everyone*. People he'd known, people he just read about in the newspapers, people he thought could help him, people it might just be nice to chat with. Ruby would phone Oscar Smith in Portland, Maine. The next day, an FBI agent would show up at Mr. Smith's front door. Ruby spent a lot of the FBI's quarters and the FBI spent a lot of time checking on the people that Ruby had called. As far. as we know, the FBI gave up that operation as a bad job.

Maybe the FBI hasn't told us all it learned. But that's another question, involving the FBI's traditional non-accountability to the American public, which I can only hope Congress will straighten out. All too often the FBI clowns around at public expense. I was sitting in my room at the Statler one day during the Ruby trial when I got a phone call from an FBI agent who wanted me to meet him in Room 621. I wondered if I couldn't meet him in the lobby, or in my room. No, it had to be Room 621. Mystified, I trotted on down to Room 621 where two FBI agents, actually in trench coats, invited me in and showed me their FBI identification. I showed them my solid-gold lifetime membership card in the Bartenders Union, San Francisco Local 410. They inspected it in all seriousness and took down the number. And then they announced the purpose of their mission.

"We think you should know," one of them said, "that

Jack Ruby has never been an agent or an employee of the FBI."

I kept a straight face. "Anything else?" I said.

"No, that's all."

I shook my head. "Tell me. Did you get this room just so you could give me this information?"

"Yes," said the agent proudly.

"Well, let's get the hell out of here," I said. "Maybe you can turn the room back in and save the taxpayers some money."

It wasn't long after Dallas that I got a notice from the American Bar Association. They didn't think it was so funny comparing membership in their august organization to membership in the Book-of-the-Month Club. And they'd rounded up eight Southern lawyers to prefer formal charges against me for my "intemperate and abusive public statements about the Dallas trial court, the jury, the District Attorney and the administration of justice."

At first, I was simply inclined to resign from the ABA. I didn't need the ABA to practice law, and about half the lawyers in the country do not, in fact, belong to the ABA. But then, I took another look at the eight lawyers who complained about my conduct and found they were all establishment lawyers, every one an insurance-company attorney. Hell, they'd have to throw me out. I wrote a twenty-six-page letter to Walter E. Craig of the ABA. "I'll be damned now if I'll resign quietly," I said, and filed a five-million-dollar suit against Craig and others in the ABA power structure to boot. (Craig was soon rewarded with a federal judgeship.)

The ABA had proved again that when it came to their own internal affairs they didn't know (or care) much about due process. Lawyers in Texas got turned down by their own Supreme Court when they tried to get me "disbarred" in Texas. Then the ABA's grievance committee said it would give me a hearing— in Dallas. I said, "You tell me when and where. I love a good fight and I'm ready. The only place I won't appear is on the top floor of the Statler Hotel, next to an open window."

"This," said the ABA's grievance committee chairman, "is not a matter of levity." They changed the hearing to San Francisco. Fine, I said. But the next thing I knew, the ABA had issued a release saying my "trial" would be in Chicago and announced that it had hired a "gang-busting prosecutor" to pursue the case against me. The obvious implication was that I was a latter-day refugee from "The Untouchables."

Appearances obviously meant more than reality to these fat cats. It was for appearances' sake that Wally Craig undertook the "official" defense of Lee Harvey Oswald before the Warren Commission (where he never really acted as an advocate for Oswald). And it was for apearances' sake that the ABA was trying to get me disbarred. In effect, they were telling the judges of America, "Hey, we're not like Belli, we won't rock the boat."

Once the ABA had tried to get that message across to the press and the people and the judges of America, that seemed to be enough. They simply and incredibly dropped the charges against me, without a hearing. For a time, at least, it would be a standoff between me and the Bar.

CHAPTER EIGHTEEN

Greasepaint

Fame was a funny thing. After the Ruby trial, I got more than fifteen hundred letters in two weeks, not the least of them from my children who had suddenly discovered that they had a daddy they didn't even know. In the spring of 1964, Yale University asked me to appear on campus for Law Day. Howard University wanted me for their commencement speaker. The 17th Annual Meeting of the Italian Sons and Daughters of America had me give their keynote address in Philadelphia and named me "Italian of the Year." I was too honored to tell them I was really of Swiss origin. I appeared on radio and television shows all over the U.S. and Canada. Tony Curtis wrote to remind me that he still wanted to play me in a movie. I wrote back, full of bluff and bravado, "Someday, we'll do a great picture, that goddamn biography of mine, that will make Darrow's life look like he practiced in Small Claims Court."

Actually, I was fed up with practically everyone and everything. My headaches were getting worse. My marriage was falling apart. Even my love affair with the law was beginning to pall. I wrote to Governor Pat Brown. I asked him for a job. I wanted a challenge. Maybe even a prison warden's job.

I snapped out of my doldrums before Pat could answer that facetious note. I got some new cases and saw some new scenery and that was all I really needed.

I helped Judge William Driscoll of Toledo get a $365,000 judgement against the Toledo *Blade* for its defamatory attacks on him on the eve of an election.* Later in the year, I represented Mario Savio and members of the Free Speech Movement in Berkeley; he was fined $525 and ninety days for creating a public nuisance. That was free speech in the 1960's. I won a $550,000 verdict for a U.S. Navy frogman in the Virgin Islands who was brain-injured late one night when his motorcycle plowed into a government car. Some silly bureaucrat had left the unlighted car parked in the middle of the road. I won a $40,000 verdict in Virginia Beach for a woman who suffered a simple back injury, the highest award there since the founding of the courthouse in 1691. I won an all-time-high verdict in Salt Lake City for a nine-year-old girl who fell from a tree and broke both her arms, and then lost one of them by amputation when the doctor botched the job by putting too tight a circular cast on the arms. †

And I won acquittals on criminal charges filed by the San Francisco police against two nightclubs that were featuring something new in modern America, bare-bosomed waitresses and show girls. The police had stopped

---

* An appeals court in Ohio reversed this judgment, basing their decision on the U. S. Supreme Court opinion of *The New York Times* v. *Sullivan*. What made me angry was seeing a newspaper picture of the chief justice of the Ohio Supreme Court arm in arm with Paul Block, the *Blade's* publisher, giving Block a good-journalism award before our case was to be argued before the appeals court. I complained about this appearance of impropriety to a television inter-

these shows just as they had stopped Lenny Bruce. But this time they didn't get to impose their morality on the public. Judge Leo R. Friedman and Judge Leland Lazarus both ordered their juries to dismiss the cases. Judge Friedman told his jury, "This is a free country. I think we have a right to pick and choose what we want to read and see. The test is not what a couple of people feel. The test is what the people of San Francisco feel. No police officer can substitute his personal feelings of what is right and wrong."

"Showtime!" I shouted after Judge Friedman's jury came back with its verdict finding the owner of the Off Broadway, Voss Boreta, and three young lovelies innocent on charges of indecent exposure and keeping a disorderly house. That night, massive crowds flocked to North Beach to cheer and celebrate the return of "topless entertainment" in a dozen nightclubs. I joined in as master of ceremonies.

Eventually, of course, the clubs did go a bit too far. The dancers ended up with nothing on except the jukebox and the courts had to agree with the cops—though why one part of the body is indecent and another not is a question that I will have to leave to the anthropologists who make a study of witchcraft and primitive taboos, and to the United States Supreme Court, which at the moment is as confused over what to do as the nightclub owners.

---

viewer in Cincinnati, Phil Donohue, and that, I thought, was the end of it. I didn't count on the bar. *Ten years later*, my own State Bar of California would try to disbar me for those remarks on television.

† After this verdict, the Utah College of Surgeons withdrew their invitation to have me speak to them at Ogden. I was sorry they did so. Maybe we all could have learned a little about medical malpractice.

As a society, we have a long way to go before we understand how to cope with freedom. It was just about this time that I found a dispatch in the Virginia Beach paper about a fifty-pound seal who had made the mistake of exhibiting his friendliness to mankind by clambering into a sailor's boat. Not content to enjoy one of God's creatures in his natural habitat, the sailor "reduced him to possession" and turned him over to the city zoo, which promptly dubbed him "Surfy." I wrote to the paper, the Norfolk *Virginian-Pilot*:

> No matter how "natural" your zoo is and made so by phony architects, I am sure "Surfy" is going to miss your wonderful ocean beaches and everything that goes with God's littoral.
> Why the hell do we always have to "lock something up" or "reduce something to possession?"
> We lock up human beings in prisons for their wild aberrations when we should be doing just the opposite to cure their aberrations and sickness. I guess it's our "human nature," at its worst, that makes us want to lock up seals, shoot the wild goose when certainly we don't need him for food with all the broad-breasted turkeys around, pin butterflies, catch the mountain trout.
> Our human population is exploding so fast that we're going to push all the wild things off the earth pretty soon anyhow, so let them enjoy it in their God-given, natural state while they can.

I found out, after the *Virginian-Pilot* printed the letter, that "Surfy" had departed this life. Appropriately, on July Fourth, Independence Day, only a short time after he arrived at the zoo.

Judge Driscoll, Mario Savio, the navy frogman, the topless waitresses and dancers had come seeking me. That was one result of the Ruby case: people with unusual problems sought me out, because they knew I didn't mind fighting authority. Another result: I had become a celebrity—which was fun about one percent of the time and a bore the rest. Being a celebrity meant getting an infinite number of appeals to donate dollars to an infinite number of causes. It meant sending a pair of my horn-rimmed spectacles to Dr. M. J. Bagley, director of the Famous People's Eyeglasses Museum of Henderson, Nevada. It meant seeing myself caricatured in a "Little Annie Fanny" cartoon in *Playboy*.

In fact, *Playboy* interviewed me for one of its long and exhaustive Q. and A.'s, and I got my own TV interview show on the Metromedia station in Los Angeles, which syndicated it around the country. The TV show was fun as long as it lasted. I met all the important newsmakers in the country, (and some who only thought they were, but even they were fun). Still, I couldn't really maintain the pace. I'd have to fly down to L.A. on a Sunday morning, do a fast study on my guests, tape the show on Sunday evening and then dash off to wherever in the country my lecture or legal business was taking me. It was exhilarating but exhausting, particularly trying to keep up with the kaleidoscopic world that provided the people and the issues for the show. Name the people who were making the news in 1964 and 1965. I interviewed them. I even made excursions abroad to film some conversations. I had an hour interview with Papa Doc Duvalier in Haiti and, among other things, asked him about Graham Greene. He said, "Mr. Greene is welcome to come back to Haiti anytime. Obviously, he was not writing [in *The Comedians*] about Haiti. He described the big holes in the main street. Do you see any big holes?"

"No," I said. "Actually, I feel safer on the streets of Port-au-Prince than I do on the sidewalks of New York."

I was surprised by the man *Playboy* sent to interview me. His name was Alex Haley, and he was as black as my mahogany bar. I'd met few black reporters in my lifetime and even fewer like Alex who were at the top of the heap. He was an editor for *The Reader's Digest* and a contributor to *Playboy* and an author of the mighty best-seller, *The Autobiography of Malcolm X*. What impressed me most about Alex was his unfailing good sense and his sensitivity. I thought, if Alex can write *The Autobiography of Malcolm X*, why can't he write *The Autobiography of Melvin Belli?* No reason I could think of.* He became a constant companion and lived there on Telegraph Hill, with me and my pet rooster and occasional visitors like The Great Imposter, Ferdinand Demara.

Demara was one of the geniuses of our time. Though he had had very little formal schooling, he had successively posed as a Trappist monk, college dean, law student, zoology grad, cancer researcher, surgeon in the Royal Canadian Navy, warden of a Texas prison and teacher in a Maine island village. He played these roles so successfully and with such panache that Robert Crichton wrote *The Great Imposter,* a best-seller about his escapades, and Tony Curtis played the guy in a pretty damn good movie—for which Fred didn't get more than a dime. By the time our paths crossed, Demara was a counselor at a boys' school in Madera, California—accused of child molesting. I got him acquitted on those trumped-up charges, but not even acquittal could remove the scars of accusation and trial on a thing like that. I felt sorry for Demara and took him in for a time. He was a brilliant guy,

* As it turned out, Alex got involved in other projects of his own, notably the writing of his epic, *Roots.*

a fantastically acute mind encased in 350 pounds of blubber. He could go through a case of Jim Beam in four or five days. One night, I tried to get into the apartment, and he wouldn't let me in.

"Mel isn't here," he said.

"Damn it, this *is* Mel." I replied.

Fred was so thoroughly drunk he couldn't understand. But he wouldn't let anyone into the citadel. I had to get the fire department to come with a ladder so I could get into my own house.

Every night was Hellzapoppin with Fred Demara. He was a real Walter Mitty. Whenever he answered the phone, he would be someone else. He might be Mary Pickford and Douglas Fairbanks on the same call. One night, he phoned the zoo, said he was just back from a big game safari and had a lion he wanted them to collect at Mr. Belli's apartment. Once, he had a curator come out from the Fleishhacker Zoo and pick up the snakes he thought he was really seeing on the walls. He would give parties at the apartment and nothing was too good that I couldn't pay for when I wasn't there. I couldn't much afford to leave him and the rooster alone for more than one day.

The rooster of Telegraph Hill became something of a public joke around town and a private joke in the legal community. Roosters in that tiny section of town were *verboten,* but I kept him anyway. That was the joke. I bet Bill Choulos, now my one and only partner, that even though the neighbors had gotten the authorities after me, I could stave off execution of the rooster for at least ten years. The neighbors tried everything, and I had a counter-move to everything they tried. They went through the sanitary board, they went through the planning commission, they went through the board of adjustment. I balked them at every turn. I started keeping a diary of the legalism game that every lawyer knows he can play.

The rooster lived a pretty good life for two years. I had four hens in the roof garden who laid fresh eggs every day, and the rooster was there to keep them happy. But he was too noisy: since he was balling those hens, he had to tell everyone in the neighborhood about it. He'd crow every morning about 5 A.M. and all day, too, and he began to bother me more than the neighbors. Finally, I had to call off the bet. Or rather, pay up. I gave Choulos ten dollars, he went out and bought a fifth of Chivas Regal with it and (while chicken simmered on the barbecue) we drank to the rooster and to the slowly grinding wheels of justice.

As a celebrity, I found that Hollywood was after me to do bit roles. Caesar and I became actors together. In 1966, Caesar was nine. I missed him a lot when he was down in L.A. with Joy, his mother, but I had him up in San Francisco as much as I could—and Joy was good about letting him come. With Caesar, I have been a good, if somewhat indulgent father. Alex Haley and his girl-friend, Rosemari, took over as his babysitters when I had to go out during an evening. The kid, they told me, was precocious. At a movie, Rosemari nudged Caesar and said, "Oh, Caesar, look at the beautiful deer."

"Those aren't deer," he said. "They're gazelles. Shut up and watch the picture."

Rosemari installed some D-cell batteries in his Erector Set. "Boy, for a dumb girl," he said, "that's not bad."

And then Rosemari showed some photos of her family to Caesar. "Do your mother and father live together?" he asked. Yes. "My mother and father see each other—sometimes." Pause. "Some of my friends' mothers and fathers live together. I miss my father during the weeks. I have more fun with him than anybody else—even other kids. He does exciting things. He'll sit right down on the floor with me and put me a train together."

Caesar and I did an episode of "Star Trek," and became members of the American Federation of Television and Radio Artists (AFTRA). I got some other parts. I played an army colonel in something called *Devil's Dolls*, with Susan Hayward and Anne Francis. I played a lawyer in *Wild in the Streets*, a fantasy about the youth takeover of America starring Christopher Jones. And I had a cameo role in *Gimme Shelter*, a movie about the rock group, The Rolling Stones, on a trip through America.

The *Gimme Shelter* role was an accident. The Stones came to San Francisco to do a free concert at Sears Point —along with two other groups, The Grateful Dead and The Jefferson Airplane—but the authorities wouldn't give them the needed permissions to do it there, so they went to Mayor Joseph Alioto and appealed to him. He told them to see me. Maybe I could help them. Instead of filing writs all over the place, I decided to go the nonlegal route and find them another place to hold their concert. Rock concerts were big in those days. Woodstock drew hundreds of thousands of youngsters, who went not only to hear the music but to be together, as kids—doing, as they said, their own thing. Sometimes, their own thing was peaceful enough: a little pot and a lot of cuddling seemed to be the popular mixture. Unfortunately, this concert of The Rolling Stones didn't quite turn out that way.

The Rolling Stones came into my office on Montgomery Street at about 6 P.M., and I started getting on the phone to find them a place. They had some movie cameras there in the office. I thought they were television cameras. They didn't bother me. I just went ahead and found them a place for their concert, Altamont, about twenty miles into the hills past Livermore, east of San Francisco.

The press had billed this concert as Woodstock West

and predicted a crowd of 300,000. They were right about the 300,000. But it was no Woodstock. Someone—not me—hired the Hell's Angels to provide "security" for the event, and the Angels came in wearing cut-off denim jackets emblazoned with their colors, and they were armed with pool cues. They ended up killing a young man who was making some noise down in front of the open-air stage. I didn't see it happen. I was up on the stage, deafened by the music and awed by the acres of kids all around me and blinded by the glare of the lights that shone down on us from temporary steel towers. Then a Hell's Angel came up to me with beer on his breath and said, "Okay, Grandpa, get off the stage." I got mad and started after him, and he raised his pool cue. Then one of his buddies grabbed him, and Bill Choulos grabbed me and we all cooled down and watched as an ambulance came whining in an picked up the young man who had been killed. The air, of course, was full of the aroma of the stuff everyone was smoking. Everyone's eyes looked like the headlights of a locomotive in the fog. The Love Generation! Unwittingly, they helped set the stage for the Nixon-Mitchell gang's landslide victory in 1972, a sweep of every state except Massachusetts and the District of Columbia, because most people of "common sense" were able to say that if Nixon promised law and order in the face of all this, then Nixon must be the one. So we got the man I'd always loathed.

Altamont gave the San Francisco Bar another chance to have at me. Herb Caen told the *Chronicle's* readers that I'd hot-wired a car in Livermore to make it to the concert that Saturday night. And for that, nothing more, the Bar wanted to discipline me. Fact was, we'd flown over to Livermore and found we couldn't rent a car so we asked a young man at the airport if we could borrow this car. "Look, I don't have the keys," he said, "but if you want to hot-wire the car . . ." So one of the musicians did, and we all piled in and drove to Altamont. We took a helicopter back to Livermore and found the owner of the car standing there. He said to me, "You took the car!" Our plane was warming up and ready to leave for the City. "Look," I said to the guy, "I'm guilty. What the hell do you want me to do? You want capital punishment or what?" With that, one of the musicians took a hundred dollars out of his pocket and gave it to the guy for the use of his car, and that seemed to satisfy him. Next thing I knew, the Bar wanted to suspend me. I had to bring people back to San Francisco to testify. The guy who hot-wired the car. The guy who paid the hundred dollars. Finally the Bar dropped the matter, but only after a hearing and a lot more harassment.

Anyway, Altamont was the backdrop for the Stones' movie, *Gimme Shelter*. I guess it is still a minor classic, a movie that helps to document some of what was happening to America during the sixties.

Being a celebrity, however, brought me more than my share of crazy cases (that didn't pay me a dime). Take, for example, the long-distance TV romance between me and the notorious Zodiac killer (who may still be at large or, more likely, on ice in a prison where his psychopathology lies mainly dormant).

In 1969 the San Francisco papers were full of a one-man crime wave called the Zodiac killer, a real loony who'd attacked three couples in lovers' lanes in the Bay area, and a cab driver, killing five of them, and leaving his mark ⊗ at the scene. He bragged about the killings in letters and cryptograms to the press which were heavily laden with zodiacal nonsense, hence his name, the Zodiac killer. Most recently the Zodiac had threatened to shoot the tires out on a school bus and "pick off the kiddies as they come bouncing out." The police were guarding the school buses and some parents were driving their kids to school in their own cars. The public was frantic, and the police were under a good deal of pressure to find the Zodiac. They got more help than they needed, scores of sincere calls and letters, nut letters and telegrams by the hundreds. Eventually the Zodiac himself decided to give them some "help" through me.

At 2 A.M. on Wednesday, October 22, 1969, a man who identified himself as the Zodiac phoned the San Francisco police and demanded that either Lee Bailey or Melvin Belli appear on Jim Dunbar's KGO-TV talk show that morning. The police called me and Dunbar immediately and made arrangements for my TV appearance at 8 A.M. When I emerged from my penthouse on Telegraph Hill I found the place surrounded by cops, even the garage was full of cops. They escorted me down to KGO. There, I also found police everywhere, even in the high, dark aeries of the TV studio, where I could see the glint of rifles at the ready.

While thousands of San Franciscans watched over their morning coffee, I had thirteen—mostly abrupt—conversations with the Zodiac. He'd call, we'd exchange a few words, then he'd hang up.

"How and where can we meet you?" I asked him, more than anxious to get this killer some help and off the streets.

"Meet me on top of the Fairmont Hotel," he said. "Without anybody else. Or I'll jump."

"Do you think you need medical care?" I asked.

"Yes," he said. "Medical, not mental."

"Do you have a health problem?"

"I'm sick," he said. "I have headaches."

I told him I had headaches, too. I told him I thought I could help him. "You won't have to talk to a soul in the world but me."

He hung up. It would be our longest chat. From then on, the Zodiac kept the conversations short—as if, if he were to talk too long, someone might recognize his voice or trace his call.

"What is your problem?" I asked the next time he called.

"I don't want to go to the gas chamber. I have headaches."

I asked him how long he'd been having headaches.

"Since I killed a kid," he said.

"Why," I asked, "do you want to talk to me?"

"I don't want to be hurt," he said.

I heard a small scream. "What was that?" I asked.

"I did not say anything," he said. "That was my headache."

It was obvious the guy was in a lot of pain and may have been one of those rare cases where one man is acutely aware of two persons living inside his skin, one of them an outlaw who can't help killing. In another call, his voice sounded muffled and I wondered what was the matter. "My head aches," he said. "I'm so sick. I'm having one of my headaches." Then he gave a little cry and he said, "I've got to kill! I've got to kill!" Then he hung up.

Next time he called I told the Zodiac we were not on the air, that Dunbar had put his call on "Silence" so we could arrange a private meeting. The Zodiac suggested we meet later in the morning at 6726 Mission Street in Daly City. It was the rummage sale of the Church of Saints Peter and Paul.

I went there without Dunbar (he had had enough) and waited forty-five minutes, but (as far as I know) the Zodiac didn't show up. I don't wonder why: An army of police from San Francisco and Daly City was there. The cops had been monitoring Dunbar's line and certainly weren't going to let this opportunity pass them by, an opportunity to catch the Zodiac and vindicate themselves before the public. That's why they called all the TV and radio stations and newspapers, who each sent film and phone crews and a gang of reporters. So it was not exactly a private meeting to arrange help for the Zodiac. I had already made a deal in advance with the S.F. District Attorney, John Jay Ferdon, not to press for the death penalty if the Zodiac turned himself in.

I figured that wouldn't be the end of it, however. The Zodiac, judging from his taunting notes to the police and the press, wanted public attention. I was sure he'd call again.

He did. On December 18, 1969, the Zodiac sent me a brief note wishing me a happy Christmas. I went off on safari to Africa. But while I was there, the Zodiac, according to my housekeeper, phoned me several times. Then, in April, the Zodiac sent a letter to the San Francisco *Chronicle*. This time he claimed he had killed ten, not five, and wanted public recognition for it. He wanted people in town to wear Zodiac lapel buttons. "I would like to see some nice Zodiac butons [sic] wandering about town," he wrote. "Everyone else has these butons like [and he made the peace symbol], black power, melvin eats bluber, etc. Well it would cheer me up considerably if I saw a lot of people wearing my buton. Please no nasty one like melvin's . . . Thank you."

As far as we know, nobody ever heard from the Zodiac again. The police stayed on the case. They felt the Zodiac may indeed have killed more persons than they'd originally believed, including one young woman in Riverside, California, in 1966 and another woman in the San Bernardino area in 1967. And then, in 1971, they had a lead that took them right to Riverside University's law school. Dean Charles Ashman phoned me to say the cops were coming into the school, under cover, to check out one of his law students, a kid who had once threatened a girl he knew and told her he was the Zodiac. But they really had nothing to check this against except the guy's handwriting —and the handwriting comparisons were inconclusive. So the police wanted me to go to Riverside and give a lecture and maybe the kid would approach me and would talk to me and I could tell whether he was the same sick person who'd called me on the Dunbar show.

I went down and gave my lecture and Ashman told me who the kid was. He sat down right in front, surrounded by a lot of strangers (cops) who had come in, ostensibly to hear The Great One. When I finished, this kid jumped up and came right over to me, shook my hand and told me how much he'd admired me. He didn't sound like the Zodiac to me, but rather than fool around, I said to him, nodding at Ashman, who was standing right there a little behind the kid, "Hey, are you the Zodiac killer?"

Shocked, Ashman* literally pissed in his pants. The kid seemed stunned. "What do you mean, sir?"

I said, "Are you the Zodiac killer? I hear you used to call yourself Zodiac."

---

* Charles Ashman is one of the best Constitutional lawyers I have ever known, quick on his feet, quick-tongued, a great promoter, a prolific author and a friend whom I have indulged excessively. He is a completely unpredictable pixie.

In 1973 I suffered Ashman to pull a fast one on *The New York Times* Sunday Book Review, at my expense. He phoned John Leonard, the editor of that review, the most important book medium in the U.S., told Leonard he was Melvin Belli, said he'd read Ashman's book, *The Finest Judges Money Can Buy*, liked parts of it, was lukewarm about other parts and saw a review assignment as an opportunity to tell some stories of his own experiences with judges who could be bought. Leonard explained later: "Because a solemn literary journal is always on the lookout for evidence of sin in high places, I said yes." Leonard published the review, on November 18, 1973, and it was, well, every author ought to get a chance to review his own book in the *Times* Book Review. It

The cops all crowded around now, anxious to see and hear the kid's answer. "No," he said. "I didn't kill anybody." I believed him. So did the cops.

Naturally, I, a celebrated lawyer, would also get the Winnie Ruth Judd case. Mrs. Judd was a notorious trunk murderess convicted in 1932, who used to escape regularly from the Arizona State Hospital in Phoenix and then finally disappeared in 1962. She showed up in 1969 as a plump, matronly cook, housekeeper and companion for the well-to-do, working under an assumed name in the San Francisco Bay area. When the California authorities found her, they clapped her into prison. I got a phone call from her in the middle of the night. "You know who this is." It was a statement, not a question.

Groggily, I said, "Yeah." And waited.

"Winnie."

"Winnie Churchill?" I said.

"No. Winnie Ruth Judd."

Through law school and beyond, W.R.J. had been a standing joke. She was over the wall more than Babe Ruth. "Oh shit," I said. "Now I've heard everything."

---

was a rave by that renowned barrister and legal scholar, Melvin M. Belli.

What could I do? I was in New York on the Saturday night this fraud hit the newsstands (just having gotten an honorary degree from the NYU Law School). Should I phone the *Times* and tell them I didn't write it? No. Wacky as he was, Ashman was still a friend. That would hurt Ashman a lot and the truth would hurt Leonard even more than the story he'd wanted to believe when New York gossips pointed out to Leonard that he'd let one of Ashman's best friends review *Judges*. Leonard ended up writing an apology in the Book Review some weeks later under the title, "Suckered," promising the *Times'* readers he'd take care in the future not to let an author's friends review his work in the *Times*. Leonard is doing other things now for the *Times*, but I assume his successors will extend that ukase to the authors themselves.

But in the morning I sent one of my younger attorneys over to the jail in Contra Costa County.

He came back and announced, "Mel, it's she and she looks like Mother C., everybody's grandmother, Barbara Fritchie and Florence Nightingale." I took the case, even when she was extradited to Arizona. I thought that the thirty-odd years she'd spent behind bars and locked gates was enough—convicted murderers only spent nine or ten —and that her record for the past eight years was proof that she wasn't dangerous. I made some labyrinthine detours through a maze of Arizona politics, and had some hearings before a parole board that looked like a Grant Wood painting. All the board members had stiff, celluloid collars, high water pants, white cotton socks, Ben Franklin glasses and hair slicked down with shoe polish. Finally, after a long personal conference with Arizona's governor, Jack Williams (who impressed my son Caesar more than he impressed me), I got her sentence commuted to time served. She now lives within fifteen miles of me.

The year of 1969 had put me in touch with enough wackos. I needed to get away. I went on an extended trip. I spent Christmas in Rome, then took the Rapido down to Naples for the military trial of a U.S. Navy commander there, a doctor, who, when he was transferred Stateside, decided to detach the hospital and bring that along with him, too. I got him off; the authorities had seized and searched the contraband without a warrant. And then, so help me, the guy said to me, "How do I make arrangements to get all this stuff home?" He thought it was his. That's what I like about most of those I've defended. They really believe in *my* defense. And he was so grateful to me that he thrust upon me an extra thousand dollars I didn't want to take.

I put the money in my pocket and grabbed the Rapido

for Rome. A pickpocket got the thousand and some other cash besides. I reported the theft to the polizia in the Stazione Termini and the colonello in charge didn't even get up out of his chair or take his feet off the desk. He just pulled out a big sheet of paper and started studying it. I shifted my weight from foot to foot and then I said, "Colonello, do I get my money back?" He looked up and, without taking the cigarette out of his mouth, said in a tone that meant he could hardly believe the question, "Certainly not, *signore.*" And I didn't.

I rendezvoused in Kenya with Danny and Joan Jones and the Countess Nieti von der — of Munich. The countess was a proud blond, patrician beauty whose father was one of the ones who had tried to execute Hitler. Danny wasn't too thrilled with the way she always let him know that she was a countess, but I didn't mind that, because I was given to the same bullshit: *I* was the King of Torts.

The safari is now a delightful memory. A surfeit of servants and service. White linen tablecloths and crystal in an equatorial jungle, boys carrying everything for the four of us on a hunting trek at dawn, caviar and champagne and ostrich-egg omelettes for breakfast when we returned. By contrast, a hotel room in revolutionary Kinshasa, rented to us by a reluctant clerk, where we could see that civilization was already growing over with weeds, one room and a double bed for four. Black mambas, poisonous snakes lying across the road, so poisonous you're dead thirty seconds after you get bit. Blue skies along some water holes that would turn black with ducks: I held my shotgun vertically in front of my face and, without looking up, I said to Danny, "Tell me when." I fired both barrels and six ducks and a goose came raining down on our heads. They had us kill about fifty more—fresh game for the boys and the game beaters. Timbuktu: no telephone, no lights, nothing, not even a can or a can opener for three or four hundred miles, all sand and the dirtiest fly-ridden kids in the world, following us like the kids of Hamelin, laughing—at our blondness, perhaps, or at my own little game of peekaboo that I played with them.

I didn't much care for the hunt—at the beginning. Once I got a gun in my land, a kind of primitive thrill took over, and I became the kind of crack shot I knew my father was back in the High Sierras. The countess turned out to be a first-class tease. She had all the normal equipment, arranged a bit better than normal, perhaps, a milky-white complexion, blond all over. But she was playing games with it. In Kenya she was cool and distant and I said the hell with it and just moved out of the tent we were sharing and got another tent down by the river. The day she burned all my credit cards she decided to go back to Munich. The countess had stayed in camp that day. Danny and Joan and I went out hunting. We had a few laughs, and Danny got himself a lion—on my permit. And then, when we got back to camp, I asked the countess where my credit cards and wallet were.

"What do you mean?" she said. She looked stunned.

"My wallet and my credit cards and all my cash were right here in this ostrich-egg box!"* I said.

She said, "You mean they were in this box with all the trash in it?"

"Trash?" I said. "My wallet, my traveler's checks, my airline tickets, my credit cards? Trash?"

---

* When I was in Africa I never did get to the great Kalahari Desert. The natives +here are amazing long-distance runners—the best in the world—but they put water in an ostrich egg and bury it at stated distances along their paths to sustain them on long hauls. Each ostrich egg has its owner's distinctive mark and anyone who takes another's egg and lifesaving water is subject to capital punishment. I bought an ostrich egg (unmarked), from the Kalahari. That didn't get me into trouble. It was the box it came in.

She said, "*Mein Gott,* I put all the trash that was in that box in the fire." She poked around the ashes for a while, in tears. And all she found was one corner of my American Express card.

Standing there in my shorts, I said to Jones: "I can't imagine anyone throwing away my credit cards, can you, Danny? You'll have to lend me some money."

"What," said Danny, "do you have for security?"

The next morning, unable to cope with all this tomfoolery, the countess was gone. *Auf wiedersehen.* The Joneses and I took off and camped at Mount Kilimanjaro. The Joneses stayed on hunting in Nairobi (I really didn't care that much for hunting) and I joined them again in South Africa, where we visited with Dr. Christiaan Barnard* and watched him perform open-heart surgery, then flew back to California, to be followed several months later by our trophies, five times as numerous, I'll swear, than what I shot, or so it seems, when I look around my office at the forest of horns.

Like W. C. Fields, I never really could trust a man who wasn't willing to chance his thoughts at random by taking a drink. And, over the years, like my dad, I've had my share. Not that it was ever a problem, but certainly, on many occasions it was a diversion.

By the same token, I can't trust a man who can't handle it. I don't care whether he's a surgeon or a lawyer. But I've

---

* Danny Jones and I admired the relaxation of this famous doctor. I didn't detect any of the tenseness I'd noticed in surgical rooms in the U.S. He talked to me during the entire operation, more than a major procedure. His nurses knew what he wanted before he asked for it, and at the end of the operation when he removed the ligatures to see if the bypass worked, everyone in the operating room yelled, "Hurrah!" Like a good trial lawyer, Barnard has extreme confidence in himself.

always felt sorry for the mild sinner who, with too much aboard, stumbled into an inappropriate circumstance. I've always tried to help him, but I've learned if there are two types of people with whom one shouldn't interfere, they are the lawyer who's engaged in a heated debate with a judge and a drunk—in inappropriate circumstances.

The trip to South America with Bill Choulos was something different. I think we deliberately set out, I know I did, to sample every kind of beverage known, brewed and concocted in South America. The wines were great, but some of the brandies, and particularly the Pisco, were both palatable and potent. We were to meet Tony Curtis in Buenos Aires, so there was really nothing to do of a business nature except to see a few senators and prominent lawyers along the way until we got there. I drank Pisco sours.

I remembered having to look at travel books and post-cards of some of the places we went in order to remember having been there. Somehow or another, we met a number of South American girls in Chili and Peru and had some delightful picnics and excursions into the lovely wisteria-blooming countryside. Particularly, do I remember meeting a chief of police's daughter. She was about nineteen and had dreams of being a motion-picture star.

Choulos told her I was just the man to introduce her to the movies. At least this is what I learned later, because I can remember coming to on the trans-Andean express from Santiago to Buenos Aires with the chief of police's daughter as company. Just Choulos and I and the chief of police's daughter.

It was explained to me by the enraptured young lady that I had agreed to take her to California to "get her into the movies." We arrived in Buenos Aires and headed for the palatial Palace Hotel, where Choulos had engaged a suite for us and a double room for the daughter. The manager had sent several buckets of champagne to our suite, and I continued the excursion. There was a general strike. I always seem to be getting into countries where there is a general strike—once in Calcutta, several times in Rome, and now in Buenos Aires.

The whole staff had walked out at the Palace Hotel and the manager called us, apologetically, to tell us that while the kitchens and elevators and maids were not working, we were free to find whatever we could eat in the sumptuous hotel kitchen. There were no taxis, no transportation, few people were on the streets and we generally stayed in the hotel—Choulos, the daughter and I. But when I went to the kitchen to get some food the bar was open, and my taste quickly transferred from the wonderful South American T-bones to bourbon and Scotches —and Piscos. I got loaded, but thoroughly loaded, such as I've never been before or since in my life. The next couple of days seem like a kaleidoscope picture, but I still have vivid memories of stalking about the palatial marble corridors of the Palace Hotel. People were staying in their rooms even though there was no service, maid, elevator or kitchen.

I suppose there's one silliest moment of a person's life, but to this day I don't know how I accomplished mine: I can remember drinking and drinking and slipping in and out of consciousness until I awoke, starkly, in complete possession of my senses, standing in the middle of a passenger elevator looking at the mirror. I guess I was having the DT's, because I had the horrible feeling that *I* was *in* the mirror, not *outside,* and I couldn't free myself! But what was worse, I noticed, in passing, that I was stark naked. I stood transfixed for several minutes until the spell was broken, then with sweat dropping from my brow, I turned to the elevator controls and ran it to the lobby. I opened the doors. I will never forget the look on the faces of a number of guests, both men and women. There I stood at the elevator controls, completely naked. I could only say (and I did), "Going up?"

But oddly enough, no one got into the elevator with me, so I shrugged, shut the doors and ascended to one of the upper floors. I had forgotten what room I was in. I had now recovered enough orientation to realize that I was stark naked in one of the upper hallways of the Palace Hotel in Buenos Aires, and general strike or no, the manager would undoubtedly call the police to apprehend the naked Americano lawyer! How I had ever gotten to her floor, I'll never know, but there, around the corner, standing in the middle of the hallway, was the "daughter." She motioned me to her room, threw a blanket around me and my most embarrassing moment ever was over. I'm sorry I was never able to get her a job in the movies. Really, she deserved it. She was one hell of a great dancer!

CHAPTER NINETEEN

Combat Boots

I like military justice, because the kind I've seen first-hand goes as far as any court in respecting the rights of the accused. Respect is an attitude that many U.S. prosecutors do *not* have for the poor unfortunates who come to the bar of justice. But in military courts (despite the harsh connotation in the word *court martial*) even the lowliest private gets respect and, generally, more than an even break. Naturally, that has made things somewhat easier for a defense attorney like myself. And the rules of military evidence are more protective of the individual than any system of law.

After my first encounter with military justice, I had my doubts. Victor M. Hungerford was a good soldier before he was caught in some North Korean artillery fire in July, 1950, a hero who won a battlefield commission for bravery under fire. Despite his good record, however, and despite the shell shock, the army gave Major Hungerford a dishonorable discharge in 1953. He was "acting peculiar"—but the official reason for the discharge was really rather slight: the record said he went AWOL, absent without leave. In 1957, Beacon Hill, a Veterans Administration hospital in Seattle, checked into Hungerford's complaints of blackouts, unaccountable falls and severe head pains, but the doctors told Hungerford his troubles were "psychosomatic." Hungerford left that hospital thoroughly confused and went out to a life of crime; nothing violent, forged checks was all, but enough to send him to prison.

He was in the California Medical Facility at Vacaville when I first saw him. But at my insistence, the doctors at Vacaville X-rayed and found a subdural hematoma, a consolidation of blood pressing on the brain, which they dated to the concussion from his battlefield injuries. An operation made Hungerford into the straight-as-a-ramrod fellow he was before Korea. In effect, the operation had excised his criminality. I tried to help restore the man's self-respect. Uncle Sam was responsible for the major's battlefield injuries and their nightmarish aftermath. Uncle Sam ought to pay. I sued the U.S. Army for discharging the man with "a time bomb in his head" and the Veterans Administration for failure to treat him properly when they examined him in Seattle.

The authorities admitted they'd made a big mistake— but pleaded immunity under the statute of limitations in the State of Washington. Hungerford, they said, should have sued within two years of his injury, or at least within two years of his discharge from Beacon Hill Hospital. We were too late, they said, and a U.S. District Court agreed with them. I appealed to the Ninth Circuit, arguing that U.S. law should govern here.

The relevant U.S. law was the Federal Tort Claims Act, but that act was unclear on the statute of limitations. We asked the court to set a precedent that would make it clear, arguing that Hungerford didn't know what his trouble was until March, 1959, when he checked into Vacaville. That wasn't his fault, it was the government's. The statute of limitations in federal cases, we argued, should begin from the date of the wrong's *discovery*. The Ninth Circuit of Appeals agreed, remanded the case for a new trial and we won a settlement of $150,000, restoration of Hungerford's commission as a major in the army with all his credits—and, by Act of Congress, $50,000 in back pay besides—and a state pardon, too. The complete apologetic works.

It wasn't until 1967 that I participated in my first military court-martial. It was in the defense of Sgt. William Woods, up for murder. But the case wasn't so much a case of murder as it was of malpractice. At least, that's what I had to prove to the military court in Germany to get an acquittal.

Sgt. Woods, recently arrived in Germany, had gotten into a fracas in a German beer garden and shot the *Braumeister* in the belly. It was during the Christmas season, the German doctor wanted to go home to his Christmas goose, and he only probed the wound halfway, didn't clean up the other half and left a remarkable instruction for the nurses: "If patient thirsty, he may have some beer." Well, the patient was thirsty and they gave him some beer; but he was thirsty because he had peritonitis, which fulminated on Christmas Day, and the patient died.

At the trial, we had to prove that the cause of the *Braumeister's* death was not the shooting by Sergeant Woods but the doctor's subsequent malpractice. I'd heard that the commanding general in Germany, Gen. Frank T. Mildren, had been given the rumors—that the flamboyant Mel Belli was going to try to make his command into a circus. We didn't do anything of the sort. We put on a very dignified case, and my star witness was AAA-111, one of the top pathologists in the United Kingdom, Dr. Francis Camps.

"What do you do?" I asked the doctor when he first took the stand.

"I work for the Queen," he said.

"What do you do for the Queen?"

"I'm the Queen's pathologist."

"Do you practice in London?"

"I practice wherever she sends me."

"Where did she send you last?"

"To South Africa, as an independent observer on a matter of some concern to the Dutch government."

"Did you fly commercial?"

"Oh, no, I go as a military man."

"Do you have a rank?"

"Yes."

"What is it?"

"General."

As soon as he said that, I could see this military tribunal sit up a little straighter. And I knew we were in. Dr. General Camps said the *Braumeister* would have lived if they had done proper surgery on him, but the care they had given him was more than reckless.

General Mildren sat in the courtroom on the last day of trial. He listened to my closing argument and then the tribunal came back with a verdict of innocent for Sergeant Woods. The general was pleased. He gave a cocktail party for me, invited me to give a lecture for his officers at Heidelberg and had me come fishing for brown trout with him near Nagold in the Black Forest. The troops gave me a beautiful black and brown Rottweiler pup. He became Caesar's constant companion—foot of the bed and all.

I told General Mildren this was my first go in the military courts. I was pleasantly surprised, I said; if I'd found the military courts were bad, I would have raised hell.

General Mildren smiled and said, "Yes, I thought you might do that."

"Well," I said, "I didn't have to. Military justice is *not* to justice what military music is to music. U.S. military courts provide more safeguards for individual rights than any system of justice in the world." I wondered aloud if the system worked as well in the fire zone, say in Vietnam.

"If you're really interested, we'll get you there," he said.

And he did. Danny Jones, my lawyer-colleague-friend who had helped me write three books, and I went over to Vietnam not long afterward as guests of the Pentagon and of General Mildren, who'd been transferred there. We had an opportunity to observe more military courts for a month all over Vietnam. Then, with that background, I tried some interesting cases there myself. I defended Air Force officer Capt. Baruch Rosen, a doctor and a kind of real-life counterpart of that Bill Holden character in *Stalag* 17. Captain Rosen was being court-martialed for something called "commercialism," which is a kind of catchall military phrase for not acting like a gentleman. I felt the reason they went after him was he was a Jew. He was selling things—everybody did. "Hell," he said, "the reason I did was I just had a lot of time on my hands. I bought a lot of stuff in Bangkok and I just had it on my bed and I'd sell it. Half the time I wouldn't make a profit. It was just to satisfy my Jewish lust for commercial ventures."

When Rosen was on the stand, I never asked him why he hadn't asked his commanding officer for approval to sell, which would have been a complete defense. "Why didn't you question me about that?" he whispered angrily when I got him down.

"Relax," I said. "You'll be asked." I knew that a military tribunal, if it's very good, usually asks its own questions. The replies to those questions are the $64,000 answers. Sure enough, and old stiff colonel sent down a question in writing: "Why didn't you ask your commanding officer to approve what you were doing?"

I put Captain Rosen back on the stand. "Answer the colonel's question," I said.

Captain Rosen, happily: "I didn't think I had to. He was buying rings from me."

Verdict: not guilty.

The next case I got in Vietnam was Sgt. Tim Kephart's. Tim phoned me from Saigon and said he needed me. The next day I got a call from his mother, who lived near Redding, California. She said she understood from her son that I wanted a cash retainer, in advance, and that she'd be down to see me. The next day, she arrived with a shoebox containing $20,000 in $100 bills.

"Is this your money?" I asked.

"No," she said, "this is some of Tim's, some he sent home."

"How," I asked, "did Tim make that much?"

"He was in the Green Berets, the Special Services."

"Oh," I said, as if that explained everything. It wasn't until I flew to Vietnam and met Tim Kephart that I began to understand. He was a fantastic soldier. He was a Daniel Boone with a tread like a panther and a marksman who was also a killer. He was six foot one, lean, handsome, spoke Vietnamese, several different dialects. He was running the goddamnedest smuggling business you ever saw, with CIA planes and Green Berets loading contraband for him. He'd go to Cambodia or Taiwan with $100,000 worth of greenbacks and, instead of coming back with an empty plane, he'd load it up with goods. Naturally, the goods would go on the Saigon black market. And the profits into Green Berets' capacious pockets.

What tripped Tim was that he fell in love with a Vietnamese girl, decided to take her with him to Hong Kong on a rest-and-rehabilitation trip. He got her on the military plane by cutting some phony orders and giving her a nurse's uniform and fitting himself out as a captain. An American woman, an officer herself, unmasked them on the way to Hong Kong (she noticed Tim's girl was wearing Parisian shoes), and Tim was in trouble, charged with falsification of records, impersonating an officer, and conspiracy to have others impersonate an officer. A possible dishonorable discharge, plus imprisonment, lay ahead.

Everyone in Vietnam told me Sgt. Tim Kephart was the greatest soldier in southeast Asia. So I said if he's the greatest, let's get some generals to testify to that. I flew in generals from all over the world, officers who had known Tim before, and they were character witnesses in a proceeding where good character, by military law, is enough to raise a reasonable doubt. The trial was in Long Binh and who should turn out to be the commandant there but General Mildren. He put me in a big air-conditioned trailer all to myself, with a resident *mamasan* to cook for me and do the laundry. He invited me to share the general's mess, which usually was steaks, and the general's movies, a different one each night, viewed from plush leather rockingchairs.

One night, I asked General Mildren if I could borrow his helicopter for a party in Saigon for the president of Shell Oil. He said I could. What I didn't tell him was that I was not going alone, I was taking Tim and his military lawyers with me. It was a hell of a party. Everybody there was in dinner jackets—and I was dressed in U.S. Army fatigues and combat boots. I made a big hit, the fighting lawyer, in from the front for a bit of forced gaiety before I had to go back and battle for a man's freedom. John Wayne would have wanted to do me.

At our hotel in Saigon at about three o'clock in the

morning, no Tim Kephart. Finally, at around four, he arrived, but without the bag that had his dress uniform in it. We had to make it back for the trial in two hours. Tim was supposed to go on the stand and all—without a uniform, without his decorations. So we went to the black market area in Saigon and started buying things: uniform, spit-polish shoes, Purple Hearts, all the decorations Tim had won and a few he hadn't. Tim paid for all this stuff from a roll of bills as big as a loaf of bread.

We made the eight o'clock trial—just barely, and neither Tim nor I looked as if we'd been out carousing the whole night before. I put on the rest of our defense, gave a good argument and got Tim off for something like one hundred dollars fine and thirty days confinement—which was suspended. In the case of a good soldier, the army takes care of its own.

The Green Berets took care of me, too. As a kind of extra reward, the head of the Green Berets flew me over Cambodia in a helicopter (about ten feet above the ground, so no one could shoot at us). We went to an artillery post and I watched them loft shells into an enemy area and then, on my return to Long Binh, they gave me a lot of material, including the AK rifle that hangs above the fireplace in my office. A silver insert on the stock says: "Presented to Melvin M. Belli by the officers and men of Co. A, 5th SFT (ADN), RVN, captured by 3rd Mobile Strike Force Command, Rang Rang, 28 January 1970."

I left on the day of the Tet offensive and I heard the shooting in the distance as I got to the airport. I had my gun with me and the army fatigues and a lot of other stuff. The guy on the plane said I couldn't take it with me. It was contraband. Tim Kephart grabbed it and laughed and told the soldier he'd keep it in Long Binh, then whispered to me, "It'll be in your office in San

Francisco before you get home." It was.

I was soon back in the Orient. I defended a U.S. Navy man charged by Japanese authorities in an Okinawa court with possession and sale of a large quantity of dope. The U.S. has a "status of forces" agreement wherever it stations troops around the globe. By means of this treaty, each host country is given jurisdiction over any criminal case occuring within its boundaries. Thus, in Japan, the accused goes first to the Japanese authorities; if they don't want him, the American military tries him. Generally, the host country's authorities decline to try the man. It saves them money. In this case, Japanese authorities did decide to prosecute and I was defense counsel.

I didn't speak Japanese (they let me try the case with an interpreter*) and I didn't think the judge or the prosecuting attorney spoke any English; they certainly never gave me any indication they did. After the prosecutor finished his opening statement (simultaneously translated into my ear by my interpreter), I launched into mine. I'd speak a few sentences, then pause while my interpreter converted that into Japanese. But after each burst from my interpreter, the prosecuting attorney would have something to inject for all the court to hear. That bothered me. The prosecutor could see that. But he kept right on with his interpolations. Finally I turned to my co-counsel, who was Japanese, and said in English, "If that son-of-a-bitch doesn't lay off, I'm going to belt him."

The Japanese District Attorney jumped up and in perfect English said to the judge, "He called me son-of-a-bitch."

The judge said, "I heard him. Proceed." We did—

* I was one of the very few American lawyers ever admitted to practice in an Okinawa court.

even though it took me a long time to get my face back to its natural color.

Japanese justice is a sort of "jumping justice." (See Belli and Jones, *Life and Law in Japan*). By this I mean, a case will go for a day or even a half a day and then be put over for a month or two. In some cases there are as many as twelve or twenty-four continuances over a period of a year. I do not understand how the judge ever keeps the facts of each case in his mind. (There are no juries.)

At any event, our judge seemed to be an excellent Japanese jurist. (I think Japanese judges are probably the most honorable judges anywhere in the world. There's never been any trace of scandal or bribery or "fixing" among them.)

When a Japanese district attorney sets the wheels in motion for prosecution, he has to be sure of his result. 99-9/10's of the cases that are prosecuted go for convictions, otherwise the Japanese district attorney "loses face." There have been many cases in which the Japanese prosecutor, after losing a case, resigns because he has lost face. The reasoning is that he shouldn't be bringing a case to trial if there's any chance that it won't go for a verdict of guilty.

I had a number of sessions in Okinawa in my case before I had to return home, but the case was only partly finished, although the major cross-examination and trial work had been done. It was almost a year later before all of the case was in, arguments were made and the result came down: "not guilty." I felt particularly good for Stan, my defendant, but I was a little concerned about my English-speaking Japanese prosecutor who, as it turned out later on, was a real good guy—as prosecutors go.

There was a Navy captain who commanded a happy

fighting ship. And an excellent one, too. Two years running he had won the coveted "E" for performance in the China Seas. But even sea captains never learn to leave well enough alone, and he wasn't satisfied that all of the smoke coming out of the stacks was from fuel oil. It wasn't. To listen to the story as it was later told on trial, there was more pot smoking (and hard drug using), on his ship than on any other warship in any navy on any ocean!

This ship sailed principally in the China Seas and put in periodically at Hong Kong. The crew seemed particularly happy after a Hong Kong visit and those fun spoilers, the shore patrol, turned in at least two dozen sailors allegedly using every type of contraband from marijuana to cocaine.

Twelve of the sailors got together and phoned me in San Francisco to ask if I'd be willing to represent them in a trial with the U.S. Navy preferring charges, at the old Japanese navy yard at Yokosuka in Japan.

I arrived in Japan about three weeks later, checked into the Imperial Hotel and immediately went to bed trying to catch up on some jet lag. It's good I did because it was the last sleep I was to get in twelve days. The next morning my sailors called for me at the Imperial and took me to Yokosuka.

Generally when I try a court-martial case, and I have tried them in the United States, in Germany, in Italy, in Japan, in Vietnam, I'm greeted almost with red bunting and at least officers' quarters. I remember when I tried a case outside Saigon. I was quartered in general's mess—housekeeper, and steaks for every meal!

The legal military brass particularly likes me because I've said that military law is the system most protective of the individual in any system of law in any country, and I mean it—or I would have said otherwise. If ever, God forbid, I was arraigned on a criminal charge, I would rather have my law from the uniform code of military justice and my jury selected from military officers than any system of law, any veniremen. There were twelve cases to try, and we were to try one a day. This meant getting up at five in the morning at my Japanese *ryokan* to prepare the day's trial, with the able assistance of the legal military officer, then waiting for the verdict, which sometimes didn't come in until after 11 P.M., grabbing a fast, late, cold supper, then a few hours sleep and then five the next morning.

The first case I tried on the first day went for a "not guilty." It was the toughest of the bunch. The next case went for "not guilty" and then, not satisfied, I put my defendant on the stand, which I hadn't done in the first two cases. This resulted in a "guilty" verdict.

It's easy to criticize a lawyer who doesn't put his defendant on by saying, "If only he'd put the defendant on to tell his story, there'd have been an acquittal." On the other way round, if the defendant does testify, those after-verdict quarterbacks will all say, "He never should have allowed his defendant on the stand to be crucified on cross-examination." I think this particularly can be said of Lee Bailey in the recent Hearst trial. He put Patty Hearst on the stand, and she had to take her Constitutional some two dozen times. This ruined her with the jury. But query: Wouldn't she have been just as "ruined" if she didn't testify?

Of course, the judge cannot comment upon the refusal of a defendant to take the stand, but lay jurors seem to demand it. Not so with the military. The military judge will instruct the military officers who sit at the bench with him and who are the jury, "reasonable doubt should warrant an acquittal and a reasonable doubt is raised by defendant's good character." So we loaded on character testimony and in the cases my defendant did not testify, the verdicts were all "not guilty." In the cases in which my defendant did testify, the verdicts, two out of the twelve, were "guilty." I had one of the same witnesses against me in each of the twelve cases. This was a seaman who had turned State's evidence, and was principal prosecuting witness. He "sang" on all of his shipmates, but the military jury did not believe him—when the accused did not take the stand. He was just short of a nervous breakdown after twelve separate cross-examinations by me!

Of all the cases I have ever tried, these twelve in a row, just last year, from time element at least, were the most difficult. Up every morning at five and to bed after one. Had it not been for the excellent work of the military officer assigned to each defendant, I never could have pulled each separate case together.

While the majority of my defendants were found not guilty, I did learn enough about drugs in the navy to be appalled. "There's nothing to do" was the principal complaint in answer to the question, "Why did you smoke pot?" Another answer was, "It's so easy and cheap to get.'

I felt particularly bitter about all of these young boys, some of them away from home for the first time, subject to the influences of dope. They had no advice or counseling from officers and most of their shipmates either were on drugs or had been at one time or another. It made me wonder whether the ration of rum, regularly ordered in the Queen's Navy, might not be an acceptable alternative.

CHAPTER TWENTY

Wedding Gown

For an old guy, however, I was doing pretty well and was still fit enough to spend most of my evenings when I was home in San Francisco engaged in strenuous horseplay with my two-year-old daughter, Melia. In 1972, I had married Lia Triff, then twenty-three; she was my fourth wife. Melia was my sixth child.

I love women and I do not like being alone, but after a while with one woman, things begin to pall for me (and maybe for her, too). Then I make a vow of perpetual bacherlorhood. Soon, though, I find adventure with someone new—and wind up married again, full of optimism that this time my own neuroses will mesh with hers. Sometimes, they do, for a while.

My marriage to Betty Ballantine lasted eighteen years, to Toni Nichols two years, to Joy Turney nine. I married Pat Montandon, a San Francisco model and the recent author of a real-life Gothic novel, in a Shinto ceremony in Japan on October 12, 1966, but it wasn't really legal because we didn't have it recorded in Japan. Pat thought I'd done this deliberately. I swear I hadn't. We split soon after our return to the U.S. Pat is a beautiful gal and a social leader in San Francisco. I still enjoy seeing her comings and goings in the press.

I met Lia when I was attending the opening in late 1971 of the Kennedy Center for the Performing Arts. I was standing around with some very important people when I noticed one of the hostesses, a dark-eyed young woman with a wide, generous mouth. I pestered her with various, inane questions about the Center, made no progress with her and returned to my group. Luckily, she had a sense of humor. She came over to me and said, "Pardon me, are you an attorney?"

"Yes," I said, sorry I could not quickly think of something clever and bold.

"Are you a famous attorney?" she asked. Now it was turning into a game.

I smiled. "Yeeees," I said, my voice deepening a bit with pride and perhaps a pinch of passion.

"Does your name begin with 'B'?"

"Yaaa-esss." I turned on all my twinkly-eyed charm.

She smiled and, pointing a mischievous finger at me, exclaimed, "F. Lee Bailey!"

I broke into laughter. She had a fit of giggles and moved on about her duties. I moved on, too, and out of the gleaming new complex. And then I went back, found the girl and asked if she'd have lunch with me on the morrow. She said yes, she'd like that. She'd read one of my books.

She told me the story of her last twenty-three years. She was Lia Triff, of Roumanian extraction, and had grown up in Dearborn, Michigan, and Bethesda, Maryland. She had put herself through the University of Maryland working as a hotel clerk in the Washington Hilton and gotten straight A's, majoring in art history and anthropology. She would graduate in June and had a Fulbright in the offing. She was for me. I laid siege. I wooed her with flowers from afar and made her exchange her graduation gown for a wedding gown. We were married in Sonora in June and had a bacchanalian feast afterward at the restaurant then owned by the father of Dan Pastorini, the quarterback from Santa Clara and the Houston Oilers.

On our honeymoon, we traveled—and took Caesar along. We went to Savannah, Switzerland, Italy, New Zealand, Australia, Madagascar, Brazil and back to San Francisco, where Melia was born. Now three, Melia is a bright, polysyllabic and imperious young lady who has the most animated and independent personality of any child I have seen. She has already learned to speak some Chinese. This may be a portent of her future, and the world's.

Lia is a multifaceted woman who can be the soul of horn-rimmed efficiency from nine to five and the warmest woman I have ever known when the sun goes down. She has become a civic presence in the City, a gal Mayor Joseph Alioto soon learned to count on when he needed someone to throw an emergency party or serve on a crash committee. She was a delegate to the UN conference on women held in Mexico City last year, she serves on the City's bicentennial commission and campaigned last year for George Moscone, the City's newly elected mayor. Every charity in town calls on her for help.

Lia wants to be a lawyer, the best preparation, she feels, for going into politics and government. She serves, in her spare time, as our new mayor's deputy director of protocol, assistant chief greeter for the City of San Francisco. The telephone doesn't ring for me anymore, it rings for Lia. If you come to San Francisco, give me a call. I'll have a lot of time to tell you some stories while Lia's out spreading her youthful charm and greeting the visiting mukluk of Patovia. I am proud of her and I love her.

Am I a romantic? Of course I am. Show me a good trial lawyer who isn't. Good trial lawyers have a zest for life, a penchant for all good things bright and beautiful, kinky and flawed, for good wines, great tables, wide travels and beautiful women. Sometimes the travel and the beautiful women go together. Once, checking into the Ritz in Paris with me, N—— laughed her agreement when I suggested we order up a whole tray of French pastries. We both roared when we saw what the waiter brought—about two dozen tortes, éclairs and Napoleons —and what we didn't throw at each other we ate. I wish we'd thrown more and eaten less: there in the Ritz, I had my first "French pastry hangover."

N—— had to return to the U.S. I flew east, unsure of my destination, just drifting by whim. About two weeks later I found myself in Teheran, lonesome. I phoned N—— and asked her if she could meet me at the Khyber Pass, at Dean's Hotel (where, in Kipling's time, British lieutenants would leave their wives and sweethearts when they went off on their assigned military adventures). She was a romantic, too: She was waiting at Dean's when I got there. From there we went on to Calcutta and found the city crippled by a general strike. Everything, but everything was closed down. There was nothing to do except go into the kitchen and get a dozen coconuts and mix the milk with some wonderful Bombay gin (with the picture of Queen Victoria on the label) in a pitcher half filled with ice. As we waited out the strike in Calcutta I had time to study the beggars in the streets and the hundred thousand or more homeless children who lay naked on the sidewalks at night or cluttered the halls of the railroad station.

N—— and I went up to Darjeeling, saw the sun rise

over the Himalayas and bought crates of Tibetan goods for my penthouse on Telegraph Hill. We reached Nepal from Katmandu and got a closer, breathtaking look at the Himalayas. We couldn't get into Tibet, but got a Royal Nepalese Air Force plane to fly quite near. Some-day—it is one of my fondest hopes—I may set foot in Tibet. We went on to Burma, Bangkok, Singapore, then flew home from Japan—but not before we enjoyed that country's hot baths, warm rice wine, raw fish and noodles, even its tea.

The only reason I relate these escapades is to try to give you some clues about the modes and means of a trial lawyer. There's a great lust for life in many of us, we are always learning, storing ideas and images in our im-aginations—from whatever source. When I stand up to argue a case, heaven knows what knowledge and what experience I will call upon to make a point. It may have been something that happened at sea years ago while I was standing watch on the foc'sle head. It may have been something I learned while riding the rods during the De-pression. In the middle of a prepared argument I may see something in an exhibit I'd never really noticed. If I can relate that to an event in my own life years before, I might help a jury to better see the central issue in a case. See it my way.*

* Picking a jury requires extrasensory perception as well as good common sense. The best test is, "If you think you like him (a juror), he'll probably like you!" I've used my and Lee Bailey's good friend, Dr. Bill Bryant, president of the American Society of Hypnosis, a resident of Hollywood, to help pick a jury on numerous occasions. To hypnotize them? Not at all. I learned that hypnosis and semanticism have a great deal in common. Indeed, I have had Dr. Haya-kawa of San Francisco State lecture several times to my Belli Seminars on the art of jury picking. Dr. Hayakawa is a semanticist. Dr. Bryant would sit in the body of the court-room and listen to the answers (these were the days when

Sometimes a single word or a phrase can win—or lose—a case. Once I had a doctor on the stand (my witness in a medical malpractice case) who was attempting to explain to my jury what had happened when a young man bled to death after a simple tonsillectomy. The doctor reconstructed the operation and its aftermath. "And then," he said, "the patient exsanguinated."

"Doctor," I said, "what is that?"

"'Exsanguinated,'" he said, "is when you seize a chicken by the legs, turn it upside-down and cut its throat. When all the blood has drained out of the chicken, it's 'exsanguinated.'"

In my final argument to the jury. I didn't have to go into any lengthy description of what had happened to my young man. The word *exsanguinated* was enough.

Another time, trying a wrongful death case in federal

---

juries were picked by lawyers, not judges who do the complete voir dire now in most state courts as well as in the federal courts) to questions he had given me to ask prospective jurors. At recess, we would go out into the hallway and he would tell me which juror's answers sounded sanguine, which reticent, which generous, who was a hangman. He did it all by semantics, language and word association. And it made good common sense, like most of these esoteric doctrins and professions when one takes the trouble to reduce them to their lowest denominator. Certain word answers give clues, and I was to learn, too, to watch "body language." I had first employed this technique on the voir dire at the Ruby case. Both Bob Considine, my late great friend and newspaper writer, and I noticed how jurors, when asked, "Do you believe in the death penalty," would either directly answer yes or no or would hesitate, fold their hands or cross their knees, then answer "yes" or "no." Those who did the latter we determined weren't quite sure about the answer they gave because their interrupting "body action" was the mirror to their mind's indecisiveness. We checked it out later and we were 90 percent right. Try it yourself in daily conversational questioning and see if the equivocators and the indecisive persons don't hesitate and do some body language before giving the eventual answer.

court in Portland, Maine, I think I won with four little words. My client was a famous little Chinese boy who had lost his mother. In my second day of trial, when it was my turn to speak, I bowed to the jury and said, *"Gung hoy fat choy."* Judge, jury and the other side's counsel were equally astounded. So I said it again. *"Gung hoy fat choy."* Opposing counsel stuttered an objection. The judge said, "What is that, Mr. Belli?"

"It is Chinese New Year's today," I explained. "My little client simply wants to wish a Happy New Year to the jury and to Your Honor. It is an ancient Chinese custom."

The judge could only beam. So did most of the jury. But during recess my adversary hustled out to the nearest phone booth in the hall. I followed, entered the phone booth next to his and heard him telling someone, obviously the "home office" of his insurance company, "Yeah, no, I'm not drunk, that's what he said, something like 'gung hoy fat choy.' He said it meant 'Happy New Year' but whatever it was, the son-of-a-bitch has won over the jury. We'd better bail out." His company authorized him to settle for $250,000—which was an extremely high award for New England in the late fifties. I think it was mostly my *"gung hoy fat choy"* that did it.

Of course, *gung hoy fat choy* is not so very arcane to me. My office is only a block away from San Francisco's Chinatown. I frequently lunch there and enjoy the celebration each year of the Chinese New Year. Knowledge is where you find it. And I find it everywhere, near and far.

CHAPTER TWENTY-ONE

Green Surgical Pajamas

Because I did get some large awards in cases of medical malpractice during the 1950's and 1960's, the medical lobby (and propagandists hired by the insurance companies) have made me a convenient whipping boy. Recently, I find that they're blaming me for the crisis in malpractice insurance. Big awards won by Mel Belli and his ilk, they say, have caused the insurance rates to go up and out of sight. That's simply insurance-company rhetoric.

In the first place, though you read an occasional headline about a million-dollar verdict, there aren't that many big awards. According to the report of the Secretary's Commission on Medical Malpractice, produced by the Office of the Secretary of Health, Education and Welfare in 1973 (with the help of many members of the medical lobby in Washington), only 3 percent of insurance-company malpractice settlements were running more than $100,000. Roughly half the cases were being settled for less than $2,000. And in the second place, all the publicity about towering malpractice premiums (which costs are passed on directly to a doctor's patients) has made it increasingly difficult for a lawyer to get a malpractice verdict of any kind from a jury. The pendulum has swung now.

In the 1950's and 1960's, I helped make it swing the other way. The courts were turning down the maimed and the crippled who had no other recourse, awards were criminally low and it was difficult to get one doctor to testify against the malpractice of another. In this, medicine wasn't so much a profession as a conspiracy, and rare was the lawyer who would sue a doctor, simply because it was so hard to win a case of medical malpractice.

I helped change all that by daring to take on doctors no one else would sue, to ask for more adequate awards —and get them. The medical conspiracy sometimes extended to hospitals, too, and the people who worked for them. Down in Fresno in the 1950's I discovered on one case that the nurses and the hospital actually had the gall to try to change their own records. (I was suing them on behalf of a family that had lost their mother after a doctor had given her the wrong type of blood following abdominal surgery.) I sensed something amiss when I saw copies of the records, so when I got to Fresno I got a court order and demanded to see the originals. The medical-records people finally found them and my suspicions were confirmed.

In trial I went right to the heart of the matter by calling a nurse as my first witness. Miss Laura Berkqvist was tall and skinny and her frightened voice was little better than a whisper. I handed her the originals and said, "You made these alterations, didn't you, Miss Berkqvist?"

"Dr. Smith made me do it," she sobbed, blinking furiously through her tears.

I was disgusted. "Miss Berkqvist," I said, "please take the hospital records from your lap and put them on the table so that your tears won't fall on them. They've been altered enough already."

Her look of infinite sweetness dissolved. She roared, "You son-of-a-bitch!" and threw the charts in my face.

It was down in Fresno, too, that I got an early education in the stick-together ways of the medical profession. In 1953 a young law student named Edward Spraker came to me with a complaint: Because of a doctor's bungling, he said, he'd lost his penis.

It happened this way. Young Spraker had noticed a small lesion on the corona of his organ and consulted a physician, who diagnosed the problem as a venereal wart. The doctor treated the "wart" with a dab of podophyllin, a tincture of benzoin, and told him the trouble would go away. It didn't. Many months and several doctors later, Spraker learned he had cancer of the penis. The doctors had to cut it off.

Denver Peckinpah of Fresno, now a judge, was the lawyer with me on the case. We sued the doctors and we asked for $500,000. "King Farouk recently bought a racehorse for seven hundred thousand dollars," I told the jury in my summation. "Had the racehorse lost his male organ, King Farouk would have no hesitancy going to court and suing for seven hundred thousand dollars. Now I am *not* going to tell you that this boy would have sired not a racehorse or even an Abraham Lincoln or an Einstein, but he could have sired a human being."

The jury awarded us $100,000, a figure I thought was exceedingly low, considering what the young man had to give up.

But the judge thought $100,000 was excessive and said the lawyers on both sides ought to sit down and work out a compromise. A compromise? *After* the jury had awarded $100,000, we were supposed to agree on less? That wouldn't have been fair to our client, so we said,

"One hundred thousand dollars is the verdict. It ought to stand." The judge ruled in favor of a new trial. He said the penectomy might have resulted no matter what the doctors had done or how soon they had diagnosed the cancer. In other words, the judge's ruling meant that all the public warnings by the American Cancer Society and others regarding the benefits of early cancer detection was just so much propaganda!

At a second trial the defendant doctors brought in a whole panoply of medical luminaries to testify for them. Each of them solemnly averred that the defendant doctors had acted in accordance with accepted medical practice. I sat there at the end of the counsel table surrounded by the most authoritative books available on the subject of cancer. Every book contradicted the testimony of these doctors on the stand. But I couldn't use the books because none of the doctors would admit they'd read them. In other words, each of them pretended he had acquired all his medical knowledge, *viva voce,* by telephone, perhaps, and had never seen or read a medical book.

I had my own medical expert, of course, who said the defendant doctors had been negligent. But at this second trial the jury was confused by the conflicting testimony and, by the verdict of 11 to 1, exonerated the defendants of all responsibility. I had one juror on my side, a corpulent Mexican woman named Mrs. Gonzalez, who, in the jury deliberations, I was told, kept repeating what was to her the essence of the case: "He losted it, didn't he?" She was so right. My mutilated plaintiff got nothing at all.

Finally I learned to do without my own medical experts; I began to use the defense doctors themselves, the expert witnesses called to court by the insurance lawyers. Asking *them* the right questions on cross-examination, I was able to draw damning testimony from their own lips.

Sometimes, I could do this on common sense alone. In one early malpractice case I had in San Diego, I remember cross-examining an expert medical witness about the maggots that had infested my client's dirty foot wound. This doctor testified that "maggot therapy" wasn't at all unusual. He cited cases where maggot-infested wounds (on the battlefield, for instance) had seemed to heal faster than wounds not so infested. What happened was that the maggots ate away the otherwise contaminated tissue. The doctor made it appear that my client was fortunate indeed to have had his unattended and dirty wound overrun with maggots. "Doctor," I said, "if maggots are such good therapy, they should be used in all of your hospitals."

I asked, "Can you tell me where you would buy them if you wanted to use them this afternoon?" The doctor couldn't answer that one, and the jury decided the San Diego doctor was negligent.

To perform the best kind of medical cross-examination, however, I needed both common sense *and* a good medical education. I began to haunt the University of California Medical School, charmed my way into autopsies and the operating rooms and donned green surgical pajamas. I tried to learn as much as I could about the human body and the kinds of things that doctors can do to foul up its normal functioning. Later, I would spend time with the famous New York pathologist, Dr. Milton Helpern, at Bellevue, and then I got a further medical education from the world-renowned pathologist, the late Francis Camps, in London, from Cesare Gerin in Rome, from Emile Brietenecker (a great friend of Erle Stanley Gardner) in Vienna and from Armand Andre in Liege. American doctors didn't want me around, but the European pathologists seemed pleased to help me get the medical knowledge that few other lawyers ever bothered to acquire.

And so, without citing here all the malpractice cases (and the awards) I have won in my lifetime, suffice it to say I helped people get an ever-increasing recompense for the horrors they had suffered. If this has meant that doctors and hospitals have to buy more protection in the form of more insurance, then so be it. Doctors and hospitals can best afford higher premiums. They do pass them on to the patients as part of the cost of doing business; the victims of malpractice can pass on their injuries to no one.

In the past year, insurance companies have hiked the premiums as much as 400 percent. Why? The insurance companies said they were losing money, but I doubt they were losing as much as they claimed or that they were losing it on the malpractice coverage. The insurance companies were taking a beating on the stock market and had to make up the losses by raising their malpractice premiums. In 1974, for example, the Argonaut Insurance Company, the company that insures doctors in the San Francisco Bay Area (and the one that tried to raise premiums 400 percent), had an underwriting loss of $83.7 million—but they still had a $7.3 million net investment gain. Spokesmen for Argonaut (a division of the conglomerate, Teledyne Industries) refused to explain the numbers to public or press, much less to the doctors. Only after an Oakland attorney, Irving J. Hurd, sued Argonaut on behalf of two doctors who claimed their contracts were canceled did the president of Argonaut, Jerrold Jerome, give some answers in a court-ordered deposition. Hurd said Jerome responded, "I don't know," "I can't recall" and "I don't remember" to most of his questions. But he did admit that Argonaut lost $11 million on the stock market in the past year.

Normally, insurance companies do make money, lots of it. The key to their profits lies in the percentage they take out of every premium dollar and put into investment reserves. When insurance companies talk about losses, they conveniently forget about reporting the earnings on these investment reserves, and I think it is unfair of them to expect that the public should subsidize these companies when they guess wrong on their gambles. This whole matter cries out for fearless investigation and public discussion. I'm sorely disappointed that Governor Brown hasn't done this yet in California. It is an opportunity for him really to do something for the people at large—and for their doctors, who are abused, I believe, by the insurance companies.

Up to now, insurance companies have avoided showing their books to outsiders. This is one of those areas where the public has a right to know. Then, maybe we will all be able to figure out why the rates have risen so drastically. I cannot believe it is because all that many people are suing their doctors. Very few sue for malpractice. One reason why: Personal-injury lawyers like me weed out the phonies. We cannot afford to take even marginal cases.

Kent Russell, an associate in my office, has done some pioneering work in this regard. When a prospective client appears at my door with a story of some doctor's malfeasance, Kent goes into consultation with a lawyer-M.D. to help us decide whether we have a case. His expert, a kind of medical detective, works with nothing but the medical records of the case. If the records do not give some clues indicating medical malpractice, there's no much point in going ahead. We tell the prospective client and do not bill him for our advice.

In the old days, a personal-injury lawyer could come into court with a mangled plaintiff and win a jury's easy sympathy. Today, that's no longer true. Juries know now that when they give someone a large malpractice verdict, their own doctor bills will rise correspondingly. They don't want that. All over the country now, the word has gone out: Juries are not sympathetic, and malpractice suits aren't worth trying. Last year, more than 80 percent of jury verdicts went in favor of the doctor-defendants. In light of this, our sober acceptance of only the most valid malpractice claims helps us accomplish the substantial ends of justice. When we have found solid evidence of negligence in the medical records, we have had little difficulty in bringing the other side to a good settlement: we're advocates, but instruments of justice, too.

Once, I was preparing a suit against a doctor whose patient had been given some contaminated blood. That doctor took the extraordinary step of coming to see me. "It's unfair to sue me," he said, "and I'll tell you why." It took him about an hour to explain what had happened to my client, his patient, how the infusion of contaminated blood had occurred and why it wasn't his fault. He convinced me that it is frequently impossible to rule out some blood contaminants; blood is one of the most complex substances we know. And I dropped the case against him.

Ninety-nine percent of the doctors I've met are great guys, doing their best and working hard. Young doctors I've met recently seem particularly dedicated. But the individual doctor has a far higher code of ethics than the physician acting in convention, through his association. With lawyers *and* doctors, it seems there's some sort of collective amorality, a callous mob psychology, that takes over the individual practitioner's ethics and honesty. Doctors as a group seem to resist measures that could improve the quality of medicine for all. Individually, they'll tell you they'd welcome all kinds of reforms.

The American Medical Association's Principles o
Ethics say: "A physician should expose, without fear o
favor, incompetent or corrupt, dishonest or unethical con
duct on the part of members of the profession." In theory
then, a doctor who does not report the incompetence o
another doctor to his medical society or to a state licens
ing agency is unethical himself. Morally, a doctor whose
training was given to him in trust, by society, owes more
to mankind than he does to the AMA and the insurance
companies who underwrite his practice. In reality, how
ever, doctors have mostly kept mum. Dr. Roger O. Ege
berg of the U.S. Department of Health, Education and
Welfare and Dr. Robert C. Derbyshire, a past presiden
of the National Federation of State Medical Boards, the
agencies that grant and revoke doctors' licenses, have es
timated that 5 percent of the nation's 320,000 physicians
are incompetent or unscrupulous. If that estimate is cor
rect, then there could be more than 16,000 practicing
physicians in the U.S. who should not be licensed to prac
tice. But, according to figures from the Federation o
State Medical Boards, state licensing agencies through
out the country have revoked only 291 medical licenses
in the past four years, an average of 73 a year.

Clearly, doctors are not doing a very good job of polic
ing themselves. They look the other way when they come
across evidence that one of their colleagues doesn't know
what he is doing. They say they don't want to run the
risk of being sued themselves for slander if their charges
do not stick. Some states will grant immunity to the re
porting doctor in a case like this. In Arizona, once that
immunity went into effect, reporting of unfit doctors
quadrupled. For the most part, however, in most parts
of the country, doctors keep quiet about their incompe
tent colleagues, and that's the major reason why there
is a "malpractice problem" at all.

Some say that if doctors don't police themselves more effectively, state or federal government will have to do so. Personally, I'd rather see doctors involved in the self-policing effort. (But I also agree with Governor Brown of California; some laymen ought to sit on every licensing board.) Still and all, those boards can deal only with the most flagrant cases of medical malpractice. I'd rather see the profession upgrade the quality of medicine practiced by the vast majority of competent doctors.

So far, the profession hasn't much insisted on continuing medical education for every doctor, but it should. Medicine is getting more and more complicated; there are about twelve hundred different drugs on the market today, many more than most doctors can know well. No drug is completely safe; all have potential side effects. Each drug is intended for a specific use, and many are not supposed to be given except under very carefully controlled conditions. Yet any licensed doctor is free to use any drug in any way he cares to, regardless of how well or how long ago he has been trained or how diligently or poorly he keeps his knowledge up to date.

Boyce Rensberger, a medical writer for *The New York Times* and an M.D. in his own right, has reported the results of an international study of drug usage that revealed that American doctors wrote twice as many prescriptions per patient as Scottish doctors do and that the rate of adverse side effects was also twice as high in the U.S. The director of that study, Dr. Herschel Jick of the Boston University Medical Center, has estimated that about 500,000 people are hospitalized in the United States annually because of a drug reaction, making this one of the ten leading causes of hospitalization in the country.

One anonymous doctor told Rensberger, "Look, some of these guys who practice all by themselves don't even recognize an adverse reaction. They treat it like just another symptom and prescribe another drug for it."

✓ Keeping up with the legal literature is absolutely necessary in my profession. It seems even more necessary in medicine, where a person's very life is at stake. Yet only a few states require evidence of continuing education as a condition of relicensing. During every three-year period between license renewals in New Mexico, for example, a doctor must attend at least forty hours of approved postgraduate courses, forty hours of sessions at a regional, national or international scientific conference and forty hours of local medical meetings. If a doctor fails to meet this requirement, his license is no longer in good standing, and he may not practice medicine. The New Mexico medical board decides on an individual basis whether to let doctors redeem licenses by making up the missed educational time. But no state has gone so far as to require that doctors pass an examination for license renewal, as Senator Edward M. Kennedy has proposed on a national level.

The times, of course, are changing. Doctors should recognize that they occupy positions of public trust just as surely as any elected official. And, like elected officials, that they, too, are accountable to the public at large. Up to now, most doctors have withheld information from even their own patients. There is no reason a patient shouldn't be permitted to look at his own chart, have a copy of his own records and be able to discuss the contents of those records with his doctor. Many persons have filed suit just so they can get a look at their own records.

If doctors were more accountable, I think they'd practice better medicine. In fact, the threat of a malpractice suit has already helped produce better doctors. I just wish that the threat of a suit wouldn't also make some doctors shy away from "good Samaritan" situations. A commission report of the Secretary of Health, Education and

Velfare has declared that legal risks are "minimal if not nfinitesimal" in giving on-the-spot emergency care to ccident victims. But roughly half the doctors in the coun-ry, according to the same commission report, say they vould not give such aid in any case.

Ultimately, doctors want to be able to insure them-elves against a ruinous lawsuit in any situation. They *hould* be able to. Which gets us right back to the nsurance companies—again.

What about the insurance companies? No one wants hese companies to stay in business solely as a public ervice. I'd like to see them make money. If they really re losing money (or not making enough to make it vorthwhile), then the solution may lie in working out, s some doctors are doing in some parts of the country, kind of cooperative insurance pool. Almost twenty ears ago in a talk in San Francisco to the Insurance rokers Exchange of California on February 6, 1957, I uggested they might have to do something like this:

> Any brokers dealing in malpractice insurance have the duty of warning their clients of their ex-posure: It can be tremendous. For plastic surgeons, X-ray men, neurosurgeons, and, indeed, all medical men, verdicts of $300,000 are now a distinct pos-sibility. [Now verdicts of $3 million are a possi-bility!] You say coverage in this amount presents prohibitive premiums? Well, if the private insurance company can't do it, then the doctor is going to have to look elsewhere—to state insurance, to coopera-tive insurance, or to a change of the system of law under which we live.

even went so far then as to suggest a form of insurance olicy paid partly by the doctor with the major share

paid by the patient as he goes into the hospital, to cove
him for "unanticipated medical result," with no imputa
tion of negligence on the part of the doctor. Few doctor
ever *intend* a bad result.

As another partial solution to the malpractice insur
ance crisis, some doctors—and, no surprise, the Califor
nia Medical Association—have urged the legislators t
outlaw the plaintiff's lawyer's contingency fee. I don
see how that would change the economics of the situa
tion, and it would certainly give less worthy representa
tion to truly deserving victims. For all their work o
medical malpractice cases, plaintiff's lawyers get only
fair recompense. One recent study done by the Califor
nia Department of Insurance shows that plaintiff's law
yers get twenty-two cents out of each premium dollar
while insurance lawyers get twenty-four cents.

These defense lawyers contribute their share of risin
costs of litigation. Defense lawyers start their meter run
ning on a case long before the plaintiff's lawyer reall
gets going on it. And they run up their expenses to suc
an extent—with all sorts of phony investigations, re
searches, depositions and motions and interrogatories—
that a reasonable settlement soon becomes impossible
Stockholders in these companies ought to take a close
look at how much money they are spending on litigation
Much of it is unnecessary.

Of course, people could insist that lawyers (on both
sides) get out of the business entirely and hand it ove
to a state commission—and then we would have the stat
intruding into one more aspect of our lives. I'm sure th
doctors and the insurance-company lawyers will be th
last ones in our society to applaud that. Even so, I believ
that doctors' efforts to have the states bail them out nov
with public funds will drive them into their chamber o

horrors, socialized medicine, faster than anything else they could do.

Until the state takes over entirely, I'll argue for the contingency fee. In the long run, I'd probably make just as much money either way. I never protested laws setting up public boards for workmen's compensation, nor have I argued against legislation in some states that have introduced no-fault auto insurance (which obviates court trial and the adversary system in the *smaller* cases). I will always find some legal pies to get my fingers into and meaningful work to do for people who need me. But removing the contingency fee—until we socialize the whole thing—would be a disaster for the little people. For them, the contingency fee is a free ticket to the courtroom. They cannot afford to hire a lawyer at a hundred dollars an hour or more. Taking away the contingency fee at this time would take away lawyers from the many and leave them in the hands of the few.

But the contingency fee doesn't affect the establishment. Corporate lawyers, such as those who work for Standard Oil or Bell Telephone, manage to hire whole rafts of young lawyers who will run their retainer "meters" far into the night. You and I eventually have to pay for them—by paying higher prices at the gasoline pumps or higher rates for our phone calls.

CHAPTER TWENTY-TWO

Soledad Stripes

I am at a stage in my life when most of the money I earn (after rather substantial taxes) goes to support the army of lawyers, secretaries and researchers that fill my offices around the world. In my darkest moments (forgetting the San Francisco office alone has about two thousand cases in the works at any given moment) I ask myself why I continue to work to support *them*. I'd have more fun as a lone wolf, I think, trying an occasional case in warranty or malpractice to bring in the $350,000 or so that I need to live and travel on each year and then, in my extra time, taking on causes hitherto unrepresented: defective children, mental patients, women, minorities, consumers, environmentalists. (This doesn't make me a radical, but a conservative—conservative because I'm not overthrowing the system, I'm just changing it to work for those who haven't been using it.)

In a small way, of course, I already do this. I have always taken on some cases *pro bono publico* and I have encouraged the younger attorneys in my office to keep at least one case in the public interest on their back burners at all times. Kent Russell, editor of my own Boalt Hall

Law Review, spent months of his time in 1974 and 1975 doing the legal research and brief-writing necessary to get Tim Leary out of state prison. He saw Leary as a man undone by his own flamboyance, persecuted by state and federal authorities and given a sentence not for the ostensible charge of bringing two marijuana cigarettes into the U.S. from Mexico, but for supposedly corrupting the minds of our youth. Meticulous Robert Ingram, a graduate of William and Mary Law School, took on the case of Lt. Col. Edison Miller, a marine flyer who spent five years in a North Vietnamese prison camp only to return home to Orange County in 1973 and find he'd been charged with *mutiny,* aiding the enemy and other prison misconduct. Miller's only "crime" was refusing to go along with the right-wing propaganda generated by his fellow prisoners to further the 1972 reelection campaign of Mr. Richard Nixon.*

Jim Garlock who came from the Michigan Law School is putting together a multimillion-dollar lawsuit against various state agencies on behalf of more than three hundred persons whose homes and prime farmlands were ruined when a levee on the San Joaquin-Sacramento Delta broke on June 21, 1972. Syd Irmas of the Los Angeles office is deeply involved in a number of civil rights cases while trying to reform the grand jury system. All of us can continue this kind of work (in addition to our regular litigation) because Bill Choulos handles office logistics.

---

* Ingram and I went to Washington together to talk to the Secretary of the Navy about Colonel Miller. The Secretary, John Warner, took me out into the hallway and tried to "plea bargain" a settlement that would have denied the principles the colonel was fighting for. We turned him down. He seemed offended, and our budding friendship was even more traumatized when we won the case completely for Colonel Miller.

That one turned out better than my previous visit to a

Choulos is my good right hand, administrator of the San Francisco office and coordinator of my other law offices in the U.S. and abroad. Without Choulos, we would all be lost in a morass of detail. He's loyal and a damn good, fearless lawyer in his own right. Occasionally, we get to travel together, sometimes abroad. He always, invariably, finds a Greek friend—or relative—wherever we go, and soon they're off in their native language. Bill really loves the poor, but thankfully for me, he himself (we'd) rather be rich. A true Greek, Choulos loves liberty—of all kinds.

In 1975, I found my career was coming full circle. I had been a hero at San Quentin in my early days and now I found I was a hero again inside the California prisons—to the prisoners, if not the guards.

I have never found it difficult to hold compassion for men languishing in prison. For Mickey Cohen, for Alvin Karpis, a client and a friend whom J. Edgar Hoover had fraudulently used to catapult himself to national fame, for Dyke Simmons and Joel Kaplan, Americans who had each spent long years in a Mexican prison. Each had something good in him, and I didn't have to go out of my way to find it.

For many in jail today, I hold an equal measure of compassion. Modern jails are a far cry from the old prisons where men lay on damp stones, had no light, little air and a bucket for human waste. Now, prisoners have visits, mail, fair food, clean cells, recreational op-

---

long-gone (and forgotten) Secretary of the Interior. I went to see him on behalf of Evel Knievel, who wanted Interior's permission to jump the Grand Canyon on his motorcycle. The Secretary greeted me cordially when I arrived unannounced but frowned deeply when I told him what I wanted. He couldn't quite believe his ears, and finally, when he realized that I was serious, he stammered, then rose abruptly and ushered me out of the office without another word.

portunities that would have been laughed at in the old days. Few "holes" are left, but it is impossible for those of us on the outside to know for sure everything that happens in our prisons. Physical conditions may be better, but some sadistic prison guards still exist—and some of them are racists. They enjoy persecuting the blacks who make up such a shocking percentage of our prison population.

Theoretically, prisoners have had an opportunity to seek civil redress from sadistic, racist guards. But they hardly knew they had these rights, nor were they bold enough to use them. Until W. L. Nolen came along. In the summer of 1969. Nolen was an inmate at Soledad Prison near Monterey, California. He was a handsome young black in his early twenties who had become a prison boxing champion. He dared to file civil suits against the warden at Soledad, the State Department of Correction and several guards. Nolen charged that the guards helped foment racial strife in the prison and helped white inmates in the ongoing vendetta in a way Nolen admitted would be hard to prove in a criminal proceeding. (The guards would leave a black's cell door open so white inmates could enter in the middle of the night and kill or maim him. That's called "setting him up.") Nolen swore in his complaint that Soledad officials were willfully creating situations that made him and other blacks fear for their lives.

Nolen's suit never came to trial. Four months after he wrote the petition, on January 13, 1970, he was shot to death by a prison guard. So were two other black inmates, Cleveland Edwards and Alvin Miller. The guards set them up, putting eight whites and eight blacks into an exercise yard, a 40-by-150-foot concrete rectangle, that had been closed for six years because of racial war in the prison. The guards waited for the inevitable fight to start, then one of them, O. G. Miller, a mean, corpulent fellow with twenty years' army service, opened fire from eighty feet away on the blacks below. In that shooting gallery, he couldn't miss. He shot through the heart. Three *blacks,* no *whites,* lay dead.

The District Attorney's office in Monterey investigated the shooting and its aftermath and brought no charges against O. G. Miller, the sharpshooter in the tower, or against any other guard. Within an hour after the D.A.'s announcement of that decision had reached Soledad, a prison guard, John V. Mills, lay dead on the concrete pavement in a wing of Soledad. It was a retaliatory killing, the first time a guard had ever been killed at Soledad. It resulted in the indictment of three black inmates, George Jackson, Fleeta Drumgo and John Cluchette. Their case (they were called "the Soledad brothers") became a cause célèbre in California and the nation and led to an all-out war inside the entire California prison system and the killing of some forty persons, including three blacks and a judge* taken hostage in a daring escape from the Marin County Courthouse in August, 1970. Also dead: George Jackson himself, along with three guards and two inmates, in a shootout at San Quentin on August 21, 1971.

Naturally, I got involved. Although the authorities in Monterey County never filed criminal charges against the guards at Soledad,† I found I could file a civil law-

---

* The same Judge Harold Haley whom I had opposed as a Marin County prosecutor in my earliest San Quentin cases.

† Too often have I seen grand juries in small towns near the state prisons whitewash the prison establishment for all sorts of provably horrendous misconduct. Usually the small-town District Attorney is at the center of the judicial conspiracy. A true bill, though frequently warranted, rarely reaches the county judge.

suit under the Civil Rights Act of 1871. The suit couldn't bring Nolen, Edwards and Miller back to life, but it would establish some truth for the record and recompense the families of the murdered men.

This was not one of those cases lawyers fight to get. It had *pro bono publico* written all over it. It took five years to prepare, and I was afraid it would go down in defeat. John Hill, a tenacious young lawyer in my office, did most of the investigation and preparation in the case, along with a dedicated young law student named Scott Hansen who passed the bar·just in time to help me try it. In April, 1975, Hansen and I appeared before Federal Judge Samuel Conti in San Francisco. (Hill was engaged at the same moment in the defense of six inmates from San Quentin on criminal charges stemming from the San Quentin shootout of August, 1971).

We got an all-white, three-man, three-woman jury in our trial, and things didn't look good for us. We couldn't prove clearly and convincingly an actual "conspiracy" on the part of the guards to set the black militants up for a kill. You just don't go into a prison and get the guards to cop out one against the other. It's like getting doctors to testify against one another in a case of medical malpractice. And most cons are afraid of retaliation from the guards. We had one witness, an ex-inmate named John Martin who testified he had heard the sergeant in charge of O Wing, Richard Maddix, tell the guard assigned to the tower, O. G. Miller, "Can you do it? If you can't, we'll get someone who will. And be sure you get Miller, Nolen and Edwards." But the Deputy Attorneys General defending the guards (who had also been working on the case for five years) threw a good deal of doubt on Martin's testimony when they demonstrated that he wasn't even in the ready room where Maddix was supposed to have given those orders. At least Martin had not signed into the logbook that day (not the logbook we saw in court) and the evidence indicated that O. G. Miller, the guard, wasn't even in O Wing that morning. We had another witness, an inmate named Bob Gardner, who testified that O. G. Miller had bragged about his commitment to the Ku Klux Klan, but the Deputy Attorneys General cast some doubt on the disinterested character of this testimony when they brought in evidence that my colleague, John Hill, agreed to help Bob Gardner get a job after he left prison. Of course, there was nothing wrong with helping a guy get a job. We even gave a night watchman's job to another Soledad witness, Tomas Meneweather, a black from the Caribbean who was an expert in the martial arts (he could take your head off with the side of his hand). But Meneweather didn't help the case either. He tried too hard, and the opposing lawyers tripped him up in important inconsistencies.

Finally, the inmates on O Wing weren't what anyone would call ideal clients. Prison officials used O Wing for the worst troublemakers, both prisoners and problem guards (one of whom—officer Dykes—was caught pouring urine in the men's milk on at least one occasion). Its slain inmates, not exactly the Hardy Boys at Camp, were sure to win little sympathy from this middle-class jury.

I said as much to the jury in my closing argument: "I know it must be difficult for you to relate to them. You had a crew here of cutthroats, you had a crew here of murderers, you had the very bottom of the barrel. All they are are—human beings!"

But I was also able to introduce some uncontradicted facts into the record. The guards knew there'd be a fight; they subjected the sixteen men to a thorough skin search before they went into the yard on the fatal day (making sure they had no weapons), and some ten guards got "ringside seats" for the anticipated battle while a sharpshooter was sitting up in the tower ready for "anything." I argued to the jury that if the guards were not conspiring against the blacks, they were at least guilty of a reckless disregard for the men in their charge. And it was a damn strange coincidence that the very men killed, shot at eighty feet through the heart, were blacks.

I pointed out that conspiracies, like Watergate, aren't easy to prove. "They act in stealth. That's the nature of a conspiracy." But I wasn't going to push it. I reminded the jury that Raymond Procunier, the chief of the California prison system, had told John Hill in a deposition: "We should have done it differently." I brought up the testimony of the State's own criminalist, David Burd, who said after his investigation that the shots were "fired directly at the chest" of two of the men, contrary to assertion of the State that Miller had fired warning shots before he started firing into the "melee" below. Shooting into a group of unarmed men (four shots in four seconds, according to E. A. Peterson, one of the Soledad supervisors) didn't seem reasonable to me.

On cross-examination, Peterson admitted that "something went wrong." I picked up that theme and played a soft symphony with it. Again and again, I asked Peterson, "What went wrong?" Finally, he put his finger on it—from his point of view.

"A gun," he said, "didn't control the situation."

Was that all? My tone changed. "Isn't 'what went wrong' that three men were killed?" I demanded sternly.

"I didn't say that," Peterson snapped back.

"That's just my point, Mr. Peterson," I said sadly.

In my summation, I didn't press and I didn't ask for the scalp of all the guards and supervisors who may have had a hand in this tragedy. "If you find that only Officers Dykes, Maddix and Miller are responsible, we'll be satisfied," I said. "If you only find Miller responsible, we'll be satisfied." I was asking damages based on a civil rights act declaring that we could seek recompense for a deprivation of rights secured by the U.S. Constitution, and one of these, the most precious, was life itself. "You're the ones responsible now," I told the jury, "for bringing the Constitution into the most odious of places, into the darkest, deepest dungeons. If you make the Constitution effective to the least of us, then it will be effective for the best of us."

I wondered whether the jury would accept this argument. I didn't wait around for their verdict, went back to the office and was so discouraged I jokingly "sold" my interest in the case to Bill Choulos for three dollars. But in a year when several Watergate participants had been convicted for in effect subverting the Constitution, I hoped that these six men and women would strike a blow for the little people against those so-called public servants who would abuse their power. It was cornball, but it's what I thought and what I wanted the jury to think. And by God, they did. They came back with a verdict against eight of the ten guards and officials we had named in the suit, including the warden himself! John Hill, just in from the Marin County trial, came leaping into the courtyard shouting, "We got eight of 'em! We got eight of em!" And in the federal courtroom, Scott Hansen was being hugged and kissed by the families of Nolen, Edwards and Miller. Someone told me that this was the same Scott Hansen who, at twelve, had written me after the Ruby trial to tell me I'd inspired him to go into the field of law. Now here he was, a winner with me, on his first case. He helped me haul our Jolly Roger up to the top of our flagpole.

According to the rules of the court, after the jury had decided on the matter of civil responsibility, we had to put on a separate case on the damage phase. We had to prove dollar damages to this same jury. I would have a hell of a time proving that these men who were killed in the yard at Soledad were worth much money. They were in for life. Given their temperaments and their propensity for getting into trouble, even behind bars, they had no hope of earning anything since they would probably spend the rest of their days in jail. And their heirs were aged parents. I ended up settling the case with the State of California for $270,000. I should have let the jury decide "quantum," too.

The money was a good thing for the families to have. But the money wasn't as important as a sense that somehow justice had been done. Addie Nolen, the mother of the boxing champ, told a reporter after the verdict: "I always felt my son was murdered. This is some measure of justice."

Furthermore, the decision would set some valuable precedents in U.S. prisons. No one had ever sued a guard for violating a prisoner's rights under the U.S. Constitution—and won. For decades, prisoners simply didn't have rights. Now, despite the reluctance of rural grand juries to indict guards on criminal charges, guards and prison officials have been put on notice. They can't pick out a prison leader and just kill him. If they do, they'll have to answer for it. In terms of its practical consequences, then, as a senior judge of the Federal District Court in San Francisco told a reporter, "This is one of the most important civil rights cases of the last thirty years."

But the rave reviews weren't unanimous. The California Correction Officers Association immediately asked the State for a public clarification of the court settlement. The legislature responded by refusing for a time to appropriate the $270,000. The bulls also demanded the State Bar disbar me from the practice of law for making "irresponsible, slanderous, fradulent and immoral" charges against all the prison guards in the state in my closing argument, which the jury just happened to agree with. I said nothing at the trial about all the guards in the state. As for the guards on trial, well, a jury found them guilty of a conspiracy to deprive some men of their civil rights, to wit, their lives. I didn't set the men up for slaughter, I just brought out the truth in a court of law.

It was all I ever wanted to do.

Epilogue

Anyone who takes an overall look at two hundred years of American history must conclude that this is a great nation, holding for the most part on course. Our friends and enemies abroad might judge from their observation of all the bickering on the bridge that the U. S. ship of state is going nowhere in particular. But they would be wrong. We are a contentious people, and as De Tocqueville observed way back in 1834, a litigious people as well. "Don't tread on me" was the legend under a coiled rattlesnake on more than one of our original state flags. But we are great precisely because we are contentious. All the arguing and litigation only make us stronger. Macaulay wasn't too far wrong when he said we obtain the best decision "when two men argue, as unfairly as possible, on opposite sides." Good ideas only get better when they have to meet a challenge in a public forum, whether that forum be in the news media or in a courtroom.

Our system is great, I believe, because it puts the highest value on open advocacy. No one has exclusive possession of "the public interest." We need an effective urging of opposing views to sharpen every issue and help identify where the public interest really lies. And for this we need lawyers, too. In the wake of Watergate (whose horrors were perpetrated by some who were, in fact, lawyers) critics are proposing the elimination of attorneys from public councils. But Richard Nixon and his gang weren't removed from office by a bloody coup. They were eased out by due process of law—in part by other lawyers who weren't politicians.

And I am encouraged by many other signs of the times. Increasingly, I see good law and good lawyering working to the benefit of all the people, thus protecting the people from the lawlessness of big business and big government. I realize businessmen and bureaucrats don't think of themselves as outlaws. Businessmen say all they want to do is make a profit. All bureaucrats want is the power to get us in line and make us march to the beat of their drums. And I'll be the first to admit I'm a capitalist and I carry insurance and use banks, the telephone and buy products from Standard Oil.

When the people at large see official lawlessness (and they do, thanks to a press which gets more vigilant every year), they do not turn to revolution and armed insurrection, they turn to the law. For every injury and injustice, there is a remedy in the law. Or ought to be. In the past, this ancient axiom worked only for those who had the money to hire a good lawyer—which hardly made for any kind of equality under the law. That's changing in America. Now, everyone who is criminally accused gets an attorney (and generally a damn good one) whether he can afford one or not. Now, every person who is civilly wronged is increasingly able to obtain counsel who will take a case for a share of the award or for a surprisingly realistic fee. Access to a good lawyer gets easier every day.

Our numbers are increasing; the law schools are jammed with smarter, more socially oriented men and women, and the last restrictions against a lawyer's advertising his availability are crumbling. And that, too, I had something to do with. The canons of the Bar have banned advertising up to now; it was unseemly and unethical to "stir up litigation." As far as I am concerned, it still is, I think there is entirely too much litigation in America today, too many people filing lawsuits against a neighbor with a barking dog, too many Redskin fans raising a legal question about a referee's decision that cost their team a victory. Twenty-eight of every thirty people who phone me on a given day don't really have a case. And I tell them so.

But advertising need not "stir up litigation." There are many, many people with good causes for legal action who never contact any lawyer. They don't know how—or whom—to call, and for that reason they are not *equal before the law*. The law and the Constitution are not self-executing. Due process is a sham unless you can get a lawyer to drive the due-process vehicle—and I think the right kind of advertising will help people find attorneys who will do that for them.

The Federal Trade Commission and the U.S. Justice Department and the courts have now come to see the logic of all this; they have reevaluated the old strictures on advertising by lawyers. Now, if I interpret the Goldfarb case correctly, lawyers *can* advertise. And so, in the past few months, I have planned a display ad in the Yellow Pages:

CONSULTATIONS
3-5 P.M.
Monday, Wednesday, Friday
Melvin M. Belli
The Belli Building
722 Montgomery Street
San Francisco

Our aim: to make due process available to *everyone*. The rich have always had legal care, and in the past ten or fifteen years so have many of the poor. But we ignore the majority of middle-class Americans. Our consultation may help change this situation. (And so will a newly emerging form of prepaid legal care, an idea Danny Jones and I espoused fifteen years ago, fifteen years ahead of time.) I have each of the lawyers in my office take turns on consultation duty and I take my turn, too. What do we get out of it? A sense of satisfaction in the thought that we are helping people. For the most part, we refer people to another public or private agency, but we are always on the lookout for something interesting—not a big, obvious moneymaker (because those cases will have been chased and lined up by others long before they come walking in my door) but a situation, perhaps, which cries out for some creative imagination and may help us pioneer a new trail in the law. As I've said in lectures to attorneys all over the land, no one ever walked into a lawyer's office and announced, "I have a case that will make legal history." A good legal mind has to see through to the core of a case, explore its ongoing legal ramifications and its social importance—and then work with all his ingenuity to make the wheels of justice turn in a new way.

This is the challenge of the law for me and the lawyers in my office. We are trying to help make a good system better, trying to help make the promises of the Constitution a reality for all.

We are not the only ones who do this. There are hundreds (I hope thousands) of lawyers in America engaged in a similar struggle, particularly the younger ones: providing counsel for those who have none, harmonizing relations between the races, assisting the consumer, protecting the environment, advancing individual rights. I am thinking of the members of my trial bar, the Association of Trial Lawyers of America, of Ralph Nader and his lawyer teams around the country, various public-interest law firms and of Morris Dees and Julian Bond of Alabama, who have involved me in their lawsuit against a family planning clinic in Montgomery and various federal agencies for sterilizing two poor, ignorant, black teenage girls without adequate consent. I was happy to get into their Relf case; it seemed like a clear-cut way to strike another blow for the rights of the individual against the potentially untrammeled power of big government. And I was happiest to think that these younger lawyers wanted to include me in their community of concern.

No matter where I go in America, no matter what accents I hear, I find that these younger lawyers and I are speaking the same language, and that our brainstorming sessions are informed by the same understanding of the Constitution. These lawyers keep me young, they teach me new applications of the law (often enough, those who teach me are the youngest, freshest faces around the table) and they make me proud to be a lawyer.

Justice Oliver Wendell Holmes once said that a man must share the passion and the action of his times—or run the risk of not having lived. I have shared. I have lived. And I expect to keep on doing so for some years to come.

ROBERT BLAIR KAISER was a prize-winning correspondent for *Time* during the 1960's and still contributes to numerous magazines in the United States and abroad. He is the author of two other books, *Pope, Council and World* (Macmillan, 1963) and *"R.F.K. Must Die!"* (Dutton, 1970). He lives in Los Angeles and Mammoth Lakes, California, with his wife, Ellen, and their six children.

Index

NON-FICTION BESTSELLERS FROM POPULAR LIBRARY

National Bestsellers from Popular Library